Occasional Publication Number 23

Traditional Knowledge and Renewable Resource Management in Northern Regions

Milton M. R. Freeman and Ludwig N. Carbyn
Editors

A joint publication of the
IUCN Commission on Ecology and the Canadian Circumpolar Institute
(formerly the Boreal Institute for Northern Studies)
1988

ISSN 000680303
ISBN 0-919058-68-X

1993
Reprinted by:
The Canadian Circumpolar Institute
The University of Alberta
Old St. Stephen's College
3rd Floor, 8820 - 112 Street
Edmonton, Alberta
Canada T6G 2E2
Telephone: (403) 492-4512
Fax: (403) 492-1153

With funds provided by:
IUCN Commission on Ecology, Working Group on Traditional Ecological Knowledge

Cover photo: Member of the Loucheux settlement of Old Crow, Yukon, preparing caribou hides for domestic
                use. Old Crow is a Native settlement situated on the banks of the Porcupine River and is located
                770 km north of Whitehorse and 112 km inside the Arctic Circle. (Photo L.N. Carbyn)

Traditional Knowledge and Renewable Resource Management

Milton M.R. Freeman and Ludwig N. Carbyn, Editors

Table of Contents

Preface

This publication includes a number of papers given at a workshop on Native Peoples and Wildlife Management, held in October 1986, during the Boreal Institute's 25th Anniversary conference on "Knowing the North: Integrating Tradition, Science and Technology."

The workshop also included three papers not printed here: one, by H.T. Lewis and T. Ferguson on traditional Native burning practices has been accepted for publication in Human Ecology, and an additional paper by T. Nudds, a bio-ecologic analysis of human hunting practices, appears in another collection of papers resulting from the Knowing the North conference (Boreal Institute of Northern Studies, Occasional Publication No. 21). A third paper, by P. Mathiesen, on aspects of Sami environmental management, was not submitted for publication. In addition to four papers (by F. Berkes, R. Caulfield, A. Gunn et al., and R. Riewe and L. Gamble) included here which were presented at the workshop, another, by H. Feit, was presented as a keynote paper at a plenary session of the Knowing the North conference, and is included here because of its relevance to the workshop theme. The paper by P. Wheeler was submitted by a participant at the workshop after the event. Papers by I. Bjorklund, M. McDonald and G. Osherenko were solicited by the editors due to their relevance to the topic and usefulness to the larger concern to which this workshop was addressed, namely the launching of a circumpolar network on traditional ecological knowledge.

The science of wildlife management was first defined by Aldo Leopold when in 1933 Charles Scribner's Sons published Leopold's Game Management. Leopold based his conclusions on careful observation and deductive reasoning. Over the years the profession has matured and increasingly relied on quantifying events. This at times has left out dimensions which had been retained by the Native or indigenous people around the world. In the recent past a number of international science-based organizations have sponsored workshops and

conferences on the topic of traditional ecological or environmental knowledge. The topic is variously labelled, sometimes as ethno-ecology or as customary law, but the new-found interest in this topic derives less from its contribution to esoteric scholarship, and increasingly toward its practical usefulness, and its management relevance. The sponsors of several recent meetings convened to examine traditional ecological knowledge, have included, e.g., the Ecological Sciences, and Marine Sciences divisions of UNESCO, the International Association of Biological Oceanographers (IABO) and the International Union of Biological Sciences (IUBS). This present collection of papers derives some impetus from another such international initiative, namely that of the Commission of Ecology of the International Union for the Conservation of Nature and Natural Resources (IUCN). The IUCN Commission of Ecology has an active Working Group on Traditional Ecological Knowledge, and several regional networks addressing this issue, of which the Circumpolar Network on Traditional Ecological Knowledge was launched during the October 1986 Knowing the North Conference. It is for this reason that the final contribution in the present volume, by T. Andrews, was included: an impressive bibliography that references over 200 studies of indigenous peoples' traditional environmental knowledge and management systems. This bibliography was originally prepared for the Dene Nation, representing the indigenous peoples of the western Canadian subarctic, and is reprinted here with permission of the Dene Nation. The report symbolizes the co-operation between non-Native researchers and the indigenous experts who increasingly share concern for improved knowledge and stewardship of the environmental resources of the Northern regions.

The other papers in this collection provide a number of case studies relating to traditional knowledge and management institutions among Inuit groups in arctic Canada, the Cree of the Canadian subarctic, Athabaskans in Alaska, and the Sámi of northern Norway. The other papers also deal with management, either traditional/indigenous, or prevailing state-mandated systems based on non-indigenous scientific perspectives. Some authors are concerned more especially to show that the traditional knowledge systems continue to function in northern Native societies to "manage" the human-wildlife interactions in ways that are equitable, sustainable, and in conformity with long-held tradition.

Not surprisingly then, several papers urge a further integration of the science-based state management system with traditional systems of self-regulation. For this to occur, it seems likely that the traditional systems will need recognition from a wide range of publics, both inside and outside of the North, and in the countries in question and also abroad, for it is perfectly evident that the sometimes uninformed environmental protests that have an impact upon domestic environmental policy formation may be influenced by foreign pressure groups. This collection of papers, one of an increasing number now appearing on the subject, is dedicated to this notion of increased understanding and a greater respect for traditional ecological knowledge. This need for recognition is not only directed to non-Native people inside and outside of the North, but also to young northern Natives who are increasingly unaware of many of the traditions that have served their ancestors for countless generations and which continue to have relevance to the environmental problems facing humankind today and in the future.

Environmental Philosophy of the Chisasibi Cree People of James Bay

Fikret Berkes
Brock University

Abstract

The ability to use resources in a sustainable manner stems from a combination of two factors: (a) the possession of appropriate local ecological knowledge and suitable methods/technology to exploit resources, and (b) a philosophy and environmental ethic to keep exploitive abilities in check and to provide ground rules by which the relation among humans and animals may be regulated. The first of these two factors, traditional knowledge, has already been discussed and documented extensively for the eastern Cree people. This paper emphasizes the second of the two, and specifically focuses on the following Cree beliefs: (a) it is the animals, not people, who control the success of the hunt, (b) hunters-fishermen have certain obligations to fulfill towards the animals to ensure a productive hunt, and (c) a continued, proper use of resources is important for sustainability. The hunter's obligation towards animals are intertwined with social obligations, so that the environmental ethic of the Chisasibi Cree is an integral part of a comprehensive philosophy of life. Cree environmental philosophy is relevant to the implementation of sustainable resource use practices. It is also relevant to the "ecosystem approach" in which human social systems need to be considered part of natural ecological systems.

Introduction

In a world made increasingly uniform by mass media and mass culture, it is easy to overlook many groups of people who have a different view of the natural environment, or to dismiss them as "irrelevant" to the world's larger-scale concerns. The fact is that not all cultures in the world share the dominant Western view of a secularized, utilitarian, depersonalized nature.

The existence of alternative philosophies of the natural environment is important as part of the cultural heritage of humankind. This "cultural diversity" is akin to biological/genetic diversity as the raw material for evolutionarily adaptive responses. It is the very stuff of human cultural evolution. While many anthropologists have argued for years that "primitive" cultures have much to teach us, it is only in recent years that there has been a surge of interest among resource managers, ecologists, anthropologists, economists and political scientists regarding traditional management systems (e.g., Johannes 1981; McNeely and Pitt 1985).

A number of international organizations have developed interests in these topics, for example, the Traditional Ecological Knowledge Working Group of the Commission on Ecology, International Union for the Conservation of Nature and Natural Resources (IUCN). As well, IUCN's Commission on Environmental Planning has pursued the subject of incorporating local concerns and involving local people in management, in the context of sustainable development. Another international thrust has been UNESCO's interest in the traditional and local-level management systems of the coastal environment (Lasserre and Ruddle 1983; Ruddle and Johannes 1985; several volumes in preparation). Yet another related development is the renewed interest in common property resources, and, in particular, the role of traditional communal property institutions in their management (National Research Council 1986; McCay and Acheson 1987).

Much of this activity can be considered as a number of steps or layers in inquiry:

(1) Documenting traditional ecological knowledge,

(2) Identifying ecologically sensible practices that can lead to sustainable resource use patterns,

(3) Identifying local-level political institutions and social arrangements in the use of resources, in particular, common property resources such as fish and wildlife.

Perhaps the next logical step to the inquiry is the investigation of the environmental philosophy of the groups under scrutiny. Stated simply, the ability to use resources in a sustainable manner cannot be accomplished merely by the possession of appropriate ecological knowledge and social institutions. There also has to be an environmental ethic to keep exploitive abilities in check and to provide "ground rules" by which relations between humans and nature may be regulated.

It is argued here that the existence of alternative environmental philosophies is crucially important in this regard, assuming that there are fundamental problems with the current environmental philosophy of the dominant Western society. If we are to question our current attitudes towards the environment, we have to know the wellspring of our present values in the first place. Our view of the world and the universe and how we relate to them is the *source* of our values, our cosmology (Skolimowski 1981). Everenden (1985) argued that humans are akin to aliens because they have a self-identity distinct from the world around them. The root of this aberration, said Everenden, is our cultural emphasis on objectivity. Skolimowski (1981) argued further that our cosmology is based far too heavily on empiricism and scientism, and is too mechanistic and analytic; it is insufficiently based on humanistic notions and morality toward nature.

These observations are not universally true for all cultures. Even some Western traditions reject the view of a secularized and depersonalized nature. But in this paper, we are not concerned with those "alternative" Christian views of nature, as with St. Francis (White 1967) and St. Benedict (Dubos 1972). Neither are we concerned with Taoist, Zen Buddhist or Sufi views, which are relevant to the debate but beyond our scope (but see Watanabe 1974; Toynbee 1972; Pepper 1984).

Rather, this paper is concerned with a group of Canadian eastern subarctic Native people, the Cree Indians of Chisasibi. These people survived three centuries of fur trade as essentially hunter-gatherers. After settling into permanent communities in the 1960s and coming into close contact with the industrial society in the 1970s (due to construction of the James Bay hydroelectric project), their present lifestyle maintains an uneasy balance between being hunter-trappers-fishermen and being lower middle class rural Canadians. Although their philosophy of the natural environment has been changing rapidly, in pace with their integration into the dominant society, they still profess and practice a distinctly different view of the world, as explored and documented in depth by Tanner (1979) for the Mistassini Cree, Feit (1978) for the Waswanipi Cree, and Scott (1983) for the Wemidji Cree.

The purpose of this paper is not to repeat the extensive analyses of these authors. Rather, the aim is to focus on Cree culture as a source of an alternative environmental philosophy. What are the philosophical underpinnings of the traditional management systems of the Cree? How does the cosmology of these people differ from ours? Further, in the context of present concerns with the animal rights movement, it may be appropriate to ask: Are these Cree hunters-trappers-fishermen engaging in frivolous and wanton killing of animals? Do the animals perhaps need the services of animal rights groups to protect their welfare against Cree Indians and other such groups of hunting peoples?

The Study Area and the People

Chisasibi is a Cree Indian community of over 2,000, located about 1,000 km north of Montreal (Figure 1). It is linked to the outside world by sea since the seventeenth century (Francis and Morantz 1983), more recently by air, and since the mid-1970s, by road. The road was built primarily for the purposes of the James

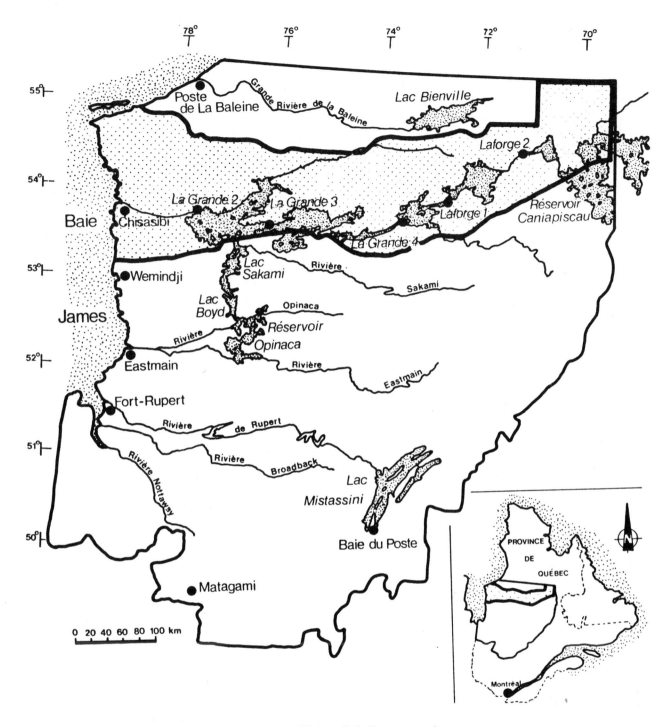

Figure 1 The hunting territory of the Chisasibi Cree people

Bay hydroelectric project. The project forced the Cree (and Inuit peoples to the North) to give up their land claims in exchange for a comprehensive agreement with the government, the James Bay and Northern Quebec Agreement, which was signed in 1975. The hunting-

trapping-fishing area used by the community is some 73,000 km^2, divided into 40 hunting areas averaging some 1,800 km^2. The subdivision of the territory into manageable units serves the purpose of sustainable utilization of fish and wildlife resources. Each of these subdivisions is under the control of a family or an individual (the tallyman). The practice of dividing community territory into family-controlled units goes back an unknown number of years. The beaver resource system, introduced over the 1930-1950 period by the Quebec government, was modelled on the existing system of Cree hunting territories (Feit 1978). In actual practice, these are hunting-trapping-fishing territories; they serve more than just beaver management.

Nearly all adult males and most adult females participate in the subsistence economy on a seasonal basis. Approximately 45 percent of the population of Chisasibi hunts as its major productive activity on an annual basis. This figure gives the percentage of the population who qualify for the Hunters' Income Security Program by, among other things, living in the bush at least 120 days of the year. Full-time trappers spend the October-December and January-March periods in bush camps, about one camp per family hunting territory. Most of the population spends May and September in goose hunting camps. The major subsistence activity in summer is fishing. In other seasons, fishing is carried out as a secondary activity to hunting and trapping.

The material presented in the following sections is based on extensive group discussion/ interviews with a volunteer working group of the local Cree Trappers Association. As a self-selected group of respected hunters, all of them tallymen, they represent perhaps close to consensus opinion. The larger report, yet unpublished, covers a number of topics on rules, traditions and practice of hunting, fishing and trapping in Chisasibi. Prepared through five sets of meetings over one-and-a-half years, and corrected by members of the group through revisions at each step, it was undertaken (a) to provide educational material on Cree culture for youth, (b) to record and strengthen traditional practice, and (c) to educate the outside world in defence of Cree culture and subsistence economy. The material is based on the actual and current practice of mature hunters in Chisasibi; it is not an elders' account of past practice. Hunters' statements are written in proper English, as requested by them, revised and corrected as necessary.

Animals Control the Hunt

In Western science and its applications to fish and wildlife management, it is assumed that humans ultimately control what happens to animal populations. In Cree philosophy, by contrast, animals control the hunt. The Cree believe that animals know everything humans do, they are aware of hunters' activities. In the past all living things talked, communicated with humans. Many Cree legends carry this theme, but it is by no means a "dead" idea:

I had a fish net out in a lake and at first I was getting quite a few fish in it. But there was an otter in the lake and he was eating the fish in the net. After a while, fish stopped coming into the net. They knew there was a predator there. So similarly game know about the presence of hunters as well. The Cree say, "all creatures are watching you. They know everything you are doing. Animals are aware of your activities." In the past, animals talked to people. In a sense, there is still communication between animals and hunters. You can predict where the black bear is likely to den. Even though the black bear zigzags before retreating into his den to hibernate, tries to shake you off his trail, you can still predict where he is likely to go to. When he approaches his den entrance, he makes tracks backwards, loses his tracks in the bush, and makes a long detour before coming into the den. The hunter tries to think what the bear is thinking. Their minds touch. The hunter and the bear have parallel knowledge, and they share that knowledge. So in a sense they communicate.

A hunter always speaks as if the animals are in control of the hunt. The success of the hunt depends on the animals: the hunter is successful if the animal decides to make himself available. The hunters have no power over the game, animals have the last say as to whether they will be caught.

Hunters have to show respect to the animals. The reason for this is that the hunter is always in pursuit of game. The game is not there for the taking. There is no guarantee of a kill; the game has to be pursued. The increase in a hunter's kill, as he reaches his prime, goes hand in hand with the increase of this respect for the animals. Another way of putting this would be that he develops respect for game as he becomes a better hunter.

Young people are taught early on to show respect to the animals. If a hunter does not follow the expected practices of respect, it happens very easily that the disrespectful individual would kill nothing. For such a person, game would be scarce. Even if he sees game in the bush, something happens, something prevents him from getting the game. And this includes all animals, not just big game and fur animals, but also small game and fish. This is a fundamental belief of all hunters. A hunter never gets angry at game. If a hunter has no luck, he looks at himself for the blame, not the animals. Quite often, the animal is only returning the discourtesy. Sometimes a hunter may be unlucky for no reason, but it is rare. This is where a good hunter comes into the picture. He shares his catch with the unlucky hunter. Sometimes a hunter is disrespectful to animals without intending to be.

> My brother was trapping otter. He had left his trap in the water a bit too long; normally, one checks traps quite often. There was an otter in the trap, but it had been in the water too long. The fur was coming off. My brother was really worried: he had caused the fur to spoil, and knew that this was a crime against the animals. He said the otter would retaliate for this by not being caught. He thought it would take perhaps three years before the otter will decide to come back to his trap again.

Since hunting success ultimately depends on the willingness of animals to be caught, a hunter who is familiar with an area often has the best success. Conversely, a stranger in an area will have poor hunting success, for, as the Cree say, "the land is unfamiliar with him."

I once invited a coaster, a good hunter, to my trapline north of the LaGrande River. He was a stranger there. Even though he was a good hunter and had done nothing wrong to the animals, he did not have much luck. There is a saying "the land and game would feel unfamiliar or uneasy with you if you are a stranger there." Such a person may have poor luck at first, but later on game will get to know him.

According to Cree beliefs, the success of a hunter increases with experience, up to a peak. After this peak, a hunter's success would be expected to decline, and his sons or other hunters in the group are thought to inherit part of an older hunter's success. When an old man passes away, some younger people inherit his animals. The whole process may be considered a cycle, from a child to a hunter at his peak, to an old man. During this cycle, the amount of animals available remain constant.

> As a hunter gains experience, he becomes better and better in hunting. He reaches a peak and after that his hunting success goes down. An old man would not be expected to hunt as well as he did when he was at his peak. It is common knowledge that an old man's hunt declines. This often happens after a man reaches 50 or 60. An old hunter does not worry about his hunting success because he knows he has had his day, that he used to kill many. My uncle was a good trapper, but in his old age he did not catch many. He used to say jokingly that "the game were letting go of him." He would say that he was being ignored by game: the game were leaving him alone. He did not care to kill any. But he set traps anyway. For him, it was a way of life.

> When an old man dies, another person takes on from him. It is almost as if that the old man's game is now passed on to a younger person in that group. It is a fundamental belief of the Cree people that a young man would inherit an old man's game.

> My father used to catch lots of game. He

used to say that once his sons started to hunt, his own hunting success would go down. And in fact, so it happened. My brother, who was an exceptionally successful goose hunter when he was young, now hunts fewer geese. But his sons make up for his losses. It can be said that his four sons inherited part of his catch.

The cyclic disappearance and reappearance of game animals is also related to the willingness of animals to be hunted. The Cree believe that almost all animals go up and down in abundance, some in shorter cycles and some in longer cycles. For Chisasibi hunters, animals known to disappear and reappear include:

* The caribou which disappeared around the turn of the century and reappeared in the 1980s,
* The beaver which were scarce in the area between about 1930 and 1950, and increased thereafter,
* The marten which declined twice since the turn of the century. In the 1980s it was very scarce in the inland traplines. However, in the coastal traplines it began to reappear in 1982-83.
* The porcupine which were last plentiful in 1960-70, and declined in the 1970s,
* The small game animals, snowshoe hares, rock and willow ptarmigan, spruce and sharp-tailed grouse, and known to have eight to ten year cycles, from one peak of abundance to the next.

While the shorter of these cycles are recognized by Western science, longer cycles such as those of the caribou are not. It is believed that management or lack thereof is responsible for the increase or decrease of caribou. By contrast, the Cree believe that animals which disappear for a time, sooner or later come back by themselves, not as a consequence of management by humans. Disappearing animals such as caribou and marten are said to go under the water or underground. This is thought to be something similar to the "disappearance" of animals such as ptarmigan, fox, lynx, and snowshoe hares in very cold weather. The belief in the return of disappearing animals is very strong:

My uncle who would have been about 90 in 1984 missed the caribou. By the time he was old enough to hunt, caribou had already declined. An old man told him not to worry, the caribou would be back some day. And they are back now. Sometimes my uncle did not believe the old men. He asked them, "Where do they go when they disappear?" They answered that it has been known in the past that caribou disappear under the water. There would come a time when they would reappear later. He was at first amazed to hear this, but believed it later on. He came to know that all the animals you see, porcupine, fur animals and others, disappeared from time to time. In his early hunting days, marten were plentiful. He saw them decline and later come back again, all in his lifetime.

He was hunting. He came to a little pond. There were fresh caribou tracks on the new snow. The tracks were leading into the lake. He walked across to the other side of the lake; he thought caribou had swum across. But here were no caribou tracks on the other side. Caribou had submerged. When he went back to the camp, the older men said, "Yes this is how big game and fur animals disappear. But they will someday come back again."

A young trapper was checking his muskrat traps in the Sakami River area. He found one of his traps had sprung underwater. He thought it was a muskrat because there was a muskrat den nearby. But instead, he found a marten in his trap. There were no marten tracks in the area; he must have come up under the water. The young trapper was scared. He thought it was unnatural, a bad omen. He returned to the camp. The old men reassured him. They said it was not a bad sign, but marten lived under the water, too. I have seen marten tracks coming out of a fish net hole in the ice. The tracks went out of the lake, around a clump of trees, as if the marten was looking for other martens, and back to the lake and into the hole again.

Obligations of the Hunters

Since animals control the hunt, lack of respect of the animals will affect hunting success — because animals can retaliate by "returning the discourtesy." The Cree say that the main reason for showing respect to animals is that man and animals are related, they share the same creator. Just as one respects other persons, one respects animals.

Respect for the animal is shown in the way:
(1) the hunter maintains an attitude of humility when going hunting,
(2) the animal is approached and killed,
(3) the animal is carried to camp,
(4) offerings are made to the animal,
(5) the meat is butchered and distributed,
(6) the meat is consumed,
(7) the remains of the animal are disposed of properly.

Hunters should not boast about their abilities. Otherwise, they risk catching nothing because they are being disrespectful of game.

While fishing with a group of people to the south of my area on the James Bay coast, I once boasted that I could catch as many trout as anyone else. It was a good area for speckled trout, and the fishermen were pulling out some 50-60 fish in each of their nets. My net was in the middle of all the other nets. But when I pulled it out, there was only one trout in it. In similar ways, many people have experienced a loss of hunting success after boasting.

Hunters should not laugh at or otherwise make fun of game, as again this will affect their hunt.

The hunter had a cord which he used for carrying black bear. But on this one hunt, he left his cord behind in the camp, laughing and boasting that he could carry any black bear without the cord. He did in fact kill a black bear on that trip. But he found out that he was not able to carry it. The moral of the story is that whatever fun you make of a black this will backfire on you.

The hunter should maintain an attitude of respect when approaching to kill game. The killing will be done quickly and simply, without mess. Hunters use a gun appropriate for the size of the animal. For example, a small bore gun is used for the smaller animals. A hunter wants an animal to look at his best. One does not want blood all over the place. If a hunter used an oversized gun and blew off the head of a beaver, this would be disapproved of.

The Cree see a great deal of similarity between social relations among humans and those among humans and animals, especially those animals which are considered particularly powerful and worthy of respect.

When a hunter visits a camp, he lets it be known that he is a visitor (*maantaau*), a person from another camp. He approaches respectfully and modestly; he announces himself simply, (*nitikushin*) "I am here." People in the camp come out to greet him as soon as they hear him. When they come out, he has already taken his snowshoes off and put them upright in the snow. People in the camp admire his snowshoes. They say, "these are beautiful snowshoes," they admire the craftsmanship, the good material and design. They note that he is a successful, able hunter.

When a hunter approaches a black bear den in winter, he does not make an exhibition of himself. He announces himself simply and with humility: "I am here." ... There is similarity between the hunter announcing himself at the camp, and the hunter announcing himself at the bear's den. The hunter shows as much respect to the bear as he shows to people. It is almost as if he is arriving at the den as a visitor, hoping that the bear will accept him.

With every animal, the first thing after killing it is to check the fat content. This is hunter's "quality control" of the game: more fat the better for it shows a healthy animal. With a goose, one pinches the fat layer under the skin (the subcutaneous fat) after removing a handful of feathers from the belly. With a black bear, one cuts the skin in front of the chest, just over the breast bone to check the fat.

There are proper ways of carrying game. For example, a beaver is normally dragged on its back in the snow. A stick is placed through the nose and a cord is attached to it. However, if there is ice stuck on the back fur, then the hands would be tied, the animal flipped over and dragged on its tummy. Similarly, there are ways to carry geese (tied by the necks and draped over the shoulders of the hunter).

With black bears, two people can carry a bear with a pole, with the bear's limbs tied. Or a hunter can carry a bear on his back, paws over the shoulder, legs held under the hunter's arms, like a child, and the limbs tied in front over the hunter's chest.

> Carrying a bear can have symbolic significance for the hunter. My friend and I killed a black bear. My friend gave me the bear. I tried to carry the bear but it was very heavy. I tried to lift it, but I tumbled and fell down. My friend said, "Now it is really yours." The point is that the human hunter is not all-powerful. Even though I tried hard, the bear prevailed over me. This way, I really earned the bear. It was now truly mine.

In the past, offerings were made to all animals including even fish. At present, offerings are made only to the more powerful animals such as black bears. A hunter who makes an offering to animals and to old men is, in effect, asking them to give him game. In the practice of Cree hunters of Chisasibi, offerings are made with tobacco and with pieces of meat thrown into the fire.

> Offerings made to an animal indicates respect. It also means that the hunters are asking the animal to provide game for them. Similarly, offerings can be made to dead men. Offerings to old men in their graves are fairly common, sometimes even to not very old men, and occasionally to women, too. There was a

respected old man who died on the point of a particular lake. He was buried there. When people went by his grave, they would make an offering to him. They rolled tobacco in tree bark and left it there. They were asking the old man to provide game for them in return for the tobacco.

A black bear is brought into camp. Hunters sit in a circle, with the bear in the middle. Someone smokes a pipe beside the bear and makes a gesture of offering the pipe to the bear. Or a piece of tobacco is placed in the bear's mouth as an offering. Once the bear is skinned, a piece of the meat is thrown into the fire. These offerings mean that the hunters are thanking the Provider.

Respect for animals is shown also in the way meat is butchered and distributed. There are special ways to cut every kind of animal, and for different uses of the animal's meat. For example, a loon is butchered differently from a goose. The pattern of cut will be different if a whitefish is going to be smoked as opposed to one that is going to be fresh boiled.

Some of the methods of cutting and preparation are related to showing respect for the animals. For example, when dismembering a goose, women are supposed to cut the wing off the body (and not break it off). Otherwise, it is said, the husband's luck in the goose hunt will be affected. In butchering a black bear, first the men cut the patterns on the bear; after that, the women skin the bear; and finally, men cut the limbs. There are special cutting patterns especially for the big game.

The owner of the game, say a black bear, decides as he cuts it, on how to distribute the meat among the families sharing the camp. He may keep the skin for the fur, and may give portions of the meat to others to distribute further. The first hunter may give the bear to a second hunter, and the second hunter may decide to pass the meat to a third owner. Commonly, a young hunter would give the meat to one of the old men or old women in the camp, who would do the honours in distributing it. Especially with big game animals, the custom was that an elder would distribute the food, thus showing respect for the animal.

Respect is also shown with the consumption of the game. The major principle is that everything is consumed and there is no wastage. A trapper says, "We are done for as a hunting society if we ever reach the point of taking only the haunch of a moose or caribou, as white hunters do."

Traditional Cree cooking uses all parts of the animals, for example:

•   goose feet, necks and head are eaten; goose fat is rendered or boiled down for later use,

•   goose intestines, heart, liver, gizzard may be cooked separately from the goose, for example, as lunch for the hunters,

•   seal intestines stuffed with seal blubber is a delicacy for some coastal people; seal flippers may be cooked separately,

•   fish heads are boiled, fish internal organs including liver, eggs, intestines (but excluding stomach contents and gall bladder) are fried,

•   fish bones are eaten, pounded into *pimihkaan* (fish pemmican),

•   blood is used in blood pudding and stews; this is a delicacy,

•   ptarmigan heads and feet are stewed,

•   however, there are certain parts of animals which are *not* eaten. For example, caribou brains are not consumed (but used in tanning skins); polar bear liver is not consumed because it is poisonous (due to the extremely high content of vitamin A).

It is said that the whiskey jack hovers about camps, checking to see that nothing is wasted. In the case of some animals, respect is shown by consuming the meat only in the camp. For example, black bear meat is eaten only in the camp; one is not allowed to take bear meat as lunch when checking traps. Similarly, lynx is shown respect by consuming the meat within the camp.

It is important that everythin killed is eaten. Killing for fi "recreation" or "sport" without eating it) is transgression. What one kills, one keeps for eating. Young boys who kill small animals when they are learning to hunt, make a gift of these animals to an old woman who prepares them; the food will then be consumed by the old woman, the boy or the whole family.

After the edible parts are eaten, hunters show respect for the animals by taking proper care of the bones and other remains. The following are hung on trees or placed on top of wooden platforms: all black bear bones, all skulls (including beaver, lynx, porcupine, muskrat, marten, otter, mink). The following are returned to water because they are water animals: bones of beaver, otter, mink. There are no general rules for the disposal of the bones of waterfowl species, but some hunters hang the throats (trachea) of geese on trees or camp posts.

Traditionally, a person eating fish collected the jawbones. After a while, he would string them and hang them on trees. Dogs are fed on fish, guts of beaver and, on the coast, seals and beluga whales. Dogs would not be allowed to eat black bear, beaver and porcupine meat or bones. Other animal remains, including fish remains, would be buried. Another recommended way of disposing of fish remains is to collect them and place them where scavenger birds can get at them. Caribou remains are burned. Sick or unhealthy animals are not consumed; the carcass would be burned.

Campsites should be left tidy and clean. All garbage would be cleaned up and burned before breaking camp. Traditionally, the only waste in the camp consisted of animal remains, bones and wood which are natural materials that easily go back to nature. Today, however, there is also plastic, metal cans, glass and paper which create a disposal problem in campsites. Good hunters take special care to burn and/or bury these materials also, so that the young generations will inherit a clean environment.

The Importance of Continued Use for Sustainability

It is the animals who control the success of the

hunt, and hunters have certain obligations to fulfill towards the animals; in addition, hunters believe that a continued use is important to achieve a sustainable, productive harvest:

> A tallyman takes care of a trapline so that the beaver continue to be productive. Taking care of a trapline means not killing too many. A trapper paces himself, killing what he needs, and what can be prepared by the women, so that there is no wastage of meat and fur, and respect for the animals is maintained. He should also make sure that the area is rested (by rotating the sectors of the hunted area). Normally a trapper should rest parts of his trapline for two or three years but no longer than four years. If he leaves it, say, six or ten years, he is not properly using his area, and the beaver will not be plentiful.

The concept of resting the hunting area is fairly well known. Many (but not all) Cree trappers, including those in Chisasibi and Waswanipi investigated by Feit (1978), divide their area into three or four units. They trap only one unit at a time, and rotate the land as in fallowing in agriculture. Feit (1986) has shown that the harvest from an area rested for two years or more is significantly greater than that from an area harvested with no rest. Over-use leads to a drop in productivity, but so does under-use.

> In an area which has not been trapped for a long time, there will be many empty lodges. This may be due to disease because of overcrowding; it may be due to beavers depleting their food supplies. The trapper knows that in an area which has not been trapped for a long time, various types of beaver food, such as aspen, would be in low supply. If there has been a fire, this also affects the beaver. Trappers know that three or four years after a fire the beaver will again begin to inhabit the area. At first, however, they would be eating more of the root foods. The trapper may resume trapping again when the willows are half grown. This may be some eight to ten years after a fire.

The Cree notion of the importance of continued use is superficially similar to that in Western science, but it probably has different philosophical roots. "Continued use" is not an obligation, in the sense of the previous section; it is simply "good management," consistent with the ideas of renewability and animal cycles. The principle that animals control the hunt takes precedence over the principle of continued use:

> From the new camp, he set out the next day with his traps. He was lucky to find beaver lodges, four or five of them, and he was quite happy about that. He sent his son to go even further east the next day. The son checked the traps set the previous day and brought in the beaver. The next day after that, the son checked the last set of traps but had no luck They waited several days and checked again: still no beaver. He took the traps out, "let them be, they will increase for the next time," he said. He was not catching anything there and there was a meaning to that. The beaver did not want to be caught yet. Next fall, he would come back to this area, and maybe then the beaver would be ready to be caught.

The principle of continued use has to be tempered also with common sense and good management. Beaver, as well as some of the other animals, can be depleted by over-hunting. Unrestrained exploitation violates the principle of respect and results in "doing wrong" to the game.

> The tallyman went to trap a part of his trapline. He had not been there for several years, but he had given permission to another group to trap it a few years previously. These people had reported plenty of beaver at that time. But the trapper knew that there would not be many beaver in that area because these other people had killed too many. He knew this because when these people returned to the village that year, their furs had not been prepared properly. Many of the furs had to be thrown out. They had killed indiscriminately —

young, old, every animal. Some of the beaver even may have been trapped out of season. The trapper visited, one after another, lakes and ponds which he knew to be good beaver lakes. There were beaver signs, but these were old signs from before that group's visit. Beaver had declined, had not produced because those trappers had not taken care of that spot. They had done wrong to the game. In such cases, game retaliates. Leave nothing behind — and it affects the later hunt. Bad management has repercussions for later years.

The general principle is that "animals are killed but not diminished" (Feit 1986), as also noted by Tanner (1979). But is this in the sense of "ecologically sustainable use" or reincarnation of a "constant supply," so to speak, of animals? Is there any accounting by numbers? Brightman (1987) has argued that the concept of game depletion by overhunting is not aboriginal but represents the influence of Western game management practice. The present study, not being historical, can neither support nor refute Brightman. In contrast to some other groups of Cree hunters, for example, those in Northern Manitoba (Brightman 1987) and those of the Waswanipi Band (Feit 1986), the Chisasibi Cree do not at present seem to have a notion of reincarnation of animals.

One point is clear, however, in hunter-nature relationships. The killing of game is not considered to be a violent act. The hunter loves the animals he kills and eats; after all, they can only be hunted if they agree to be hunted. The Cree have difficulty with the Western idea that hunting involves suffering on the part of the animals, that killing is equated with violence, and that the best conservation (as some would argue) means leaving the game alone. To the Cree, if the game want to be left alone, they would let the hunters know. Otherwise, the proper conservation of game does include the hunting and eating of game.

Discussion

The ability to use resources in a sustainable manner stems from a combination of two factors: local ecological knowledge and methods/technology to exploit resources, and a philosophy and environmental ethic to keep exploitive abilities in check. The two factors probably go together, in some kind of balance. Suitable social organization and political institutions that allow appropriate ecological practices such as territoriality in hunting are also obviously important (Berkes 1987).

The environmental knowledge of the Cree has already been documented in some detail by Feit (1973; 1986; 1987) for moose and beaver, by Berkes (1977; 1987) for fish and by Scott (1983; in press) for geese. The task in this paper is to concentrate on the second factor, the environmental ethic of the Cree. In this regard, three questions come to mind:

(1) Do the Cree have an environmental ethic, a philosophy which is distinct and different from the one(s) in Euro-Canadian society?
(2) Is the Cree environmental ethic still in existence as a viable set of beliefs after several centuries of fur trade and recent cultural change?
(3) Is this philosophy which apparently serves the sustainable utilization of resources, designed in the first place to do so?

The answer to the first question is a definite "yes." Not only the material in this paper but also the extensive work of Tanner (1979) Feit (1978) and Scott (1983) show that Cree philosophy with regard to animals is indeed distinctively different from that of Western society. This is not to say that the Cree environmental ethic is unique among the numerous cultures in the world. Cree beliefs probably share much common ground with other hunting and fishing cultures and with pantheistic/animistic traditions in general. Cree beliefs are also consistent with some interpretations of Christianity, for example, the Christian mysticism of St. Francis. Elsewhere, I have presented evidence to suggest that the Cree have developed their own Christian theology, one which permitted a belief in animal spirits and allowed them to talk to animals. St. Francis would have probably been quite comfortable with this; many of the missionaries who served in the James Bay area were not (Berkes 1986).

The second question is more difficult to answer. There is little doubt that there has been great cultural change in Cree communities, as elsewhere in the Canadian North. Cree culture has not survived intact, but it has survived. It would be almost impossible to determine how much of the original Cree philosophy (and Cree culture in general) has been lost. The concept of reincarnation, for example, may have fallen into disuse among the Chisasibi Cree. Nevertheless, the material quoted above still represents the working environmental ethic of the recognized community leaders among hunters. However, Cree leaders themselves would be the first to admit that the system is under stress, and violations of the ethic are frequent and widespread, tendencies which the leaders have been battling against for years.

The third question is also difficult to answer, and a detailed discussion of it is outside the scope of this paper. Suffice to say that Cree knowledge and ethics are aimed at the continued success of the hunt, and this is compatible with the sustainable use of resources. To the extent that the Cree take a *long-term* view of resource sustainability, their philosophy serves the purposes of conservation. The leaders among the hunters, and those sophisticated in hunting and in Cree culture in general, recognize this to be so. The Cree do not make a distinction between "economic" objectives of conservation (food, furs), and "biological" objectives (the maintenance of animal populations). Untutored in Western reductionistic science, the Cree consider these objectives to be one and the same. Note that this view parallels the concept of conservation in the World Conservation Strategy (1980): the objective of long-term ecological sustainability is one and the same with the objective of obtaining long-term economic benefits from the resource.

The three principles discussed in this paper (control the hunt by the animals, obligations of hunters towards animals, and the importance of continued use for sustainable harvests) do not cover all aspects of Cree environmental philosophy. These three principles were selected for discussion here so that certain points can be made, given that Cree environmental philosophy is distinctively different from the Western one, that it is still alive, and that it is compatible with sustainable resource use practices. These points may be summarized as follows:

(1) Cosmology of the Chisasibi Cree, their view of the world and the universe, at least the living universe inhabited by animals, is different from that of the dominant society. That is, not only are the Cree views and values of nature different, the source of these values is also different.

(2) Relations with animals parallel social relations, one does not just go and kill a black bear in the den; one approaches the den as a guest and one talks to the bear. Just as there are reciprocal social obligations, especially those involved with the sharing of food, there are reciprocal obligations between hunters and animals. Hunters' relations with nature are intertwined with social obligations, so that their environmental ethic is an integral part of a comprehensive philosophy of life.

(3) Unlike the people of Western cultures, the self-identity of the Cree is *not* distinct from the world around them, in reference to Everenden's (1985) "natural aliens." The intimate role of the natural world and natural events in the self-identity of the Cree is well known (e.g., Preston 1975).

(4) The traditional ecological knowledge of the Cree is *empirical* knowledge, as in the observations of the "disappearance of animals in extremely cold weather, the way black bears try to cover their tracks before denning, the sensing and the avoidance of (predatory) otters by the fish. However, the "sense" the Cree make of empirical knowledge is not scientific, mechanistic or analytic (re: Skolimowski 1981). That is not to say that the Cree approach is either superior or inferior to the Western scientific one, but it is different. For example, it leads to the conclusion that caribou have extremely long population cycles and that they would eventually come back, provided they are not offended by a show of lack of respect. Unscientific as it would no doubt seem to caribou biologists, the Cree model of caribou

cycles shows a better fit with the actual caribou population dynamics in Quebec-Ungava Peninsula than does the current scientific model.

(5) Unlike Western environmental values, those of the Cree are based on humanistic notions (Skolimowski 1981). Humanistic because "animals are like persons" (Feit 1986); they are intelligent beings and have powers to reason. They no longer talk to humans as they once did, but they still do communicate, as in the story of the hunter who is trying to think like a bear.

(6) Unlike Western environmental values, those of the Cree are based on morality toward nature (Skolimowski 1981). As with most if not all pantheistic/animistic tradition, one makes offerings, follows prescribed rituals, and generally placates spirits. Note White's (1967) observation: "In antiquity every tree, every spring, every stream, every hill had its own *genius loci*, its guardian spirit. . . Before one cut a tree, mined a mountain, or dammed a brook, it was important to placate the spirit in charge. . . By destroying pagan animism, Christianity made it possible to exploit nature in a mood of indifference to the feelings of natural objects."

(7) The Cree have an environmental ethic to keep exploitive abilities in check. Not only are there prescriptions for appropriate behaviour to show respect to animals, but restraint in harvesting is also built into the traditional management system, for example, in reference to the passage on the overhunting of beaver. Other examples of restraints in hunting and fishing practice are detailed elsewhere (Feit 1973, 1978, 1986; Berkes 1977, 1982, in press). This point is important in view of the controversial claim by some resource managers that Northern Native peoples have *no* tradition of restraint of harvesting effort (for an evaluation of the controversy, see Usher 1982; Feit 1984).

(8) To the Cree, animals are important as food, but they are not merely objects to be harvested. There is a large cultural complex involving animals; they have a role in social relations, legends and other elements of Cree culture, indicating that animals have intrinsic value. The respected older hunter who jokes that the "game were letting go of him" bring to mind Naess' (1986) hypothesis that "the attainment of well-rounded human maturity leads to *identification with all life forms* in a wide sense of 'life' and including the acknowledgement of the intrinsic value of these forms." For the Cree, the animals do have equal rights, but the human right to obtain food does *not* diminish the right of animals to exist — animals are killed but not diminished.

To follow Naess' reasoning further, a phrase such as "animals are killed but not diminished" is not scientific, but the context is such that the distinction between "scientific" and "unscientific" is irrelevant. The expression may be introduced into a scientific text by using the terminology of ecosystems and concepts of renewability and sustained yields.

I would like to conclude by relating this last point to two kinds of current issues in the real world, the first dealing with animal rights arguments, and the second, with sustainable use of resources and the ecosystem approach.

To the Cree and to many other groups of hunting-trapping people, it is bad enough that the animal rights movement is a threat to their already precarious way of life and subsistence economy; worse, it is also Western ethnocentric and misdirected. It is doubtful that urban-based Westerners have much to teach the Cree about the proper treatment of animals. But furthermore, as Herscovici (1985, p. 208) pointed out, "one of the most unfortunate aspects of the animal rights movement is that it unconsciously serves the interest of the mining, oil and gas and hydroelectric industries, which would like nothing better than to clear traditional hunters and trappers from the land."

For environmentalists who are concerned with the ecologically sustainable use of resources and the implementation of the ecosystem approach, the philosophy of the Cree is extremely interesting as a living, here-and-now alternative to the current Western view of nature. The hunting cultures of Northern Native peoples are part of the global heritage of all humankind.

They are part of our cultural diversity from which a new and environmentally appropriate ethic of nature may be forged. The renewed emphasis on traditional ecological knowledge and traditional management institutions, as detailed earlier, is part of this search for alternatives. In this context, the Cree concepts of renewability and sustained use are obviously important. So are the Cree principles of obligations and humility, and the linking of humanistic notions and morality toward nature — a synthesis of natural and human ecosystems which some of us refer to as the ecosystem approach.

References

Berkes, F.
1977   Fishery resource use in a subarctic Indian community. Human Ecology 5: 289-307.
1982   Waterfowl management and northern Native peoples with reference to Cree hunters of James Bay. Musk-Ox 30: 23-35.
1986   Chisasibi Cree hunters and missionaries: Humour as evidence of tension. Papers of the Seventeenth Algonquian Conference, pp. 15-26.
In press Common property resources and hunting territories. Anthropologica.
1987   Common property resource management and Cree Indian fisheries in subarctic Canada. In The Question of the Commons. B.J. McCay and J.M. Acheson, eds. pp. 66-91. Tucson: University of Arizona Press.

Brightman, R.A.
1987   Conservation and resource depletion: The case of the boreal forest Algonquians. In The Question of the Commons. B.J. McCay and J.M. Acheson, eds. pp. 121-141. Tucson: University of Arizona Press.

Dubos, R.
1972   A God Within. New York: Scribners.

Everenden, N.
1985   The natural Alien. Toronto: University of Toronto Press.

Feit, H.A.
1973   The ethno-ecology of the Waswanipi Cree; or how hunters can manage their resources. In Cultural Ecology. B. Cox, ed. Toronto: McClelland and Stewart.
1978   Waswanipi realities and adaptations. Resource management and cognitive structure. Ph.D. Thesis, McGill University, Montreal.
1984   Conflict arenas in the management of renewable resources in the Canadian North: Perspectives based on conflicts and responses in the James Bay region, Quebec. In National and Regional Interests in the North. pp. 435-458. Ottawa: Canadian Arctic Resources Committee.
1986   James Bay Cree Indian management and moral consideration of fur-bearers. In Native People and Renewable Resource Management. pp. 49-65. Edmonton: Alberta Society of Professional Biologists.
1987   North American Native hunting and management of moose populations. Swedish Wildlife Research, Supplement 1:25-42.

Herscovici, A.
1985   Second Nature. The Animal Rights Controversy. Montreal: CBC Enterprises.

Johannes, R.E.
1981   Words of the Lagoon: Fishing and Marine Lore in the Palau District of Micronesia. Berkeley: University of California Press.

Lasserre, P. and K. Ruddle
1983   Traditional knowledge and management of marine coastal systems. Biology International, Special Issue 4. Paris: International Union of Biological Sciences.

McCay B.J. and J.M. Acheson (editors)
1987   The Question of the Commons. Tucson: University of Arizona Press.

McNeely, J.A. and D. Pitt (editors)
1985   Culture and Conservation. London: Croom Helm.

National Research Council
1986   Common Property Resource Management. Proceedings of a Conference. National Academy of Science Press, Washington, D.C.

Naess, A.
1986   Intrinsic value: Will the defenders of
        nature please rise? *In* Conservation
        Biology. M.E. Soulé, ed. pp. 504-515.
        Sunderland: Sinauer.

Pepper, D.M.
1984   The Roots of Modern Environmental-
        ism. London: Croom Helm.

Preston, R.J.
1975   Cree narration: Expressing the personal
        meaning of events. National Museum of
        Man, Mercury Series, Paper No. 30,
        Ottawa.

Ruddle, K. and R. E. Johannes (editors)
1985   The Traditional Knowledge and Man-
        agement of Coastal Systems in Asia and
        the Pacific. Jakarta: UNESCO.

Scott, C.
1983   The semiotics of material life among
        Wemindji Cree hunters. Ph.D. Thesis,
        McGill University, Montreal.
In press Hunting territories, hunting bosses and
        communal production in coastal James
        Bay Cree hunting. Anthropologica.

Skolimowski, H.
1981   Eco-Philosophy. London: Boyars.

Tanner, A.
1979   Bringing Home Animals. London:
        Hurst.

Toynbee, A.
1972   The religious background of the present
        environmental crisis. A viewpoint.
        International Journal of Environmental
        Studies 3: 141-146.

Usher, P.
1982   Fair game? Nature Canada 11(1): 5-11,
        35-43

Watanabe, M.
1974   The conception of nature in Japanese
        culture. Science 193: 279-282.

White, L.
1967   The historical roots of our ecologic crisis.
        Science 155: 1203-1207.

World Conservation Strategy
1980   IUCN/UNEP/WWF, Morges.

The Contribution of the Ecological Knowledge of Inuit to Wildlife Management in the Northwest Territories

Anne Gunn, Goo Arlooktoo and David Kaomayok
Department of Renewable Resources
Government of Northwest Territories
Coppermine, NWT

Knowledge of wildlife is integral to the Inuit culture which is still essentially a hunting culture that has depended on Arctic wildlife for three thousand years. Scientific knowledge of Arctic wildlife has a time depth of about two hundred years, though scientists can draw on extensive ecological knowledge gathered elsewhere. Science has developed in a culture many generations removed from its hunter origin and, thus brings its own particular perspective to the study of Arctic wildlife. Over the last one to two centuries, historical events brought the two cultures together with far-reaching consequences for wildlife and those dependent upon it. The fur-trade, with its introduction of improved hunting technology and its incessant demand for fur, encouraged intensive harvesting of animals. The effect of those developments were aggravated by other cultural changes, such as the replacement of indigenous religions, which formerly had influenced hunting practices.

In many areas, wildlife resources were depleted by the 1950s: biologists and administrators urged conservation practices onto hunters already struggling to cope with a radically different way of life after moving to the settlements. The initial concurrence with hunting regulations (the rationale of many of which was incomprehensible to the hunters) masked misunderstanding and resentment. Those feelings were compounded by the failure to consult with and to integrate hunters' knowledge in wildlife management decisions (e.g., Freeman 1985) even although the scientific basis for those decisions was in its infancy. By the 1980s, increases in the availability of most wildlife in the NWT have engendered less confrontational and less polarized positions between hunters and biologists. The resulting more cooperative approach, set in the context of greater political influence of hunters, leads to an exchange of knowledge between biologists and hunters.

Few people who have travelled with members of a hunting culture doubt the observational powers of hunters and their perceptive sensitivity to their environment (for example, Nelson 1969, Van der Post and Taylor 1985). Competent biologists also owe their standing to long hours of observing and personal experiences with wildlife: a point sometimes conceded to by hunters who can readily detect from conversations whether a biologist has intensive firsthand knowledge. Authors such as Laughlin (1968), Nelson (1969), Brody (1975), Freeman (1979), Lopez (1986), and Nakashima (1986) have characterized Inuit wildlife knowledge. Still others have contrasted European-derived scientific knowledge with indigenous hunter knowledge (e.g., Freeman 1985, Usher 1986).

This paper reflects our different backgrounds and experiences as Inuit hunter and wildlife biologist in the Northwest Territories. We have structured our discussion of the integration of Inuit hunters' and biologists' understanding of wildlife by considering "knowledge" as having three components: (1) observations, (2) organization of observations and (3) action based on observation (i.e., conservation or management as the end product of wildlife knowledge). In each of the three sections we discuss examples which illustrate the contributions to and limitations of the two approaches to wildlife management.

1. Inuit and Biologists' Observations of Wildlife

Hunters live with the wildlife in the same habitat: acute and accurate observations make the difference between hunting success or failure not to mention safety and ease of travelling. Wildlife and landscape are also, in a sense, a source of entertainment as hunters pass away the hours discussing wildlife, the land and hunting.

Hunters are cognizant of the wildlife use of specific areas by different wildlife species usually but not necessarily in association with hunting. For example, sites traditionally used by polar bears (*Ursus maritimus*) for winter denning are known as places where bears can be hunted when they emerge in late winter. Those same sites were also regarded as food reserves in earlier times. If hunting was poor and starvation threatened, a trip to a bear denning area was almost always successful as a denned bear was a relatively easy kill once a hunter had located the blown-over mound of snow dug out by a denning bear. Long acquaintance with those places and observation of the effects of annual variations in snowfall led to predictions of whether it was worth a hunting trip to the area. Shallow snow and strong winds in fall may prevent snow accumulating in drifts deep enough to accommodate a hibernating bear. One of us (D.K.) predicted in early winter 1985 that snow drifts were too shallow for polar bears to den on Gateshead Island, off the east coast of Victoria Island — usually a high density denning area. This prediction was confirmed by a survey in March 1986. The observations of traditional maternal denning areas has proved to be a significant contribution by hunters to polar bear management. The identification of denning areas is of paramount importance in preparing for nonrenewable resource development (e.g., Stirling 1986). In fact, the aforementioned Gateshead Island has been designated a Special Management Area in recognition of its

importance as a polar bear denning area, which was first identified by local hunters.

Observations of animal behaviour are often detailed and frequently related to hunting. The concept of leadership in caribou (*Rangifer tarandus*) was used while spearing caribou at water-crossings: conspicuous human activity had to be concealed until the lead caribou had swum across so the rest of the caribou group would try to follow their leader and cross in spite of the sudden appearance of hunters (Arima 1975). Contemporary hunting by snowmachine and rifle on occasion can be made more successful by identification of the lead caribou: if the leader is taken first, the remainder of the group will mill uncertainly around and allow further shooting opportunities.

Observation of wildlife's use of area is not restricted to those species normally utilized. For example, nesting sites of birds-of-prey such as eagles and falcons are often known, and there is also an awareness of behavioural interactions such as Gyrfalcons (*Falco rusticolus*) usurping Raven (*Corvus corax*) nests. Those observations formed the basis for cooperative studies of Gyrfalcons undertaken by the Baffin Regional Inuit Association when Inuit hunters carried out the basic field work to locate and monitor Gyrfalcon nest sites (Bromley 1983). The knowledge of species not utilized may be extraordinarily detailed and extend to rare species. The Ivory Gull (*Pagophila eburna*) is a rare visitor to Cambridge Bay for example, but one of us (D.K.) not only recognizes it but also the stages of juvenile plumage.

Inuit hunters from Alaska (Nelson 1969), Victoria Island and throughout the Eastern Canadian Arctic (Freeman 1984; G. Williams, I. Stirling pers. comm. and D.K.) have reported walruses (*Odobenus rosmarus*) killing and eating ringed seals (*Phoca hispida*). Hunters dislike walruses hunting seals, not only because walruses will scare seals away but there is the danger that walruses will aggressively stalk hunters along the floe-edge (G. Williams personal communication). The observations documenting the walrus as a predator of seals illustrate the ability of hunters to relate wildlife behaviour to changes in the habitat. In Lancaster

Sound, when the thickness of the landfast ice exceeds about 50 cm., walruses can no longer maintain breathing holes and they shift to open water or moving ice. If the water is too deep to dive or too rocky for clams, some male walruses, especially older males, will hunt seals and those walruses can be recognized by their yellow-blubber stained tusks. One of us (D.K.) was able to recognize a walrus successfully hunting seals by the seal oil slick calming the choppy sea around the walrus. The walrus used its tusks to stab the seal grasped between walrus's long and maneuverable fore flippers.

Much knowledge of wildlife is acquired during the butchery of harvested animals. The detailed knowledge of anatomy includes observations of, for example, the different consistencies of the body fat and marrow fat of caribou, the appearance of pelage to interpret body condition and seasonal changes in the mineralization of bones. Frequently, biologists have independently made these same observations: in fact when it comes to anatomy and physiology, biologists and hunters make many similar observations though interpretations may differ. One of us (D.K.) believes that polar bears use their thin sheet of scapular subcutaneous muscle to help twitch the hide to shake off water but biologists allocate a role of heat dispersal to that muscle though the same muscle could serve both functions (I. Stirling personal communication).

The extensive travel of hunters during winter months leads to observations of behaviour not paralleled by biologists whose winter observations of arctic wildlife are often lacking. For example, in the Central Arctic, Arctic hares (*Lepus arcticus*) take refuge on the sea-ice along some coastal areas with few boulders or rocks as cover: the hares shelter in the wind-scooped hollows around chunks of grounded sea-ice, and move back to the shoreline at night to feed. Ptarmigan (*Lagopus* spp) also shelter in the rough ice areas and Snowy Owls (*Nyctea scandiaca*) have learned to hunt for ptarmigan in those areas.

Another hitherto unreported aspect of winter ecology is the observation that adult arctic foxes (*Alopex lagopus*) with sufficient body fat reserves shelter in snow burrows in December and January, while subadult foxes have to continue searching for food and are thus more likely to be taken in traps. Likewise, J. Tikhak's report of wolverine (*Gulo gulo*) breaking into birth lairs to take seal pups in Bathurst Inlet is unrecorded in the biological literature.

Many hunters' observations contribute to wildlife ecology and to our understanding of wildlife distribution and relative abundance. The passing on of observations of wildlife in particular areas over generations is an incomparable reservoir of knowledge of annual patterns in wildlife distribution and migration routes (e.g., Freeman 1976, Nakashima 1986). The arctic ecosystem is characterized by annual variations in the abundance and distribution of wildlife — a single or two seasons' observations can be misleading. The observations of hunters can be a valuable guide to some of those longer-term changes in wildlife distribution and behaviour. Hunters do not however usually have observations on wildlife that migrates to a different area or uses habitats inaccessible to them such as below the ice surface (Stefansson 1921). Biologists have the advantage of greater technological resources, and can observe wildlife over large areas or beneath the ice or water.

Hunters' contributions to ecology are sometimes ignored because they fall outside the biologist's first hand experience, or the incredibility of the explanation is allowed to bias belief in the fact. Across the Arctic, there is a pervasive belief by hunters in two types of polar bear. The "weasel" bear has longer limbs and a slimmer head compared to the more common type — a shorter, more rounded bear. In the Eastern Arctic, mythology enters the picture to describe a bear type that is exceptionally large and strong. One of us (D.K.) has seen both types of bear though his observations have not yet been paralleled by biologists. Nevertheless, as others such as Nelson (1969) have noted, observations are rarely wrong even if the interpretations may be.

Freeman (1985) described the divergence of scientific knowledge from hunters' knowledge at the point of whether the observations were qualitative or quantitative. Hunters' knowledge is primarily based on qualitative observations because there is no need for them to absolutely quantify their observations. That is not to say, however, that hunters do not have a relative idea of the frequency or some other measure of an observation. Scientific knowledge is not based only on quantitative observations though they tend to dominate. Qualitative observations have a different role but, nevertheless, do contribute to scientific knowledge. We suggest that the divergence of hunters' knowledge from scientific knowledge is not in the type of observation (quantitative vs. qualitative) but in the organization of the observations and the physical recording of them which for the scientist usually has to be sufficiently detailed to be repeatable or comparable.

2. Organization of Observations

Inuit hunters rarely question observations related by others and do not always ascribe more importance to multiple than single observations: both those characteristics are vital in small social groups and in preparing a hunter for even rare contingencies (e.g., Nelson 1969). The same characteristics are, however, the antithesis of science: science is the stepwise attainment of knowledge based on questioning of observations to fit them into or modify the pattern formed by other observations. Scientific knowledge accommodates natural variation by seeking to collect enough observations to measure it hence the preoccupation with quantitative observations.

Hunters make observations in the course of their travelling and hunting and the intensity of their vigilance can be awe-inspiring. New observations are also acquired through discussion with other hunters. There is not the narrow focus on collecting specific observations to answer a certain question which so often motivates scientific information gathering. Hunters' observations are loosely organized in an informal and flexible system which may equally include a spiritual or mythical interpretation. The organization of the observations is akin to a mental encyclopedia used for successful hunting and travelling. The accumulated observations are not ranked nor

value ascribed to them, and they do not dictate the acquisition of subsequent observations which is in contrast with the scientific organization of observations. There is no particular beginning or end to the collection of observations and natural variation is accepted as it is observed.

Science takes one set of observations and uses them to determine what subsequent observations are needed to answer the questions or refine the points posed. This predilection for the collection of scientific observations to be directed toward the answering of a particular question is further compounded by the project-specific context of most inquiries, and their restricted duration.

Each system evolved for specific reasons and limitations become apparent only when the original context is changed. Both knowledge systems seek to answer questions and use observations to modify subsequent behaviour. The hunters use their accumulated knowledge to interpret events and make the appropriate hunting or travelling decisions based on observations already acquired. Biologists, like hunters, are deeply aware of the intricacies of biological systems but, nevertheless, their collection of observations and the questions raised are often directed to untangling cause-and-effect relationships within those systems.

Science tends to impose an objective and rigorous interpretation of observations which is necessary to establish cause-and-effect relationships. The simultaneous observation of two events is not necessarily sufficient evidence to assign a relationship between them. For example, the disappearance of caribou from an area at the same time that there was aircraft traffic or seismic activity in the area does not either prove or disprove that the two observations were related as the role of other factors was not considered. The observations are not in dispute but their interpretation requires a more systematic testing, as is inherent in the scientific approach.

The organization of the observations in both scientific or indigenous knowledge systems is sufficiently different as to impede integration of the two systems at this level. Either organizational framework is, however, sufficiently flexible to accept individual observations.

3. Actions based on observations

The knowledge of hunters is directed toward successful hunting and travelling on the land. Freeman (1984) suggested that the existence of hunters with their food species over a long period of time is an *a priori* proof for conservation practices but, in reality, there is little information on the conservation practices that culminated from the intimate observations of wildlife by hunters during the eras preceding European contact. The complex system of kinship and food-sharing practices included taboos against wildlife wastage. This notion was also a tenant of the prevalent religion (e.g., Rasmussen 1930) and would have encouraged a conservation attitude. It is unrecorded as to whether there were conservation systems with a feedback from observations during the then current harvests to regulate future harvesting behaviour. Spiritual and earlier religious practices emphasized a regard for the perpetuation of food species but do not relate, if in practice, hunting effort or location were adjusted in line with the status of the hunted population. Regulatory harvest strategies in the sub-arctic for moose and beaver (Feit 1986) developed where neither the hunters nor the beaver and moose were migratory. Non-migratory behaviour may facilitate the development of such regulatory systems: Inuit were more seasonally nomadic as they depended on migratory wildlife. We know of no evidence in the NWT currently available for the regulation of harvest that involved adjustment of harvesting behaviour according to some measure of abundance as described by Feit (1986) for beaver.

There was, and still is, especially among older hunters a strong sentiment against unnecessary harvesting or wastage, which is a conservation measure in itself. Berkes (1981) describes socially-regulated strictures on the hunting of migratory waterfowl by the Cree people in James Bay which functioned as conservation practices. Also, there is recognition that reduced levels of wildlife abundance may not justify harvesting effort, and again this harvesting behaviour can be construed as a

conservation practice. Many wildlife species traditionally concentrate in certain areas even when populations are reduced (e.g.: polar bear denning areas, caribou calving grounds) with the result that those conservation practices may not alone have been sufficient over the longer term.

Wildlife biologists direct their knowledge toward wildlife management, which is a recent innovation in North America and as such is still evolving and reevaluating its basic concepts and techniques. The broad objective of wildlife management is the wise and sustained use of wildlife which includes both consumptive use and non-consumptive use. The management prescriptions nominally have a scientific basis but the rigorous use of the scientific method has lagged behind intuitive management practices to the detriment of wildlife management (e.g., McCullough 1979, MacNab 1983, Fraser 1985).

The pressures to accomplish precise management are increasing as harvesting levels rise in response to the growth of the human population and development of the renewable resource-based economy. The shortfalls of relying solely on intuitive practices in wildlife management would be paralleled by relying only on the intuitive knowledge system of hunters. More stringent and demanding wildlife management will require both ecological observations from hunters combined with other facts, such as the age of first breeding, mortality and reproductive rates, that require the application of wildlife technology. The interpretation of the information and subsequent predicting and testing of the results has to follow the discipline of the scientific method.

One basic premise of wildlife management, namely, that level of hunting is related to levels of loss and gain in any one population, is already familiar to hunters. For example, experienced bear hunters do not argue with biologists that as polar bears do not breed until adult (5-6 years of age) and cubs stay with their mother for 2 or 3 years, the likelihood of hunting more bears than can replace themselves is significant. Hunters sometimes accept that the economic pressures to hunt bears can now deplete a population if the hunting is unregulated. They have contributed their knowledge to evaluating the effect of hunting on bears even when it led to reduced quotas (Lloyd 1986).

Usher (1986) has declared that the real challenge to wildlife management in the NWT is to integrate the indigenous and scientific wildlife management systems, though without specifying examples of how to achieve that integration or the extent of indigenous systems. Berkes (1981) described wildlife management practices of the Cree people in the James Bay area and he also concluded that some hybridized form of scientific management and indigenous management is necessary. Berkes (1981) also commented that the inclusion of indigenous knowledge and Native participation in scientific studies is insufficient if it is only used to serve scientific management rather than some hybrid between the indigenous management system and scientific management. In the NWT, we are still at the phase of integrating the two systems of wildlife knowledge. The two systems have common objectives in the promotion of the wise utilization of wildlife and the differences are partly a problem of language (including jargon) and gaining access to each system, as well as the organization of the information and under-standing and valuing the relative contribution of each other's system.

Access to each other's knowledge is time consuming — a brief interview, meeting or written report is not always the most fruitful way to exchange knowledge. Indeed, the late and as yet relatively small contribution of hunter's knowledge to scientific wildlife management has stemmed more from a communication failure than any inherent limitation in either system of knowledge. The failure is not just a reflection of not taking enough time to appreciate and learn each other's knowledge. An aware-ness of each other's culture eases the exchanges: an obvious example is the questioning of observations — normal for a scientist but rude for a hunter. There are, of course, other examples of differing social graces or attitudes that are relevant to communicating between cultures (e.g., Black 1973, Darnell 1981). A further added complexity is that thinking processes can vary between cultures and the subsequent organization of observations reflects the differ-ent cognitive styles (Gladwin 1964).

One of the most frequently expressed cultural differences relates to the handling and marking of wildlife, without which certain wildlife facts are impossible to obtain. Yet many hunters maintain that to capture and mark wildlife is to show a lack of respect (e.g., Wenzel 1986) and change the animal's "wildness." Problems such as this are not easily resolved and can substantially hamper the subsequent exchange of knowledge between hunters and biologists.

The Department of Renewable Resources (Government of the Northwest Territories) has taken two significant steps in promoting the integration of scientific and hunter's know-ledge. Experienced hunters are hired on staff as Assistant Renewable Resource Officers; more recently, their knowledge and longtime experience of their area and its wildlife has come to be valued as much as their abilities as guides. The second step that facilitated exchange of knowledge was the placement of Regional Biologists into the major settlements, effectively increasing the opportunities for knowledge exchange. Biologists in the Department of Renewable Resources have, in the 1980s, started to design projects to systematically rely on the hunters' observations. The projects depend on local skills for travelling on the land as well as observations of wildlife distribution and behaviour. Hunters' knowledge of wildlife distribution (e.g., Freeman 1976), or behaviour (e.g., Smith and Stirling 1976) have been previously used by biologists, but Renewable Resources is attempting to increase the frequency of integration of hunters' knowledge. For example, polar bear denning surveys have been conducted in areas identified by hunters and such studies are now investigating annual variations in the location of dens. Likewise, observations of caribou distribution and abundance in the living memory and from stories of the previous two generations of hunters are being gathered by Renewable Resource Officers in the Baffin Region. That compilation may help to document the hunters' contention that caribou numbers follow a 60-70 year cycle — a contention that strongly influences their views on the utility of caribou studies and hunting regulations (G. Williams pers. comm.).

Other surveys conducted for wildlife management purposes that describe sex and age composition of caribou and muskoxen (*Ovibos moschatus*), especially in the Central Arctic, are being planned as ground-based, rather than aerial surveys. Ground surveys involve and depend on local knowledge and skills, and the biologists have more opportunities to experience wildlife habitat and to exchange their knowledge with that of the hunters.

The extent to which the government has intervened and made wildlife decisions is, in the 1980s, being reversed through granting greater responsibilities to Hunters and Trappers Associations (HTAs) and establishment of specific management boards such as the Kaminuriak and Beverly Caribou Management Board. Renewable Resources, usually after discussion with the HTAs, establish the level of the quotas for polar bears and muskoxen but leaves the decision of who actually harvests the animals to the HTA. The HTAs often make their decisions concerning the allocation of the quota according to traditional values. Questions of wastage are also sometimes left to the HTA to resolve with its members.

There is currently some urgency to the interchange of knowledge as so much of the traditional knowledge is held by the elder hunters. As the Inuit themselves are aware, there is a generation growing up which has little experience of living on the land to continue and develop the traditional knowledge. For example, in Cambridge Bay, there are Inuit children who have never seen a live caribou although in winter there are caribou within a few kilometers of the hamlet. The rapid changes in life-style also limit the observational opportunities to acquire knowledge: a hunter travelling slowly sometimes for weeks with dogs (who extend the hunter's awareness through their acute vision and sense of smell) would have more opportunities than a wage-earning Inuk hunting by snowmachine only on weekends.

Further progress in integrating the traditional knowledge of the Inuit and the scientific knowledge of biologists in order to develop an appropriate conservation system for the modern arctic, will depend on the identification and description of the indigenous management systems (regulatory feedback systems) as well as traditional conservation practices. These will likely vary in the extent of their development between areas and wildlife species as the models described by Berkes (1981) and Feit (1986) for the James Bay Cree for example, may have limited applicability to areas above the treeline. The identification of the existence and extent of those indigenous management systems will require cooperative studies between wildlife biologists, hunters and anthropologists. The key to the description and integration of the indigenous and scientific systems in the NWT may be more effective communication with anthropologists as well as between hunters and wildlife managers.

Acknowledgements

Earlier drafts of this paper benefited from reviews by S. Fleck (Department of Renewable Resources, Government of Northwest Territories), M. Strachan (Arctic Bay), I. Stirling (Canadian Wildlife Service) and G. Williams (DRR, Arctic Bay). The time and trouble they took is appreciated.

References

Arima, E.Y.
1975   Views on land expressed in Inuit oral traditions. *In* Inuit Land Use and Occupancy Project. M.M.R. Freeman, ed. pp 217-222. Ottawa: Indian and Northern Affairs Canada, Vol. II.

Berkes, F.
1981   The role of self-regulation in living resources management in the North. *In* Proceedings of the First International Symposium on Renewable Resources and the Economy of the North. M.M.R. Freeman, ed. pp 143-160. Ottawa: Association of Canadian Universities for Northern Studies.

Black, M.
1973   Ojibwa questioning etiquette and use of ambiguity. Studies in Linguistics 23: 13-29.

Brody, H.
1975   The People's Land: Eskimos and Whites
        in the Eastern Arctic. London, England:
        Penguin Books.

Bromley, R.G.
1983   1982 Raptor Studies. NWT Wildlife
        Service File Report No. 35, 47 pp.

Darnell, R.
1981   Taciturnity in Native American
        etiquette. Culture 1: 55-60.

Feit, H.
1986   James Bay Cree Indian management
        and moral considerations of fur-bearers.
        In Native People and Renewable
        Resource Management. pp. 49-66.
        Edmonton: Alberta Society of
        Professional Biologists.

Fraser, D.
1985   Piggery perspectives on wildlife
        management and research. Wildlife
        Society Bulletin 13(2):183-187.

Freeman, M.M.R. (editor)
1975   Inuit Land Use and Occupancy Project.
        Indian and Northern Affairs Canada,
        Ottawa, Ontario, Vols. I-III.

Freeman, M.M.R.
1979   Traditional land users as a legitimate
        source of environmental information. In
        Canadian National Parks: Today and
        Tomorrow, Conference II. J.G. Nelson,
        R.D. Needham, S.H. Nelson and R.C.
        Scace, eds. Volume 1: 345-361.
1984   Arctic ecosystems. In Handbook of North
        American Indians. D.J. Damas and
        W.C. Sturtevant, eds. Volume 5:36-48.
        Washington, D.C.: Smithsonian
        Institution.
1985   Appeal to tradition: different perspectives
        on arctic wildlife management. In
        Native Power: the Quest for Autonomy
        and Nationhood of Indigenous Peoples. J.
        Brøsted, J. Dahl et al., eds. pp. 265-281.
        Oslo: Universitetsforlaget.

Gladwin, T.
1964   Culture and logical process. In
        Explorations in cultural anthropology:
        essays in honour of George Peter
        Murdoch. Ward Goodenough, ed.
        McGraw-Hill.

Lloyd, Kevin
1986   Cooperative management of polar bears
        on Northeast Baffin Island. In Native
        People and Receivable Resource Man-
        agement, pp. 108-116. Edmonton: Alberta
        Society of Professional Biologists.

Lopez, B.H.
1986   Arctic Dreams. New York: Charles
        Scribner's Sons.

McCullough, D.R.
1979   The George River deer herd. Ann Arbor:
        University of Michigan Press, 271 pp.

MacNab, J.
1983   Wildlife management as scientific
        experimentation. Wildlife Society
        Bulletin: 11: 397-401.

Nakashima, D. J.
1986   Inuit knowledge of the ecology of the
        Common Eider in northern Quebec. In
        Eider ducks in Canada. A. Reed, ed. pp.
        102-113. Canadian Wildlife Service,
        Report Series 47.

Nelson, R. K.
1969   Hunters of the Northern Ice. Chicago:
        University of Chicago Press.

Rasmussen, K.
1930   Observations of the intellectual culture of
        the Caribou Eskimos. Report of the Fifth
        Thule Expedition 1921-24, Copenhagen,
        Vol. VII.

Smith, T. G. and I. Stirling.
1975   The breeding habitat of the ringed seal
        (Phoca hispida). The birth lair and
        associated structures. Canadian Journal
        of Zoology 53(9): 1297-1305.

Stefansson, V.
1921   The Friendly Arctic. New York: Mac-
        millan

Stirling, I.G.
1986   Management and research on polar
        bears Ursus maritimus. Polar Record
        23(143):167-176.

Usher, P.
1986   Devolution of power in the Northwest
        Territories: implications for wildlife. *In*
        Native people and renewable resource
        management. pp. 69-80. Edmonton:
        Alberta Society of Professional
        Biologists.

Van der Post, L. and J. Taylor.
1985   Testament to the bushmen. Harmonds-
        worth, Middlesex, England: Penguin
        Books Ltd, 176 pp.

Wenzel, G.W.
1986   Resource harvesting and the social
        structure of Native communities. *In*
        Native People and Renewable Resource
        Management. pp. 10-22. Edmonton:
        Alberta Society of Professional
        Biologists.

The Inuit and Wildlife Management Today

R. Riewe, University of Manitoba
and
L. Gamble, Winnipeg, Manitoba

Abstract

The Inuit and their ancestors have been competent managers of wildlife for thousands of years, but their traditional management systems have been disrupted by Euro-Canadians. Despite the outside interventions, Inuit have continued to employ some of their traditional management techniques; in this paper, the controlled spring harvest of geese and eggs is described as one example. In spite of an increasing Inuit population equipped with modern hunting technologies, hunting pressures on caribou in the Keewatin are probably lower now than they were in the pre-contact era — and the caribou are abundant on the barren grounds. Recently the Inuit have endeavoured to manage their wildlife, by means of both traditional and modern techniques, through a system of regional wildlife associations. These attempts, however, have often been frustrated by government agencies which limit the effectiveness of these associations. Inuit are now preparing to assume, once again, an active role in wildlife management following the recently signed Nunavut Wildlife Agreement.

Introduction

In aboriginal times the Inuit actively managed their wildlife resources through a complex set of beliefs and taboos, harvesting and storage techniques, sharing systems, and by adopting a dispersed and mobile settlement pattern that served to decrease their impact upon wildlife resources. With the introduction of European culture in the Arctic many traditional Inuit management techniques were disrupted, altered or abandoned. The Euro-Canadians who disrupted this delicate balance between the hunter and his prey have often spoken out against the Inuit for poor hunting practices and wastage of game. Since the 1950s the white biologists and wildlife managers have been amongst the most vocal critics of Native hunting practices.

In typical colonial fashion the Euro-Canadians have attempted to manage the Northern wildlife via their own belief systems based on the scientific method and certain political overtones. Scientists believe they can control wildlife population behaviour and attain management objectives if they can gather the correct data, such as information on species distribution, habitat requirements, population size, structure and discreteness, reproductive potential, and natality and mortality rates including those occasioned by domestic and commercial harvesting. Unfortunately, this comprehensive data base is rarely attained in the south, and has never been obtained for any northern species (Davis, et al. 1980, Dickinson and Herman 1979, Freeman 1985a).

"Wildlife management" is actually a misnomer — it should be referred to as "people management" because most wildlife populations are actively manipulated by managing the harvesters, by setting seasons, quotas, bag limits, etc., and not by manipulating the wildlife species.

The state wildlife management system in the North has often created strong animosities and distrust between the managers and the users and hence poor management of wildlife. Most of this distrust stems from misunderstandings. Biologists usually are well-trained in zoology, botany, ecology, statistics and computer sciences but they are inadequately trained in the social sciences: anthropology, linguistics, psychology, and sociology. When a southern-trained biologist accepts a northern position he or she usually arrives without any cross-cultural experience and replete with southern cultural myths of the North and the Native peoples. All too often these southerners believe that traditional Native management of wildlife was based merely on the fact that their hunting technology was so crude that they were unable to over-exploit their environment (Macpherson 1981; Theberge 1981). This myth can be dismissed by merely examining the vast anthropological literature on hunting societies (see Andrews, this volume).

Today another myth commonly held by southerners is that all Inuit males are extremely competent hunters. This is no more true than is any other generalization. In reality a majority of the Inuit population is not adult hunters at all, but rather is comprised of children and adolescents. In Eskimo Point for example, over half the Inuit population is under the age of 16 years. Some of these youths are becoming competent hunters. Many children, however, don't have the interest or the opportunity to travel and hunt because of the southern schooling system and other pervading influences of the non-Native populations in the North and as a consequence, they are not gaining the skills of a hunter.

Most adult males participate in hunting activities as frequently as possible, but because of such inhibiting factors as employment, disabilities and, shortage of cash, very few men are able to hunt on a full-time basis. One of the foremost factors inhibiting full-time hunting is the high cost of hunting equipment and the low economic returns from the hunt, and hence the need for the hunters to hold wage-earning jobs in order to provide the cash necessary to hunt. The basic hunting gear, including a snowmobile, 24-foot freighter canoe, 50 horse-power outboard motor, rifles, shotgun, three-wheel all-terrain vehicle, etc. costs between $20,000 and $30,000 if purchased at a northern store. Most hunters, however, usually don't own all the required equipment on a year-round basis, but rather, they are constantly trading, loaning, borrowing and buying the appropriate equipment when it is required. Many hunters hold wage-earning jobs just so they can acquire the cash necessary to hunt. Despite the fact that hunters having a job have very little time to hunt, while those with the

time to hunt lack the necessary equipment, the importance of hunting has remained, to this day, the continuing basis of the Inuit culture (Freeman 1985b; 1986) and continues to provide many Inuit with the bulk of their nutritional needs (Schaefer and Steckle 1980).

Despite the alien management institutions imposed upon the Inuit, they continue to employ some of their traditional management techniques as well as adapting their traditional systems to the state-management paradigm.

Spring Goose Hunt

The spring goose hunt is an example of a traditional hunt which is conducted despite the Migratory Birds Convention Act which bans the activity. As the snow and Canada geese migrate north they are well-endowed with nutritious fat reserves. The Inuit hunt these birds intensively for the first few weeks after their arrival. The fat birds provide an important diversity to the Inuit's otherwise traditionally lean diet (Schaefer and Steckle 1980). Once the geese begin to nest the Inuit curtail their hunting activities because the bird's fat reserves have been depleted. Goose eggs are then harvested. Usually all the eggs are taken from a nest, but due to the huge numbers of geese present, this harvest has a negligible effect upon the populations. For example, between Eskimo Point and the McConnell River there are an estimated 300,000 nesting snow geese (MacInnis, C. personal communication, 1986). The community of Eskimo Point, however, only harvest from about 1000 nests, for a total of about 6,000 eggs.

Another Keewatin community harvests about 10,000 goose eggs annually. In this community almost one third of the eggs are harvested by a single hunter who fills his moss-padded freighter canoe with eggs. The hunter distributes the eggs throughout the community. The community realizes that one careful person will cause far less disturbance to the nesting grounds than would many people individually collecting eggs. After the brief "egging" period the geese are no longer disturbed; because the geese have been depleted of their fat reserves, they are no longer sought as food. The spring goose hunt is culturally important, makes nutritional sense and has a negligible effect upon the goose populations, and, incidentally, would be exceedingly difficult to suppress with enforcement.

Caribou Management

No aspect of wildlife management in the North has sparked more controversy than the status of the barren-ground caribou. Biologists and managers have often accused the Inuit of over-harvesting and wasting caribou since the introduction of the rifle (Kelsall 1968). By the 1970s biologists believed that the rapidly expanding Inuit population could not continue to be maintained by the dwindling caribou herds. The biologists estimated that the caribou in the Keewatin in 1979 numbered approximately 214,000 animals from four distinct herds (Dickinson and Herman 1979). The largest herd, the Beverly herd, was estimated at 124,000 animals; this herd supposedly occupied the western edge of the Keewatin and was available only to the Keewatin community of Baker Lake. The biologists admitted that they lacked adequate harvest data but their best estimate was that 4100 caribou were being harvested annually by the Keewatin communities (Interdisciplinary Systems Limited 1978; Gates, C. personal communication 1980).

The Inuit did not believe these census estimates, for they were sure the biologists were missing caribou on their surveys. By 1982 the biologists' assertions of over-harvesting and imminent "extinction" of the herds were thrown into serious question, when the supposedly most-endangered herd, the Kaminuriak herd, exploded from an estimated 40,000 animals in 1980 to 200,000+ in 1982. Today it is estimated that there are about 1,000,000 caribou in the Keewatin broken down as follows: Kaminuriak Herd 300,000; Beverly Herd 300,000; Wager Herd, 100,000 to 300,000; Melville Herd 50,000 to 100,000; Bathurst Herd 300,000; Coates Island 3,000 to 10,000 and Southampton Island 2,000 (Heard, D. personal communications 1978-1986). These recent caribou estimates have tempered the biologists' criticism of the Inuit harvest and have forced them to question their own scientific methodologies: aerial surveys, statistical

analyses and computer models. These recent estimates also forced the biologists to question their understanding of caribou biology. No longer could it be assumed that caribou herds were discrete populations with the females displaying strong fidelity to discrete calving grounds. Biologists are also beginning to realize that there may be caribou cycles or fluctuations which can not be attributed only to hunter kill and wolf predation. Further, migration patterns may shift over time, influenced by range quality, variable snow conditions, and other environmental factors. Forest fires may also influence habitat availability and migration patterns (Thomas, D. personal communication 1986).

Just as the apparent vast increase in caribou numbers was becoming known, the Inuit began to monitor their own harvest. In September 1981, a preliminary study of the Inuit wildlife harvest in the Keewatin Region was initiated (Gamble 1984). This study which was conducted until 1986 (Gamble 1987, 1988, in press) was administered by the Keewatin Wildlife Federation (KWF), which hired a southern biologist to design and organize the study. The harvest study was funded by the Federal Department of Supply and Services on behalf of the Canadian Wildlife Service, Fisheries and Oceans Canada, Indian Affairs and Northern Development, the Government of the Northwest Territories (GNWT) and the KWF. This study encountered a number of unanticipated problems, many due to the cross-cultural nature of the inquiry. For example, it attempted to elicit statistically valid harvest information by survey methods common in Euro-Canadian society, yet fundamentally foreign to the traditions of the Inuit. Nonetheless, the harvest study has been rated as the most credible study of its kind conducted in the Northwest Territories to date (Usher et al. 1985).

This harvest study demonstrated the continued dependence of Inuit on wildlife harvests. The Keewatin Inuit harvest of caribou for example, approximately 12,000 annually, is almost three times as great as the number earlier estimated by the biologists.

Prior to 1981, biologists felt strongly that it was primarily over-hunting, perhaps augmented by wolf predation, that had precipitated the apparent decline of the Kaminuriak caribou herd. However, despite the use of modern hunting technology by the Inuit, their high birth rate and hence rapidly expanding population and their continued dependence upon country foods, the Inuit caribou harvest is possibly much lower at the present time compared to the harvest in pre-contact or early contact times. If we assume a very small pre-contact Inuit population of about 500 people inhabiting the Keewatin, and a harvest of 50 caribou per person per year (Lawrie, in Kelsall 1968), then the Keewatin harvest may have been 25,000 caribou, or more than double what it is today with an Inuit population eight times as large. The Keewatin caribou number about 1,000,000 today and could probably sustain a five percent harvest level, or 50,000 animals per year compared to the present harvest of about 12,000 animals.

Biologists and managers have also decried the wastage of caribou by the Inuit and have pointed out the difficulty of enforcing the anti-wastage regulations. There is no doubt that there has been wastage and it is likely this may continue in the future; however, the Inuit have demonstrated their concern about this wastage and applied pressure in order to control the problem. As an example, recently a large herd of caribou appeared in the community of Baker Lake. The young men in town who seldom hunt went on a shooting spree and killed a large number of animals. The Renewable Resource Officers realized the difficulty of attempting to press charges. Instead, they collected the wasted carcasses and piled them in the centre of town. Realizing the magnitude of the waste, the elders, Hunters and Trappers Association (HTA) and the Hamlet Council applied pressure to the youths in order to prevent the incident from recurring.

Elders Waste Committee

In Igloolik a similar situation to the one in Baker Lake prompted the formation of a community organization to deal with waste (Allen, R. personal communication 1986). By the mid-1970s the high price paid for walrus ivory and the reduced demand for dog food created a situation where walrus were often hunted only for their ivory. The lack of need for dog food also resulted in considerable wastage of beluga and narwhal meat. The local Fisheries Officer talked to the offending hunters, hoping to convince them to halt their wasteful practices. The hunters admitted that they were wasting meat but they did not see a problem. The officer also talked to the local HTA, but it too could not put effective pressure on the offending hunters, because all active hunters who were members of the association may have wasted meat themselves at one time or another. In exasperation the Fisheries Officer took pictures of the wastage and posted enlarged photographs of the scenes in the local Co-op store. The community became very embarrassed; the hunters then realized that the wastage was not merely a few isolated incidents but rather that it had reached epidemic proportions and was a problem that had to be faced. In 1979 a committee of elders and higher status hunters was established to deal with this problem.

Igloolik is proud of its traditional ways and the elders are highly respected members of the community, as they were in the past. The elders who no longer hunted were in a particularly good position to solve the dilemma because they had not wasted meat in the past nor would they do so in the future. The HTA now reports any person who has wasted meat to this committee which in turn disciplines the offenders. The committee also employs the local radio as an effective means of reviving the traditional anti-waste ethic. The committee makes regular broadcasts which cover everything from encouraging the hunters to harvest only what they require, to techniques for utilizing animals by-products, to offering assistance to anyone who might need help in locating a lost meat cache. This system has virtually eliminated wastage in Igloolik.

In Coral Harbour on Southampton Island, hunters who have wasted meat are dealt with even more harshly by their community. A few years ago three men who had taken their allotted quota of walrus had wasted the carcasses. The local HTA heard of the incident and immediately summoned the Fisheries Officer from Rankin Inlet. The HTA pursued the case and took the three offenders to court and had them prosecuted. The fines were awarded to the HTA by the judge and the offenders had their hunting rights to harvest walrus revoked for a number of years by the courts. Of course once the offenders' rights are reinstated by the courts, the HTA can itself consider whether or not to allow those hunters to hunt walrus, for the allocation of harvest rights remains with the community.

Ptarmigan Hunting Seasons

During this decade the Inuit have adapted more of the southern concepts of wildlife management and enforcement to their own situation. The setting of ptarmigan seasons in the Keewatin is a good example of southern-style wildlife management initiatives adopted by the Inuit on behalf of Euro-Canadian residents. In the NWT the ptarmigan hunting season for residents extends from September 1 to April 30. In the vicinity of Coral Harbour, Baker Lake, Whale Cove and Eskimo Point, ptarmigan can be found year-round. However at Rankin Inlet ptarmigan do not migrate into the area until the end of April and are in the area only until mid-May. The birds then migrate up the coast to Chesterfield Inlet where they can be found only between May 15 and 30. The birds do not arrive in the area of Repulse Bay until early to mid-June and then they begin nesting. In other words, ptarmigan are not available in Rankin Inlet, Chesterfield Inlet and Repulse Bay during the legal resident hunting season. In order to overcome this problem, the KWF and the communities decided that the seasons had to be changed to allow resident Euro-Canadians in these three communities to legally harvest ptarmigan. The GNWT preferred an extended season through the Keewatin to solve the problem. However, the KWF desired a more restrictive season to prevent excessive hunting: in Rankin Inlet the season extended to May 15, in Chesterfield Inlet the season was extended to May 31, and in Repulse Bay the season was extended to June 15, with the other four Keewatin communities retaining the early closure date of April 30.

Cooperative Wildlife Management

Most Native groups in Canada are demand-

ing an active role in wildlife management. The Inuit are no different; in fact, in 1982 the Nunavut Wildlife Agreement was the first Agreement in Principle negotiated by the Tungavik Federation of Nunavut during land claims negotiations with the federal government. This agreement formalized in 1986 (but not yet financed) provides Inuit a direct participatory role in wildlife management.

Cooperative management can not simply mean an advisory role for the Native users; rather the users must be fully involved in the design and production of the wildlife management schemes. This has always been the intent of Native associations. In times of financial restraint, however, government frequently provides only sufficient funds to obtain advice on matters where Native input appears to validate and thereby provide public support for government programs, or for obtaining data which is not available through regular government channels. The role of Native associations in the design and interpretive phases of research often are not funded, nor, unfortunately, are they even considered by some government agencies.

In October 1980 the KWF, comprising the presidents of the seven local HTAs, was established. Since 1982 in the Keewatin, wildlife agencies have complete studies on muskox and narwhal, and on an arctic char test fishery; currently caribou surveys using radio telemetry, a polar bear study in Foxe Basin, a beluga whale study and a walrus study are on-going. These research programs often resulted from pressure exerted by KWF or through active support from the federation. KWF has circulated copies of its harvest study internationally and has presented materials at the CITES meeting in Argentina.

Native wildlife associations should be encouraged and be provided with sustained financial resources in order to provide the cultural perspective on wildlife in their regions including the routine and necessary collection of harvest data.

Conclusion

The Inuit were effective wildlife managers for thousands of years but their management systems were disrupted by the Euro-Canadians. Once again, however, the Inuit have adapted to a changing environment. They are prepared to reassume their responsibilities as managers of the wildlife upon which they still depend, but they are prepared to share this management responsibility equally with the Euro-Canadians who have moved into their lands.

References

Allen, R.
1986   Personal communication. Department of Fisheries and Oceans, Iqaluit, NWT.

Davis, R., K. Finley, and W. Richardson
1980   The Present Status and Future Management of Arctic Marine Mammals in Canada. Report No. 3. Yellowknife: Science Advisory Board of the Northwest Territories.

Dickinson, D. and T. Herman
1979   Management of Some Terrestrial Mammals in the Northwest Territories for Sustained Yields. Report No. 4. Yellowknife: Science Advisory Board of the Northwest Territories.

Freeman, M.M.R.
1985a   Appeal to tradition: different perspectives on Arctic wildlife management. In Native Power: The Quest for Autonomy and Nationhood for Indigenous Peoples. J. Brøsted et al., eds. pp. 265-281. Bergen and Oslo: Universitetsforlaget.
1985b   Effects of petroleum activities on the ecology of Arctic man. In Petroleum Effects in the Arctic Environment. F.R. Engelhardt, ed. pp. 245-273. London: Elsevier Applied Science Publishers.
1986   Renewable resources, economics and Native communities. In Native People and Renewable Resource Management. pp. 23-39. Edmonton: Alberta Society for Professional Biologists.

Gamble, L.
1984   A preliminary study of the Native harvest of wildlife in the Keewatin Region, Northwest Territories. Canadian Technical Report of Fisheries and Aquatic Sciences. No. 1282. Winnipeg: Department of Fisheries and Oceans.

1987   Native harvest of wildlife in the Keewatin Region, Northwest Territories for the period October 1983 to September 1984. Canadian Technical Report of Fisheries and Aquatic Sciences. Winnipeg: Department of Fisheries and Oceans.
1988   Native harvest of Wildlife in the Keewatin Region, Northwest Territories for the period October 1984 to September 1985. Canadian Technical Report of Fisheries and Aquatic Sciences. Winnipeg: Department of Fisheries and Oceans.
In press Summary of Native Harvest of Wildlife in the Keewatin Region, N.W.T.: October 1981 to March 1986. Fisheries and Aquatic Sciences Data report No. 688. Central and Arctic Region. Winnipeg: Department of Fisheries and Oceans.

Gates, C.
1986   Personal communication. Department of Renewable Resources, Government of the NWT, Fort Smith, NWT.

Heard, D.
1978-86 Personal communications. Department of Renewable Resources, Government of the NWT, Yellowknife, NWT.

Interdisciplinary Systems Limited
1978   Effects of exploration and development in the Baker Lake area. Volume one: Study report. Prepared for the Department of Indian Affairs and Northern Development, Ottawa.

MacInnis, C.
1986   Personal communication. Ontario Ministry of Natural Resources, Maple, Ontario.

Macpherson, A.H.
1981   Commentary: Wildlife Conservation and Canada's North. Arctic 34(2):103-107.

Theberge, J.B.
1981   Commentary: Conservation in the North: an ecological perspective. Arctic 34(4): 281-285.

Thomas, D.
1986   Personal communication. Canadian Wildlife Service, Edmonton.

Schaefer, O. and J. Steckle
    Dietary Habits and Nutritional Base of
    Native Populations of the Northwest Ter-
    ritories. Yellowknife: Science Advisory
    Board of the Northwest Territories.

Usher, P., D. DeLancey, G. Wenzel, M. Smith,
    and P. White
1985 An Evaluation of Native Harvest Survey
    Methodologies in Northern Canada.
    Report No. 004. Ottawa: Environmental
    Studies Revolving Funds.

State and Indigenous Fisheries Management: The Alaska Context

Polly Wheeler
University of Alberta

Introduction

Over the past twenty-five years increasing attention has been directed at what has been labeled by some scientists as the "Global Predicament" (Orr and Soroos 1979; Segerstedt and Nilsson 1974). In general, this term has come to be associated with human over-population and subsequent over-utilization of resources. In partial response to this dilemma, as well as to the apparently insufficient existing management schema, additional consideration has been increasingly devoted to alternative theories and models of resource management (Firey 1960; Segerstedt and Nilsson 1974; Orr and Soroos 1979; O'Riordan 1971). Other studies of alternative resource management institutions have arisen out of interest in and a concern over, federal, public and privately held lands (Clawson 1983; Firey 1960). Native of indigenous resource user groups have been considered peripherally if at all in most of these studies. Admittedly, in many areas indigenous user groups do not comprise a majority of the total user-group category. However, while they do not comprise a majority, indigenous user groups tend to be a consistent, and until recently, silent population; yet a population that is often most directly affected by nation-state management decisions.

By the latter 1970s the existence of indigenous systems of self-regulation and/or management was beginning to be directly considered and addressed (Berkes 1977, 1979; Feit 1979) although for the most part discussion of this topic was less than sympathetic. Until that time, indigenous self-management systems were not usually recognized, such that the inevitability of over-use, as postulated in Hardin's (1968) "tragedy of the commons" essay, was seen to be the inescapable outcome unless state management was enforced.

More recently, indigenous self-management and regulation, and conservation practices have been considered more directly (Berkes 1982, 1983, 1985, 1986a; Brody 1980; Feit 1983, 1986, 1987; Flowers et. al. 1982; Foin 1984). In the Canadian Arctic and Subarctic, where Native and non-Native interests in resources increasingly conflict and compete, research has focused on possibilities of indigenous self-regulation of fish and game resources (Berkes 1979, 1983, 1985, 1986a, 1986b; Feit 1983, 1986, 1987). In Alaska the situation differs considerably; competition for resources is both more acute and political as a result of an active sport and commercial lobby which does not exist in the Canadian North. Few studies have directly addressed the question of indigenous self-management in Alaska, although several studies have discussed various ideological practices and self-regulation in the hunting of land mammals (Nelson 1982, 1983). Additionally, several historic accounts mention self-regulation as an (indirect) result of ideology (Loyens 1966; Jette 1911; Sullivan 1942). In general however, few studies have directly considered the existence or possibilities for Native self-management of fish and game resources in Alaska.

In response to the lack of data concerning indigenous self-management systems in Alaska, the present paper will provide a case study of the Koyukon Athabaskan fishing system in which both commercial and subsistence fishing occur. I contend that subsistence fishing represents a self-regulating system, one that is regulated on the basis of need through a number of different social, cultural and technological mechanisms. In contrast, regulation of commercial fishing is not attempted by local fishermen, who regard regulation as being a state management responsibility. It should be noted that both commercial and subsistence fishing are regulated according to the same indices; this is dealt with further below. Local management abilities are not a consideration in establishing regulatory schema.

The commercial fishery will be described as a contrastive situation in order to argue that Lower Koyukon Athabaskans maintain their subsistence fishery through a definitive system of self-regulation. This follows a model introduced by Berkes (1977) where he argues in a similar fashion that self-regulation among the Cree is practiced, following the use of the null hypothesis that "the Cree of Eastern Canada fish haphazardly."

The subsistence fishery in Kaltag shows many elements of a self-regulated system; specifically, social and cultural practices exist and are followed which optimize resource harvests without stock depletion. The practices employed in maintaining this system parallel those practices presented by Berkes (1877, 1981a, 1981b, 1986a), Feit (1979, 1983, 1986) and Usher (1981, 1982). These will be discussed later in the paper. In contrast, these same Lower Koyukon Athabaskans exhibit little effort at managing the commercial fishery by self-regulation. Instead, the commercial fishermen tend to view the commercial fishery as appropriately managed by the state, the rationale being that it is a western introduced, and not an indigenous, system. Therefore, the subsistence fishery and the commercial fishery clearly illustrate a self-regulating and non-self-regulating system respectively. It should be stressed that while not necessarily arguing for a conscious management system (as that implies conscious recognition of a western model of cause and effect), it is argued that a system of resource management exists, manifested in social, cultural, economic and ideological aspects of Lower Koyukon Athabaskan life.

The following sections focus upon state and Koyukon Athabaskan management of both the subsistence and commercial fisheries of a self-regulating mechanism. The paper will be presented in three parts. First, a review of management from the state perspective. Second, the dominant anthropological perspective of state and indigenous systems of resource management will be reviewed. Following that, local perceptions of state management will be presented in conjunction with evidence for self-regulation among the Lower Koyukon Athabaskans. The paper concludes with a discussion of the issues presented.

Alaska State Management of Fish and Game

History

In 1940, the Alaska Native population represented 45 percent of the total state populations (Rollins 1978). While the Native population continued to maintain itself over the next forty years, the influx of large numbers of non-Natives to the state decreased the Alaska Native population relative to the total state population so that by 1980, it represented only 16 percent of the total state population (U.S. Bureau of Census 1980).

The 1970s witnessed several events which directly affected the issue of subsistence. A large increase in the overall state population occurred, and the Alaska Native Claims Settlement Act (ANCSA) was passed in 1971. ANCSA did not provide explicit protection for the right of Alaska Natives to harvest fish and game resources, thus providing the basis for continued conflict between Alaska Native and other users of wildlife (Shinkwin 1985). In addition, an inevitable corollary of the former event was the increased use of fish and game resources by all three user groups, namely: subsistence, commercial and recreational users. This raised the possibility that subsistence use would be diminished.

In 1975 and again in 1976, the state legislature passed laws addressing the authority of the Boards of Fisheries and Game to provide for subsistence uses (Case 1984). The state legislature passed a law in 1978 that gave priority, under certain conditions, to subsistence use over other uses. The Madison Decision was passed in 1985, which ruled that the 1978 Subsistence law was unconstitutional in that it discriminated against non-Natives. It called for subsistence use to be determined on the basis of rural or urban residence: if a community is determined to be rural, then residents are entitled to subsistence use of fish and game resources.

Models Utilized In State Fisheries Management

As with other renewable resources in Alaska, fisheries are managed on the basis of sustained yield. More simply stated, the state is responsible for ensuring the perpetuation of the species of fish in Alaska and to maintain optimal populations of these species (Alaska Department of Fish and Game 1981). Additionally, the Department of Fish and Game is responsible for protecting and providing for the human use of the fish resources for commercial, subsistence and sports or recreational users. This is accomplished through monitoring salmon populations and harvests. On this basis, regulations are established which control the use and harvest of salmon. For each species of salmon, fishery regulations cover seasons, periods, technology (types and kinds), quotas, and even work groups. Regulations are set for commercial, subsistence and recreational interests, although all fisheries are regulated within parameters set for the commercial fishery (Wheeler in press).

Despite the fact that commercial and subsistence salmon fisheries are regulated within the same context, the two fisheries are quite different. In the local view, subsistence and commercial fishing are seen as entirely different empirical and ideological systems.

Anthropological Perspective

Rather than focusing on indigenous systems of resource management and conservation, anthropological research on the use of wild resources by Alaska Natives has been primarily descriptive (cf. Kari 1983; Thomas 1982; Caulfield 1983; Behnke 1982). These baseline studies have provided data on general resource use, in contrast with other, also basically descriptive, studies which are issue-related (cf. Stokes and Andrews 1982; Braund 1980; Fall, Foster and Stanek 1983; Marcotte 1982). Several other studies have focused on specific research problems, such as the relationship of cash to subsistence activity (Wolfe 1981; Wolfe et al.

1984), variations in wild resource use (Wolfe and Ellanna 1983), the relationship between traditional socio-political arrangements and contemporary subsistence activity (Shinkwin and Case 1984), and the effect of technological change on the social organization of modern hunting activities (Ellanna 1983).

The fact that the state of Alaska is mandated to protect the rights of subsistence users has been partially responsible for the lack of research on indigenous self-regulatory systems. As a result of 1987 Subsistence Law, the Division of Subsistence of the Alaska Department of Fish and Game was established. The goal of the Division of Subsistence (many of whose employees are anthropologists) has been to conduct base-line resource use studies in all rural communities in the state. These reports are utilized in the process of establishing resource-use regulations. Thus the role of anthropologists hired by the Division of Subsistence is, in part, one of advocate in the presence of regulatory regimes. Self-regulation clearly does not factor into this process in any way: the Department of Fish and Game sets regulations for both subsistence and commercial user groups. Thus, the system is not established or mandated to consider the presence or efficiency of indigenous self-regulatory systems.

I contend that the paucity of data concerning Alaska Native self-management also originated from several other related issues. First, since 1959 the State of Alaska has been responsible for management of all fish and game resources; this responsibility was strengthened by the Subsistence Law of 1978. As a result, a large number of individuals (mostly biologists) were hired to regulate and manage fish and game resources through the Department of Fish and Game and its Divisions (each of which represents a different user group). The majority of individuals hired by the Department of Fish and Game are trained biologists, well schooled in resource management; it is in these officials best interests to maintain existing management perspectives, rather than considering indigenous self-regulating mechanisms which could potentially threaten their position. In addition, many of these individuals maintain that in general, Natives exhibit flagrant abuse of resources, and they willingly cite cases in support of this contention. While abuse clearly takes place, those that abuse appear to be the vast minority. In any case, a more constructive approach would be to focus on those who treat resources with respect, and who regulate their use of resources accordingly.

This is not to say that the need for state regulation does not exist; it does, as evidenced by the tremendous impact of commercial fishing on salmon stocks. Since 1918 when the commercial fishing industry began operating on the Yukon River, salmon stocks have been seriously depleted, resulting more than once in closure of the river to either commercial fishing or both subsistence and commercial fishing (Pennoyer, Middleton and Morris 1963; Gilbert and O'Malley 1920). Not surprisingly, commercial fishing alone has been responsible for threatening salmon stock as a whole, which has obviously been detrimental to subsistence harvests (Pennoyer, Middleton and Morris 1963). In 1985, 84 percent of the total salmon harvest on the Yukon river was commercially harvested (Alaska Department of Fish and Game 1986). The nature of the commercial fishery is such that if commercial fishermen were left to harvest in an unregulated fashion, they would endanger the stocks immediately, demonstrating the "tragedy of the commons" (Hardin 1968). In effect, the importance of maintaining and regulating commercial fishing has tended to monopolize regulatory interest in almost all Alaskan fisheries. As a result, subsistence fisheries are regulated within the context and confines set for the commercial fishery.

Given this situation, at one level it is not surprising that indigenous management systems have not been considered seriously. However, several other facts point to this as a regrettable omission on the part of state resource managers. In 1959 (when Alaska became a state) Alaska Natives comprised the biggest user group of fish and game resources (with the exception of commercial fishermen) in the State of Alaska. The same holds true today, although the Alaska Native population is only 16 percent of the total

state population (Rollins 1971; U. S. Bureau of Census 1980). In addition, subsistence economies have traditionally been and continue to remain in effect among Alaska Natives, as among all hunter-gatherers (Leacock and Lee 1982). Not only are subsistence systems characterized by tremendous time depth, but traditionally (and to various degrees today) subsistence systems remain dependent upon fish and game harvests. In general, subsistence systems based upon the harvest of wild resources support and are dependent upon local economic, social, cultural, and spiritual values and institutions.

As Berkes (1977) suggests, the ability to over-exploit stocks has always existed, but dependent populations appear to have managed to maintain themselves and the resources stocks for thousands of years. Proponents of the acculturation model presume that limited technological capabilities have kept indigenous peoples from over-exploiting resources. However, increasingly, more effective technology has been available since the time of first contact, yet over-use and over-exploitation has not occurred on a regular basis.

This is not to deny that over-exploitation may not have happened at different times or locations but it has not been a persistent problem. Resources have been maintained in part through indigenous self-regulation, whether through recognition of direct cause and effect, or by following certain traditional unquestioned prescriptions that served to limit harvesting levels. Since the latter can potentially reinforce a causality-directed understanding however, one can argue convincingly for self regulation.

A distinction needs to be made here regarding conservation and self regulation. Conservation is a conscious act which reflects an awareness of human consumption and its effect on resource system. Self-regulation can occur both consciously and unconsciously. More important than the above distinction however, is an identification of the critical underlying question: whether self-regulation is directed to conservation (as defined above) or conversely, whether self-regulation merely coincidentally results in that end. On this basis, the local fishery will be considered.

The Local Fishery

Introduction

While the subsistence fishery in Kaltag has substantial time depth, the commercial fishery is a relatively recent development (Loyens 1966; Marcotte 1982; Sullivan 1942). Whereas the Lower Yukon River has had a commercial fishery for almost 70 years, the Middle Yukon has been involved in a commercial fishery only within the past decade. The commercial fishery in Kaltag takes place only in summer, and is directed to the roe obtained from female chum salmon. Local people are interested in the commercial fishery for the monetary returns it provides. It is viewed as a western system introduced, maintained and regulated by non-Native people. It is considered as an opportunity to be exploited. This perspective is critical when looking at regulation.

In certain respects, the role of the state is one and the same for both subsistence and commercial fishing insofar as both systems are regulated according to the same indices, e.g., open and closed seasons and periods, gear types and locations. It should be noted here that while the commercial fishery focused on female summer chum salmon, the subsistence fishery targets silver and king salmon of both sexes.

Commercial Fishery

In general, the commercial harvest is far greater in terms of numbers and weight of fish than the subsistence harvest of salmon. This is due to several factors, including the intensity of the summer chum run (in comparison to the king and silver salmon runs), the technology utilized in harvesting, and the source of motivation and subsequent effort directed at the fishery. The major motivating influence in the commercial fishery is financial gain. Thus, not only are needs externally defined but they are also theoretically limitless—bounded only by the capabilities of the processors. In practice, however, limits are set by the state in the form of quotas and regulated seasons and permissible fishing periods. With the exception of transfer payments, commercial fishing provides the largest source of cash to the village economy.

Commercial fishing provides one of the few opportunities for local people to successfully participate in the market system. In light of this, commercial fishermen do not consciously set limits on their commercial harvest; basically they attempt to harvest as much as possible.

Subsistence Fishery

In 1985, the subsistence harvest accounted for only seven percent of the total salmon harvest (in numbers). While the above mentioned factors all contribute to this phenomenon, the substantial variance between commercial and subsistence harvest levels is also a reflection of the basic difference between the two fisheries, and specifically, underlying values and motivations. While the needs of the subsistence fishery are internally defined, with the harvest directly reflecting the needs of the group, the commercial harvest essentially reflects an attempt by local people to maximize harvests. It is important to note that processing the subsistence harvest is extremely labor intensive, and as a result subsistence is bound by labor capabilities. Therefore, while the subsistence harvest is only a small part of the overall harvest, it represents far more of a cultural, social, economic and ideological investment than is indicated by the quantitative measure of this harvest.

Associated Value Systems

Two separate value systems underlie the two fisheries. I contend that values associated with the two fisheries are directly reflected in social, economic and technological aspects of the fishery; for example, utilization of different technologies, perceptions surrounding the different gear types, varying composition of work groups (in terms of number and sex), and separate economic and social goals of the two fisheries.

The predominant gear type in Kaltag is the fishwheel. Twelve of the 14 commercial permit holders have fishwheel permits and two have set net permits. Reflecting this, 94 percent of the commercial harvest was taken with fishwheels. Local people view fishwheels as the ideal commercial technology; if continually operated it efficiently harvests the fish, virtually limited only by weather factors and abundance of the fish run. To ensure an even greater harvest, individuals are stationed at the fishbox to remove males, as only the female fish are commercially valuable because of the roe. In theory then, fishwheels provide the opportunity for an indefinitely large harvest (although it is recognized that numbers of salmon are finite, therefore the harvest could not be infinite). The only self-imposed limit on the commercial fishery is the speed and skill of the processors (since only the roe is sold). External limits are set by state regulations through open and closed periods and by quotas. Social values of commercial fishing are illustrated by the fact that basically anyone can and does process summer chum for roe, though men are the primary cutters; in fact, quite often commercial fishing work groups are composed of men only. Finally, if there are not enough people within the family or extended family, workers are often hired and paid in cash.

In contrast, subsistence fishing is closely monitored by its participants. Harvest levels are set by the needs of the group. Set and drift gill nets are the major subsistence technology, accounting for 99.9 percent of the total harvest. Fishwheels are not utilized for subsistence fishing, although occasionally silver or king salmon caught incidentally with the commercial harvest will be utilized in the subsistence economy. Set and drift gill nets are the preferred subsistence gear because they enable careful monitoring of the harvest: only that which is needed, and more importantly, that which can be effectively processed, is harvested. In reference to questions regarding subsistence harvesting and processing, local fishermen reiterated the statement that "we only take what we need, there is no waste." In contrast to commercial fishing, only women, and preferably older and more experienced and skilled, process fish for subsistence, an important subsistence social value. Thus subsistence fishing work groups are female dominated and directed. Finally, and without exception, subsistence fishing work groups are kin-based, reinforcing one of the most important social values among Koyukon Athabaskans.

Management Perspectives

In the local view, residents believe that they manage and should manage subsistence salmon fishing and that they maintain a viable system of resource management through self-regulation. Regulation is effected by various means. In general, subsistence fishermen employ rotational use of salmon streams, although explanations for this activity vary. Some individuals claim that the "fish are hiding" and thus it is not profitable to fish in certain locations. Other fishermen explain that it is bad luck to fish certain areas consistently, so different streams are used at different times. In either case, there does not appear to be a clear articulation of management for "sustained yield."

Historically, fish camp bosses controlled summer salmon fishing for the Lower Koyukon Athabaskans by controlling access to specific fishing territories and locations (Sullivan 1942). These fish camp bosses generally worked at one fish camp, and directed all fishing and hunting activities occurring there. By inviting certain individuals and families to fish at "their" camp, they effectively controlled access to the fish camp as well as to the associated fishwheel sites.

A parallel can be drawn between the tradition "Fish camp Bosses" and the Cree "Goose Bosses" or "Beaver Tallymen" as discussed by Berkes (1982) and Feit (1982). These bosses control access to hunting or trapping territory under their domain, they hold rights to that land, and control the number of hunters/trappers on the land. In this way they effectively manage the land and protect against over-exploitation of the resources.

Contemporary structure and composition of Lower Koyukon Athabaskan fish camps has clearly changed. However, traditional ideologies of fish camp use have not changed all that dramatically, and I maintain that some critical aspects remain intact, especially aspects that directly affect regulation of the resource. Specifically, individuals are recognized as being heads of camps, and thus in charge of certain fish camp and fishwheel sites. That right is recognized and respected until the individual expresses other intentions.

Additional means of self-management exist in contemporary local ideologies concerning subsistence harvest levels, with definite moral and social prescriptions discouraging over-exploitation of the resource. Taboos against over-harvesting subsistence resources exist and are strongly observed. Punishment for waste of or disrespect towards, resources results in bad luck occurring in almost any area of life. Similarly, encountering bad luck in resource harvesting is usually explained on the basis of an individual wasting or treating resources with disrespect. Rituals to protect the resources and to ensure their return are also practiced. No such similar set of social rules exists in reference to commercial fishing.

Discussion

These local perceptions of self regulation and resource management are not necessarily based on western models of cause and effect. However, the evidence clearly suggests that subsistence fishing is a functional, self-regulating system both directed at and resulting in "conservation" and sustained yield. Because it is such a highly valued system, internal mechanisms of control which operate at both an individual and community level serve to "conserve" and essentially manage the resource. State regulations pertaining to subsistence fishing are thus perceived as intrusive and totally unnecessary. Additionally, state regulations are seen to interfere with a system of which the state managers know very little. In light of local knowledge and ongoing traditional mechanisms of self-regulation, state regulation of subsistence fishing is deeply resented.

In contrast, commercial fishing is viewed as an externally introduced activity, which is understandably regulated by the state. Commercial fishing is perceived by local residents as being open to all fishermen, within limits set only by state regulations. As a result of this commonly held perception, regulations are seen as a necessary and expected aspect of commercial fishing.

At this point it should be evident that two very different management paradigms exist: that upon which the state and local commercial fishery operate, and that upon which the subsistence fishery operates. Underlying each of these two management paradigms are fundamentally different thought processes, value systems, and perceptions of the environment. In principle, the paradigms are similar in that their purported goal is maintenance of sustained utilization of the resource. Ideologically and empirically, however, the paradigms are diametrically opposed. The state utilizes an economic model of resource management, whose overall goal is to maximize economic return on a resource. However, as a result of this orientation, managers often focus attention upon one resource to the exclusion of others. By attempting to manage a single resource on a sustainable basis whilst ignoring all other resources, managers are ignoring ecological realities. Thus the economic model of resource regulation essentially fails to acknowledge the role of different resources within an ecological system.

In contrast the Lower Koyukon Athabaskans generally operate within an ecological framework, where the management unity in this case is the entire fish world, not just an isolated species or salmon stream. In actuality, the management unit is essentially the perceived universe, because every human or animal action, every natural or supernatural event occurring, causes an effect. Resource management is thus part of all-encompassing behavioural influences acting upon the overall system; individuals work within that system, not as an external entity operating on an isolated aspect of the entire system.

As stated in the introduction, waste and over-exploitation occurs on many different levels. The introduction of the commercial fishery and the subsequent tendency to view resources as a commodity has clearly illustrated this point. However, subsistence resources are associated with an entirely different realm compared to commercial fishing resources, and as such as effectively managed by means of a viable self-regulating system. Though stating that a functional system of self regulation exists, it cannot be concluded whether conservation is the unintentional goal or merely the fortuitous by-product of self-regulation. Further field work in this area is needed to shed light on this important question. However, regardless of whether or not this regulatory regime is conscious or unconscious, empirical or mythical, it merits attention. Management schemes of western scientists currently engage the attention of nation-states, and are thus considered legitimate by the dominant system, despite varying levels of management success. Rather than viewing these different management schemes as alternatives, in some circumstances a synthesis of the two perspectives may potentially result in a superior management paradigm.

References

Acheson, J.M.
1981   Anthropology of fishing. Annual Review of Anthropology 10: 275-316.

Asch, M.
1986   Wildlife, Domestic Animals and the Dene Aboriginal Rights Claim. Paper read at the 4th International Conference on Hunting and Gathering Societies, London, September 1986.

Berkes, F.
1977   Fisheries resource use in a subarctic Indian community. Human Ecology 5(4): 289-307.
1979   An investigation of Cree Indian domestic fisheries in northern Quebec. Arctic 32(1): 46-70.
1981a   The role of self-regulation in living resources in the North. In Milton M. R. Freeman, ed. Proceedings First International Symposium on Renewable Resources and the Economy of the North. pp. 143-160. Ottawa: Association of Canadian Universities for Northern Studies.
1981b   Alternative styles in living resources management: the case of James Bay. Paper presented at the Sixth Commonwealth Conference on Human Ecology and Development. May 24-28, 1981.
1982   Waterfowl management and northern Native peoples with reference to Cree hunters of James Bay. Musk-Ox 30: 23-35.
1983   The Ontario Native Fishing Agreement in perspective, A study in user-group ecology. Environments 15(3): 17-26.
1985   Fishermen and "The Tragedy of the Commons." Environmental Conservation 23(3): 199-205.
1986a   Environmental philosophy of the Chisasibi Cree people of James Bay. In Traditional Knowledge and Renewable Resource Management in the North. Milton Freeman and Ludwig N. Carbyn eds. Occasional Paper 23. Edmonton: Boreal Institute for Northern Studies.
1986b   Common property resources: ecology of a management dilemma. Workshop on Ecological Management of Common Property Resources. IV International Congress of Ecology, Syracuse, New York.

Behnke, S.R.
1982   Wildlife Utilization and the Economy of Nondalton. Alaska Department of Fish and Game, Division of Subsistence, Technical Paper No. 47. Anchorage, Alaska.

Braund, S.R.
1980   Cook Inlet Subsistence Salmon Fishery. Alaska Department of Fish and Game, Division of Subsistence, Technical Paper No. 54. Anchorage, Alaska.

Brody, H.
1982   Maps and Dreams. New York: Pantheon Books.

Case, D.S.
1984   Alaska Native and American Laws. University of Alaska Press. 586 pp.

Caulfield, R.A.
1983   Subsistence Land Use in the Upper Yukon-Porcupine Region, Alaska. Alaska Department of Fish and Game, Division of Subsistence, Technical Paper No. 16. Juneau, Alaska.

Clawson, M.
1983   The Federal Lands Revisited. Washington D.C.: Resources for the Future.

Ellanna, L.J.
1983   Technological and Social Changes of Marine Mammal Hunting Patterns in Tyonek, Alaska. Alaska Department of Fish and Game, Division of Subsistence, Technical Report No. 105. Anchorage, Alaska.

Feit, H.A.
1979   Political articulations of hunters to the state: anthropology and the James Bay Cree. *In* Politics and History in Band Societies. E. Leacock and R. Lee, eds. pp. 373-412. Cambridge: Cambridge University Press.
1983   Conflict areas in the management of renewable resources in the Canadian North: perspectives based on conflicts and responses in northern Quebec. pp. 435-458. National and Regional Interests in the North. Third National Workshop, Ottawa: Canadian Arctic Resources Committee.
1986   James Bay Cree Indian management and moral considerations of fur-bearers. *In* Native People and Renewable Resource Management. pp. 49-65. Edmonton: Alberta Society of Professional Biologists.
1987   North American Native Hunting and Management of Moose Populations. Swedish Wildlife Research, Supplement 1:25-42.

Firey, W.
1960   Man, Mind and Land. Illinois Free Press.

Flowers, N.M., D.R. Gross, M.L. Ritter and D.W. Werner
1982   Variation in swidden practices in four central Brasilian Indian societies. Human Ecology 10(3): 203-217.

Foin, T.C. and W.G. Davis
1984   Ritual and self-regulation of the Tsembaga Maring ecosystem in the New Guinea Highlands. Human Ecology 12(4): 385-412.

Gilbert, C.H. and H. O'Malley
1920   Investigation of the salmon fisheries of the Yukon River. *In* Alaska Fisheries and Fur Seal Industries in 1920. pp. 128-153.

Hardin, G.
1968   The tragedy of the commons. Science 162: 1243-1248.

Jette, J.
1911   On the superstitions of the Ten'a Indians. Anthropos VI:95-108; 241-259; 602-723.

Kari, P.
1983   Land Use and the Economy of Lime Village. Alaska Department of Fish and Game, Division of Subsistence, Technical Paper No. 80. Anchorage, Alaska.

Leacock, E. and T. Lee (editors)
1982   Politics and History in Band Societies. Cambridge: Cambridge University Press.

Loyens, W.J.
1966   The Changing Culture of the Nulato Indians. Ph.D. Dissertation. University of Wisconsin.

Marcotte, J.
1982   The King Salmon Drift Net Fishery on the Middle Yukon: An Overview of the 1982 Season. Alaska Department of Fish and Game, Division of Subsistence, Technical Paper No. 18. Anchorage, Alaska.

Nelson, R.K.
1983   Make Prayers to the Raven. Chicago: University of Chicago Press. 292 pp.
1982   Tracks in the Wildland. Anthropology and Historic Preservation. Cooperative Park Studies Unit. University of Alaska, Fairbanks, Alaska.

O'Riordan, R.
1971   Perspectives on Resource Management. London: Pion Ltd.

Orr, D.W. and M.S. Soroos
1979   The Global Predicament. Chapel Hill: University of North Carolina Press.

Pennoyer, S., K.R. Middleton, M.E. Morris
1965   Arctic-Yukon-Kuskokwim Area Fishing History. Juneau, Alaska: Alaska Department of Fish and Game, Division of Commercial Fisheries.

Rollins, A.M.
1978   Census Alaska: Numbers of Inhabitants, 1792-1970. Manuscript on file at the Elmer Rasmusson Library, University of Alaska, Fairbanks.

Segerstedt, T. and S. Nilsson, (eds.)
1974   Man, Environment, and Resources. Stockholm: The Nobel Foundation.

Shinkwin, A. D.
1985   Native Alaskan Development: Nenana
        Village. Laurentian University Review
        Vol. XVIII(1): 134-145.

Shinkwin, A.D. and M. Case
1984   Modern Foragers: Wild Resource Use in
        Nenana Village, Alaska. Fairbanks,
        Alaska: Alaska Department of Fish and
        Game, Division of Subsistence, Tech-
        nical Paper No 91.

Stokes, J.W. and E.A. Andrews
1982   The Subsistence Hunting of Moose in the
        Upper Kuskokwim Controlled Use Area,
        1981. Fairbanks, Alaska: Alaska De-
        partment of Fish and Game, Division of
        Subsistence, Technical Paper No. 22.

Sullivan, R.
1942   The Ten'a food quest. Catholic Univer-
        sity of America Anthropological Series
        No. 11. Washington, D.C.: Catholic
        University of America Press.

U.S. Department of Commerce
1980   American Indian Areas and Alaska
        Native Villages: 1980. Census of
        Population. U. S. Department of Com-
        merce: Bureau of Census.

Usher, P.J.
1981   Sustenance or recreation? The future of
        Native wildlife harvesting in Northern
        Canada. In Proceedings First Inter-
        national Symposium on Renewable
        Resources and the Economy of the North.
        M.M.R. Freeman, ed. pp. 56-71. Ottawa:
        Association of Canadian Universities for
        Northern Studies.
1982   Fair Game. Nature Canada 11(1): 5-11,
        35-43.

Watkins, M. ed.
1977   Dene Nation: the Colony Within.
        Toronto: University of Toronto Press.

Wheeler, P.
In press State Fishing Regulations and an
        Indigenous Fishing System: A Case
        Study of Kaltag, Alaska. Alaska Depart-
        ment of Fish and Game, Division of
        Subsistence, Technical Paper No. 156.
        Fairbanks, Alaska.

Wolfe, R.J.
1981   Norton Sound/Yukon Delta Sociocultural
        Systems Baseline Analysis. Bureau of
        Land Management, Outer Continental
        Shelf Office, Anchorage, Technical
        Paper No. 72. Juneau, Alaska.

Wolfe, R.J. et al.
1984   Subsistence-Based Economies in Coastal
        Communities of Southwest Alaska.
        Alaska Department of Fish and Game,
        Division of Subsistence, Technical Paper
        No. 89. Anchorage, Alaska.

Wolfe, R.J. and L.J. Ellanna, eds.
1983   Resource Use and Socioeconomic
        Systems: Case Studies of Fishing and
        Hunting in Alaskan Communities.
        Alaska Department of Fish and Game,
        Technical Paper No. 61. Juneau, Alaska.

Sámi Reindeer Pastoralism as an Indigenous Resource Management System in Northern Norway— A Contribution to the Common Property Debate*

Ivar Bjorklund
Tromsø Museum
University of Tromsø

It is commonly believed that pastoral management systems necessarily imply periods of ecological breakdown and loss of animals through famine. According to conventional knowledge, the reason for this development is to be found in the combination of individual ownership to animals and common ownership to land which characterizes a pastoral economy. The management implications of such a situation, as it is believed, is the "tragedy of the commons" (Hardin 1968): Every single herder will try to maximize his individual gain by putting more animals on the pasture, which ultimately leads to overgrazing, diminishing herds and economic loss for all herders.

This paradigm, which was presented as an abstract model of human behaviour, has recently been met with critique from different scholars interested in common property resource management (Berkes and Farvar in press, McCay and Acheson 1987, National Research Council 1986). In particular, in Canada there is a growing literature on the ethno-scientific character of Native management systems (Freeman 1985, Usher 1987, Usher and Bankes 1986) in regard to resources like fish (Berkes 1977, 1979, Berkes and Farvar in press), beaver and moose (Feit 1973, 1984, 1987). These case studies, mainly among subarctic Indian groups, are focusing upon the cosmology and organization among the people exploiting the resources, and

thereby stressing the fact that people are mediating their relation to nature through social arrangements. This dimension — man as mediator — is more or less absent in the above-mentioned theories of man as predator, maximizing his profits regardless of the social fabric he is a part of.

Pastoralism is often presented as the classical illustration of this predator form for human behaviour, and the core of the problem is believed to be in the existence of *common* ownership to land. Although it has been shown that privatization of pasture is not the only solution available to prevent overgrazing and that people are capable of acting collectively to protect common pastures (Gilles and Jamtgaard 1981), there are few studies of how pastoralists actually manage their pastures in relation to the interests of the collective. There seems to be an underlying assumption in the literature that pastoralism is the very condition under which the "tragedy of the commons" is likely to occur.

Now, as the following presentation will try to demonstrate, this paradigm of the commons has to be modified also when it comes to pastoralism. This is because pastoralism is by its very definition a situation where man is mediating the relation between land and animals, while Hardin's paradigm presupposes a social vacuum where the only relation of interest is the one between animals and pasture.

The domestication of reindeer is at least a thousand years old among the Sámi of middle and northern Fennoscandia, and as a pastoral

---

* This paper is to be published in *Development and Change*, The Hague.

adaption reindeer herding is known back to the 16th century (Anderson 1958, Ingold 1980). Ownership of the animals is individual and the main production unit is the household. The owners keep their animals together in herds, which size and composition reflects strategies of both herding and husbandry (Paine 1964, 1972). The households move around with the herd in a yearly cycle between inland (winter) and coast (summer) according to the seasonal grazing conditions. Legally speaking, pasture is a common resource for all herders. The pastoral production reflects the consumption needs of the production unit (meat, milk, sinew and skins) and conversion through an always existing market for meat has provided the unit with cash when necessary.

The viability of this pastoral ecosystem then, depends upon the relations between the three factors of production: personnel, herd and pasture. These relations have up until recently been mediated exclusively by the herders themselves and thus within a Sámi cultural framework. Culturally speaking, reindeer pastoralism has been a very autonomous system of production. None of the Scandinavian countries have, until recently, tried to interfere much with these ecological relations. The only exceptions being reducing pasture areas through regulations and land encroachments. The size and management of the herds, access to herding and pasture — these are all decisions which have been more or less left to the Sámi pastoralists themselves. In the last decades however, the pastoral ecosystem has been gradually integrated into governmental institutions, as the relations between the different factors of production became controlled by national laws and regulations. This development took place in Sweden in the 1970s (Beach 1981) and is today on the governmental agenda in Norway.[1]

This administrative integration was to a large extent justified by the authorities, by referring to economical and biological arguments. Being social democracies, well embedded in the ideology of the welfare state, the governments in both countries argued that reindeer herding was a very anachronistic undertaking in its traditional form, because of its uneven distribution of animal wealth among the herders. Statistics were presented to prove this pastoral matter of course and regulations were introduced to equalize these differences in animal wealth.

But even more important were the biological considerations; according to the biologically trained experts in the governmental administration, it was of the utmost importance to regulate the number of reindeer before overgrazing and an "ecological catastrophe" became a reality. In Norway, for instance, departmental economists and agriculturalists[2] would stress what they regarded as a classical situation of the "tragedy of the commons": Grazing is a "free" resource, and "unrestricted" access will inevitably lead to overgrazing and poverty for all herders (Odelstingprop 1976-77, Government of Norway 1985). The authorities have therefore in the last decade introduced a law and a set of regulations which are supposed to stop "overgrazing" and make herding more "profitable" by a) reducing the number of animals and b) the number of herders, thus increasing the weight of the animals and consequently the income of the remaining individual herders.

Now, presupposing the non-existence of any system of resource management among the Sámi pastoralists, this governmental approach is a good example of the conventional wisdom when it comes to pastoralism: Individual herders, unrestricted by restraints or responsibility, are each pursuing their own interests, regardless that it brings ruin to all. Let us therefore, examine more closely the traditional pastoral ecosystem of the Sámi in view of questions of resource management. As a starting point, we can go straight for the crucial question — paraphrased by both biologists and bureaucrats —

[1]The development in Finland has been somewhat different because of the intrusion of Finnish reindeer herding farmers in Sámi pastoral areas in the last century (see Ingold 1983).

[2]In Norway, the administrative responsibility for reindeer herding lies with the Department of Agriculture.

and ask: is pasture a free resource and does it (inevitably) result in overgrazing and mass starvation of reindeers?

The first and very important statement is given by the historical sources: There is no historical evidence of overgrazing in a general sense in Sámi pastoral areas. In fact, if overgrazing is to be understood as the destruction of pastures, consequently reducing the number of animals being able to persist, this is not known as a general characteristic of the pastoral conditions any time in Sámi history. Overgrazing in such terms seems to be a more apt description of the tragic development among Sahelian pastoralists in Africa (Swift 1977). The abrupt breakdowns in reindeer populations often cited by biologists (Kosmo 1984), are all examples referring to wild reindeers — cases when man is not mediating their relation to pasture.

The relatively few disaster-like breakdowns (*S. nealgidalvi*, Nwg. *vår*) we know in Sámi pastoral history, seems to be of quite another kind. The climate of the winter pastures in northern Fennoscandia — especially in the mountain plateau of northernmost Sweden, Norway and Finland (*S. duoddar*) — is extremely stable. The winters are dry and cold, and the relatively small amount of precipitation (compared to the coast) makes it possible for the reindeer to find the lichen through the snow without too great efforts. Twice this century (1917/18 and 1967/68) did quite irregular climate destroy the grazing conditions in the winter pastures of Guovdageaidnu, the most important pastoral area in Norway. Rainfall early in the winter was followed by series of freeze and thaw. The reindeer were consequently not able to break through the ice cover for food. Mass starvation was the result, and in 1918, for instance, this reduced the reindeer population in Guovdageaidnu by a third.

But events like these did not reduce the lichen as such — like for instance drought in Sahel would do with the plant production — and could accordingly not lead to overgrazing.[3] The

problem succeeding such winters as not related to the grazing conditions, but to the rebuilding of the herds.

The fact that there are no recorded cases of breakdowns of the reindeer population due to overgrazing, undermines the pessimistic prophecies we have seen put forward by biologists and economists and begs some questions about the nature of Sámi pasture management. One way to answer these questions is to focus upon what actually seems to be the case of the matter, namely the concept of *carrying capacity*.

Now, for the biologist this concept is a question of the relationship between animals and pasture. For the pastoralist, however, this concept puts him in the middle of this relation. For him, the carrying capacity of the given pasture is a reflection of his capacity to mediate the relation between herd and pasture. Because of the climatic and biological variations which characterize the yearly cycle of the reindeer, it makes little sense to the herder to define the question of carrying capacity in relation to a certain type of pasture at a certain time of the year. Abundant grazing by the coast in the summer is, for instance, not so much of interest if lichen pastures are not available to keep the herd alive through the winter. Or one might have access to large winter pastures, but that might be a value of less interest if the area available in the calving season does not have the corresponding capacity.

The main challenge for any pastoralist then, is to manage his herd in such a way that he can overcome these seasonal variations (and maybe also fluctuations) in pasture capacity. The way the Sámi perform this mediation is by dividing and combining their herds throughout the year to obtain the optimum relation between the size of the herd and the capacity of the given pasture at any time (Paine 1964, 1970). To exercise this mediation, the herder must possess a certain amount of *control* and *knowledge* of these two factors of production. He must have an intimate knowledge of animal behaviour in relation to climate and pasture and he must be able to control the reindeers *and* the pasture in correspondence with this knowledge.

---

[3] But grazing reserves, like lichen on rocks and trees, which is not grazed in normal years, were almost extinguished after winters like these.

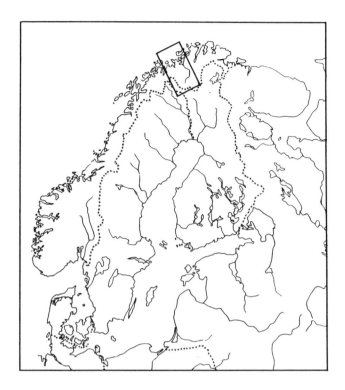

The pastoral area of Guovdageaidnu,
Finnmark.

This knowledge and control is organized
and exercised by the Sámi pastoralists through
the cultural institution called *siida*. This is a
form of cooperation between reindeer owners
organized bilaterally through kith relations
(Blehr 1964) but the sibling group being most
important (Pehrson 1957, Paine 1970). The term
refers to the group of reindeer owners who live
and migrate together and to the herd of reindeers
owned and herded by them. As the herds differ in
size through the year according to the varying
grazing conditions, so does also the demand for
herding tasks and labour. Consequently, the
siida changes size and composition through the
year, as the pastoralists are dividing and
regrouping their herds. Today, this may take
place up to three times a year, the implication
being that the pastoralists' society is constituted
according to three different seasonal sets of
organization: winter, spring and summer/fall.
The siida is then, in other words, an alliance
bilaterally recruited through cognatic and
affinal kinship relations, based upon the mutual

herding strategies among its members. The
bilateral principle of organization provides any
reindeer owner with potential access to pasture
and herding partners over a large area.[4]

One consequence of this form of resource
management is that overgrazing does not occur
as a general characteristic in the Sámi pastoral
area. As a general principle, the size of any herd
(i.e., siida) will not exceed the carrying capacity
of the corresponding seasonal grazing area. The
strategies underlying the composition of the
siida as a pastoral management system are to
never be in a position where the herd is not in
proportion with the pastures. If such a situation is
approaching, individual owners will withdraw
their animals from the common herd and join
other herding units according to kinship
relations and available pastures. The often
harsh competition which might be involved in
such regrouping must not overshadow the basic
point that the pastoral system, as such, is a
genuine system of indigenous resource
management — keeping a balance between the
number of animals and the carrying capacity of
the pastures as a whole.[5]

Not surprisingly, a characteristic effect of
this pastoral ecosystem is its permanent
centrifugal dynamics. The occupation with
dividing and regrouping in order to keep the
production units viable tends over time to propel
people and animals into any area where grazing
is available. This effect is, of course, at its

---

[4]The richness of Sámi kinship terminology reflecting
this flexibility has been demonstrated by Pehrson (1957).
[5] Ingold (1978:123), on the contrary, ends up with the
opposite conclusion, arguing that: "reinder pastoralism
is inherently unstable, carrying the seeds of its own
destruction in the contradiction between the
accumulation of deer and the ecological foundations of
pastoral controls." The problem is that Ingold's
fieldwork is done in an area (Salla, Finland) where
pastoral institutions for mediating the relations between
pasture, reindeer and humans no longer exist (see note
8) and Ingold defines this situation as "predatory
pastoralism." In drawing his conclusions, he seems to be
unaware of the fact that reindeer herding in northern
Norway still is a *pastoral* undertaking, organized and
exercised through the cultural institution of the *siida*.

strongest in periods when the growth of the herds is at its peak. Sámi pastoralists from Guovdageaidnu have, for instance, over the centuries migrated to Russia, Northern Finland, Northern and Central parts of Sweden and Norway, Greenland, Alaska and the Northwest Territories in Canada.[6]

Another effect — traceable through the last three or four centuries — is the shedding of non-viable units. If the number of animals is below the level necessary to keep the production unit viable, the owners settle down for a sedentary life as a farmer, fisherman or some kind of paid occupation.[7]

The preceding passage through Sámi pastoralism sheds a new light on the statements put forward by biologists quoted earlier in this article. So far, reindeer pastoralism has not led to any known case of the "tragedy of the commons." The two cases this century of abrupt decrease in the number of animals seem to be due to climatical fluctuations over a large area temporarily causing the grazing conditions to diverge seriously from the otherwise extremely regular seasonal cycles. Any other case of disproportion between herds and pasture — for whatever the reasons might have been — seems to have been solved in the sense that it did not lead to overgrazing, destruction of pasture and large loss of animals.

The reason for this lack of ecological breakdown is to be found in the management of relations between herds and pasture. Sámi pastoralism presupposes the individual control of animals, expressed through the seasonal dividing and combining of herds and organized through the social organization of the siida. Exactly *how* this control is exercised — degree of domestication, use of fences, mechanical facilities etc. — is of less interest.[8] It is in the social organization of herding that pastoralism differs from the conventional idea of a common pasture where everybody has free access. There is, thus, no "free access" to reindeer-grazing, as the biologists are postulating. The access is regulated through a culturally designed distributive institution, thereby regulating the carrying capacity of the pastures.

The conventional view recognizes only man's capacity as harvester and not as mediator. As the latter, herders are constituting management units which are mediating the relation between herds and pasture within a cultural framework implying strategies, negotiations, rules and sanctions (Paine 1970). The idea of the "tragedy of the commons" does not seem to take into consideration the social arrangements designed by the pastoralists to manage their relations to animals and pasture. As a paradigm, it reduces man to a predator, unrestricted by collective strategies and responsibilities. Not surprisingly, the examples cited to demonstrate this view are all from the biological literature on wildlife populations. But pastoralism implies human control, as the case of the Sámi pastoralists exemplifies, and thereby also the possibility of mediating the animal-pasture relation in the interest of the social group — and not only in the maximization of individual profit.

---

[6]This migration seems to a certain extent to have occurred in waves, as around 1690-1710, in the 1860s, around 1900 and in the last two-three decades. This indicates probably periods of strong growth of the reindeer population.

[7]The North Norwegian fiords with their abundance of fish — and, earlier, sea-mammals — have always represented a viable alternative for Sámi pastoralists who had to leave reinder herding. The only restriction has been the market sale of fish, which gave a very fluctuating return, as it was all controlled by Norwegian merchants. The technology and knowledge necessary for this kind of adaptation were more or less common property.

---

[8]Ingold (1980) gives an interesting account of a situation where control over individual reindeer no longer exists and the extent of pasture available to the management unit is fixed (through legislation). Thus the owners are not able to mediate the carrying capacity of the pasture; they are not able to divide and regroup their animals and legal restrictions define their access to pasture. Ingold coins this mode of adaption *ranching*.

References

Anderson, R.T.
1958   Dating reindeer pastoralism in Lapland. Ethnohistory 5(4):361-391.

Beach, H.
1981   Reindeer herd management in transition: the case of Tuorpon Sameby in northern Sweden. Uppsala Studies in Cultural Anthropology 3. Uppsala: Almqvist and Wiksell.

Berkes, F.
1977   Fishery resource use in a subarctic community. Human Ecology 5(4): 289-307.
1979   An investigation of Cree Indian domestic fisheries in Northern Quebec. Arctic 32(1): 46-70.

Berkes, F. and Farvar, M.T. (eds.)
In press Community-based sustainable development: the ecology of common property resources. Cambridge University Press.

Blehr, O.
1964   Action groups in a society with bilateral kinship: a case study from the Faroe Islands. Ethnology 2:269-275.

Feit, H.A.
1973   The ethno-ecology of the Waswanipi Cree, or how hunters can manage their own resources. In Cultural Ecology. B. Cox, ed. pp. 115-125. Toronto: McClelland and Stewart.
1984   Conflict arenas in the management of renewable resources in the Canadian North. In National and Regional Interests in the North, pp. 435-458. Ottawa: Canadian Arctic Resources Committee.
1987   North American Native hunting and management of moose populations. Swedish Wildlife Service, Supplement 1:25-42.

Freeman, M.M.R.
1985   Appeal to tradition: different perspectives on Arctic wildlife management. In Native Power. J. Brøsted et al., eds. pp. 265-281. Oslo: Universitetsforlaget.

Gilles, J.L. and Jamtgaard, K.
1981   Overgrazing in pastoral areas. The commons reconsidered. Sociologia Ruralis, Vol. XXI-2.

Government of Norway
Forskning, veiledning og utdanning i reindriften. Tilrådning om langtidsplan for reindriftens fagtjeneste 1985-1995. Landbruksdept. mai 1985, pp. IV-21-31.

Hardin, G.
1968   The tragedy of the commons. Science 162:1243-1248.

Ingold, T.
1978   The rationalization of reindeer management among Finnish Lapps. Development and Change 9:103-132.
1980   Hunters, Pastoralists and Ranchers. Reindeer Economies and their Transformations. Cambridge: Cambridge University Press.
1983   Farming the forest and building the herds: Finnish and Sámi reindeer management in Lapland. Production pastorale et société 12:57-70. Maison des Sciences de l'Homme, Paris.

Kosmo, A.J. og Lenvik, D.
1984   Resurstilpasningen i reindriften. Landbruksokonomisk Forum, Hefte 2, Ås-Norsk Landbrukshøgskole.

McCay, B. and Acheson, J.M. (eds.)
1987   Question of the Commons. Tuscon: University of Arizona Press.

National Research Council
1986   Proceedings of the Conference on Common Property Resource Management. Washington, D.C.: National Academy Press.

Odelsting prop. nr. 9 (1976-77). Om lov om reindrift. Landbruksdept. pp. 39-45.

Paine, R.
1964   Herding and husbandry, two basic concepts in the analysis of reindeer management. Folk 6(1): 83-88.
1970   Lappish decisions, partnerships, information management, and sanctions — a nomadic pastoral adaptation. Ethnology, vol. IX(1).
1972   The herd management of Lapp reindeer pastoralists. Journal of Asian and African Studies, 7(1-2).

Pehrson, R.
1957   The Bilateral Network of Social
        Relations in Könköma Lapp District.
        Indiana University.

Swift, J.
1977   Sahelian pastoralists: underdevelop-
        ment, desertification and famine.
        Annual Review of Anthropology 6:457-
        478.

Usher, P.J.
1987   Indigenous management systems and
        the conservation of wildlife in the
        Canadian North. Alternatives —
        Perspectives on Society, Technology and
        Environment, 14(1).

Usher, P.J. and Bankes, N.D.
1986   Property, the basis of Inuit hunting rights
        — a new approach. Ottawa: Inuit
        Committee on National Issues.

The Role of Subsistence Resource Commissions in Managing Alaska's New National Parks

Richard A. Caulfield
University of Alaska, Fairbanks

Introduction

When the United States Congress enacted the "Alaska National Interest Lands Conservation Act of 1980" (ANILCA) it sought not only to protect outstanding natural landscapes and fish and wildlife resources, but also to provide for continued subsistence harvest opportunities on federal lands in Alaska (Atkinson 1987). Moreover, it sought to establish an administrative structure for management of public land resources which would enable "rural residents who have personal knowledge of local conditions and requirements to have a meaningful role in the management of fish and wildlife and of subsistence uses on the public lands in Alaska" (ANILCA, sec. 801(5)).

Enhancing the role of Native people in renewable resource management is of concern in many areas of the North (Osherenko 1988, Alberta Society of Professional Biologists 1986, Freeman 1985). Yet there seems to be little consensus about the most effective strategy for accomplishing this goal. In Alaska, there is an extensive process for involving the public in managing fish and wildlife resources, although its effectiveness in responding to rural concerns has been questioned (Lonner 1984). Other strategies (Langdon 1984; Berger 1985; Pamplin 1986) focus upon formal cooperative Native self-regulatory regimes such as the Alaska Eskimo Whaling Commission, the Alaska Eskimo Walrus Commission, the International Porcupine Caribou Commission, and the Yukon-Kuskokwim Delta Goose Management Plan.

This paper examines the role of seven "subsistence resource commissions," created under section 808 of ANILCA, in incorporating local knowledge and expertise in the management of new national park units in Alaska. The commissions — comprised principally of local resource harvesters — are each required to devise and recommend to the Secretary of the Interior a "subsistence hunting program" for their respective parks.

These commissions are unique because of their congressional mandate requiring the Secretary of the Interior and the National Park Service to promptly implement their recommended program for subsistence hunting unless it:

> violates recognized principles of wildlife conservation, threatens the conservation of natural and healthy populations of wildlife..., is contrary to the purposes for which the park ... is established, or would be detrimental to the satisfaction of subsistence needs of local residents. (U.S. Congress 1980)

Thus, the commissions have the potential to incorporate traditional knowledge of Native and other rural people into management systems founded upon Western scientific principles.

However, this process is not without serious obstacles. Agency reluctance to share decision-making power, management perceptions of protecting a broader "national interest" against "narrower" local interests, community mistrust of management efforts, and lack of administrative and budgetary support could undermine cooperative efforts. For these and other reasons, the commissions are at a crossroads.

This paper focuses first upon the effect of ANILCA's subsistence policies on Alaska's new national park units. Next, it examines dilemmas facing the commissions in striving to protect both park values and subsistence opportunities, with examples drawn from deliberations of the Subsistence Resource

Commission for Gates of the Arctic National Park. Finally, it analyzes the role of the commissions in light of difficulties raised by Usher (1986) in melding "indigenous systems" of Native resource management with "state systems" of management.

ANILCA and Subsistence in Alaska

Protecting subsistence on federal lands in Alaska was a key provision of ANILCA. With its passage, Congress sought to fulfill the final elements of a major political compromise which emerged nine years earlier, from the Alaska Native Claims Settlement Act of 1971 (ANCSA). ANCSA extinguished aboriginal land claims and hunting and fishing rights in exchange for 44 million acres of land and $962.5 million (Berger 1985). Congress assumed that protection of subsistence would thereafter be a joint responsibility of both federal and state governments. In adopting ANCSA, Congress noted that it expected "both the (Interior) Secretary and the State to take any action necessary to protect the subsistence needs of the Native" (Langdon 1984:11).

In the ANCSA negotiations, environmental interests also included a provision (commonly referred to as "D-2") which required the study and recommendation of up to 80 million acres of land for new national conservation units (parks, preserves, forests, wildlife refuges, and so forth). When ANILCA was enacted nine years later, it incorporated these recommendations and added 104 million acres to national conservation systems (University of Alaska 1985).

However, by the late 1970s many Native leaders concluded that ANCSA's reliance upon weak state and federal protections for subsistence was insufficient (Case 1985:297-9). Subsequent political battles over the state's "subsistence law," which had been adopted in 1978, served as a potent reminder that the federal government's "trust" relationship with Native people needed to be reasserted as a means of protecting subsistence.

As a result, Native leaders convinced Congress to include provisions in ANILCA requiring the state to enact a law to guarantee a subsistence priority on all public lands. Failure of the state to do so would lead the federal government to reassert control over fish and wildlife management on its land (approximately 60 percent of Alaska's total). Protection for Native subsistence opportunities was strengthened when Congress confirmed its federal trust responsibility to protect those rights under the "commerce clause" of the United States Constitution (Langdon 1984:11-12).

Thus, ANILCA's Title VIII provided protection for "customary and traditional" subsistence uses by Native and non-Native "local rural residents." The state was authorized to develop a subsistence management regime mirroring federal requirements in order to retain management authority over federal lands. Federal approval of the state program required the state to include three key provisions found in ANILCA: 1) definition of "subsistence uses" by local rural residents; 2) preferences of those uses over others in case of resource shortages; and 3) adequate provision for rural public input in decision-making.

ANILCA further specified that utilization of public lands in Alaska was to cause "the least adverse impact possible on rural residents who depend upon subsistence" (section 802), and that federal land use decisions must take subsistence uses and needs into account (section 810). Access to subsistence resources was also to be provided rural residents (section 811), and the federal government was required to monitor implementation of the state subsistence management regime to ensure its compliance with Title VIII (section 806 and 813). Finally, ANILCA mandated the creation of "subsistence resource commissions" for each new national park unit in which subsistence uses are permitted (section 808).

Subsistence in Alaska's New National Park Units

ANILCA extended National Park system management to ten new areas in Alaska, totalling over 43 million acres (Willis 1985:239-249). In contrast to most other National Park system units in the United States, consumptive uses of wild resources for "traditional" subsistence purposes were permitted in all of these new areas, with only one exception. In this respect, Congress recognized that these park units were different from those situated elsewhere in the United States. The congressional committee agreeing to the final bill noted that it:

> believes that the establishment of these units should protect the opportunity for local rural residents to continue to engage in a subsistence way of life. The Committee notes that the Alaska Native people have been living a subsistence way of life for thousands of years, and that the Alaska Native way of life in rural Alaska may be the last major remnant of the subsistence culture alive today in North America. In addition, there is also a significant non-Native population residing in rural Alaska which in recent times has developed a subsistence lifestyle that also is a cultural value (U.S. Congress 1979b).

Protection of subsistence resources was specifically included as a designated purpose for three of the new areas — Kobuk Valley National Park, Cape Krusenstern National Monument, and Bering Land Bridge National Preserve. Political compromises with environmental advocates led to simply "permitting" subsistence uses in other park units, including Gates of the Arctic National Park and Preserve, Aniakchak National Monument and Preserve, Lake Clark National Park and Preserve, Noatak National Preserve, Wrangells-Saint Elias National Park and Preserve, Yukon-Charley Rivers National Preserve, and additions to existing Katmai, Denali and Glacier Bay parks. In Gates of the Arctic National Park — touted as Alaska's "ultimate wilderness park" — and several other units, a further limitation was imposed, requiring that subsistence uses be allowed only "where such uses are traditional" (ANILCA, sec. 201(4)(a)).

Since the passage of ANILCA, controversy surrounding subsistence in these new park units has centered upon the definition of key terms and phrases used in the legislation. The two most controversial phrases have been "customary and traditional" and "natural and healthy." While

ANILCA provides for "customary and traditional" uses in the new parks, the phrase was not further defined in the statute. Thus, managers and users alike have had to interpret legislative intent. One such section notes that the phrase refers to resource harvest patterns which:

> ...have played a long established and important role in the economy and culture of the community and in which such uses incorporate beliefs and customs which have been handed down by word of mouth or example from generation to generation (U.S. Congress 1979b:269).

ANILCA appears to recognize the desirability of a broad and flexible definition of "customary and traditional uses." Since its passage, the state has adopted a set of eight broad criteria for identifying these uses, which emphasize the importance of evaluating "patterns" of use by rural residents for whom subsistence harvests provide substantial economic, cultural, social, and nutritional benefits. The state's program also sought to establish "a dynamic process for the regulation of subsistence resources and uses which will enable rural people to participate in the decision-making process ... on a case-by-case basis to meet the needs of a particular management situation in a particular area" (ibid.).

A second critical concept in Park Service management of subsistence pertains to maintenance of "natural and healthy" population of fish and wildlife (this requirement differs from other conservation units, which must only maintain "healthy" populations). Many observers view the additional proviso regarding "natural" populations as prohibiting intensive wildlife management techniques, such as predator control. In ANILCA, Congress noted that "the National Park Service recognizes, and the Committee agrees, that subsistence uses by local rural residents have been, and are now, a natural part of the ecosystem serving as a primary consumer in the natural food chain" (ibid). Nevertheless, concern has been expressed that the "natural and healthy" requirement could be interpreted to unduly limit or even exclude subsistence uses (Hall 1985:11-14).

Role of Subsistence Resource Commissions

As noted previously, ANILCA provided the subsistence resource commissions considerable decision-making authority, beyond that of most "advisory" committees. Congress mandated that the Secretary of the Interior must "promptly implement" the commission's program as long as it meets legislated standards. The commissions were directed to "devise and recommend to the Secretary and the Governor a program for subsistence hunting within the park ... (and) each year thereafter ... (to) make recommendations to the Secretary and the Governor for any changes in the program or its implementation which the commission deems necessary" (ANILCA, sec. 808).

The commissions were to be established within eighteen months of the passage of ANILCA and were to have nine members; three appointed by the Governor of Alaska, three by the Secretary of the Interior, and three by the state's "regional fish and game advisory council" for the region(s) in which the park unit(s) was situated. However, delays in appointing commission members within the eighteen month period meant that they did not begin meeting until May of 1984, more than three years after ANILCA was enacted.

Membership of the commissions was drawn largely from local residents most intimately familiar with the needs of subsistence users and with resource populations. As of June of 1986, commission membership was 67 percent Native and 33 percent non-Native. Most of the commissioners had a long history of involvement with fish and wildlife issues in their respective communities, both as harvesters and as members of local fish and game advisory committees.

Each commission was allocated a budget of approximately $10,000 a year for preparation of their initial subsistence hunting program. As required by law, commissions held meetings in communities adjacent to the park unit to gather input from subsistence users for inclusion in the hunting program. The National Park Service maintained final authority over all expenditures for the commissions, and also provided logistical and secretarial support.

By fall 1986, all of the commissions had completed their draft subsistence hunting program and several had actually submitted their final program recommendations to the Secretary of the Interior. Recommendations from most of the commissions dealt with two major topics: 1) *access* to local resources; and 2) *eligibility* requirements for utilizing those resources. Other topics addressed included improving communication between managers and harvesters, hiring of additional Native people to work in park areas, predator control, greater public oversight of Park Service permit policies and decisions, comments on State fish and game regulations, and identification of future research needs.

Developing a Subsistence Hunting Program: The Case of Gates of the Arctic National Park and Preserve

The eight million acre Gates of the Arctic National Park and Preserve was created under ANILCA to maintain the "wild and undeveloped character" of the mountainous landscape in the central Brooks Range of Alaska. It was also intended to provide opportunities for wilderness recreational activities, and to protect habitat for arctic wildlife including caribou, grizzly bear, Dall sheep, moose, and furbearers. While "traditional" subsistence harvests were allowed, sport hunting was prohibited in the park (U.S. Department of the Interior 1985).

The park's southern boundary lies in the boreal forest zone of Interior Alaska, a land inhabited largely by Koyukon Athabascan Indians in the communities of Evansville, Allakaket, and Hughes, and a smaller group of Inupiat Eskimo in Alatna and Evansville (Nelson et al. 1978). To the west, in the upper Kobuk River drainage, are the Kuuvangmiit Eskimo communities of Ambler, Kobuk, and Shungnak (Anderson et al. 1977). On the eastern boundary is the recently-opened Dalton Highway, which bypasses the old gold-mining communities of Wiseman and Nolan and has spawned a new community at Coldfoot. To the north, on the edge of the treeless arctic slope, the Nunamiut Eskimo community of Anaktuvuk

Pass is situated within the boundaries of the park (Hall 1985). The village of Nuiqsut, near the mouth of the Colville River, lies to the north. Population of the region's communities was approximately 1650 in 1983 (U.S. Department of the Interior 1985:12). All of these communities (with the exception of Coldfoot) have a documented tradition of using resources within the park or preserve.

The idea of creating a park in the central Brooks Range dates back to the 1930s when adventurer Bob Marshall first proposed protecting the "ultimate wilderness" he found there. Early National Park Service studies also emphasized the national significance of the region, and proposed creating a major national park (Willis 1985:53). Significantly, the Nunamiut Eskimo residents of Anaktuvuk Pass also supported a park which would preserve opportunities for continuation of their way of life (ibid: 133). This Native band, which had a brief but rich history of collaboration with Western scientists on wildlife research projects (Stephenson 1982), supported a proposal for creation of a joint Gates of the Arctic Park and Nunamiut National Wildlands to be managed cooperatively by the National Park Service and the Arctic Slope Regional Native Corporation (Willis 1985:133).

Creation of the park and preserve in 1980 signalled the beginning of recurring disagreements between local residents and the Park Service over implementation of subsistence policies, many of which have been voiced through the subsistence resource commission. An early controversy had to do with the proposed designation of mapped "traditional use areas," which would limit local residents to specific zones for harvesting wild resources. The Park Service interpreted ANILCA's allowance of subsistence uses only "where those uses are traditional" to mean that traditional use areas should be mapped and incorporated into regulation. In 1984 they began the process of identifying on topographic maps the specific areas used for seasonal harvest activities. Maps drawn by Park Service staff showing known summer and winter use areas for each community near the park were distributed to the commission and to the communities themselves for comments, with the intention of using the maps in subsequent federal rule-making.

Reactions of local residents to the proposal were uniformly negative; they argued that park managers would use the maps as a means of placing further restrictions on their way of life and pointed to language in ANILCA's legislative history which suggested that:

> ... if the subsistence zone concept is to be applied to any park areas, fundamental fairness seems to require that the designation and boundaries of those zones be made by the subsistence resource commissions ... rather than by park planners and researchers, and that if there is any doubt as to whether subsistence hunting should be permitted within a particular area, that the decision be made on the basis that subsistence hunting should be permitted rather than restricted (U.S. Congress 1979a).

Harvesters stressed the need for access to resources such as the Western Arctic caribou herd which varied in numbers over time and had changing migratory patterns. This testimony coincided with conclusions of a North Slope Borough report on Nunamiut subsistence patterns which concluded that "three factors are absolutely crucial to a continuation of (Anaktuvuk Pass) subsistence pursuits: mobility; the ability to find suitable subsistence alternatives when primary resources fail; and free access to necessary subsistence resources" (Hall 1985:80).

After hearing considerable testimony, the Commission concluded that traditional use zones would be "culturally inappropriate, administratively cumbersome, and unduly arbitrary" (Subsistence Resource Commission 1986). The Commission drew upon local knowledge in recommending that park values be protected by managing access and eligibility, and by allowing local geographic constraints (e.g., water levels on rivers) to provide de facto limits on use. It also suggested that local communities themselves be encouraged to deal with any potential conflicts over use of hunting or trapping areas rather than having the Park

Service do so.

A second major controversy concerned the use of new technology in subsistence pursuits, especially that of all-terrain vehicles (ATVs) on park land by residents of Anaktuvuk Pass. Until the early 1950s, the Nunamiut frequently moved their settlements to maintain access to local resources, but they were now permanently situated within park boundaries. Unlike most other rural Alaskan villages, Anaktuvuk Pass was not situated on a river or ocean; summer access to local resources (by boat in other communities) was limited. As cash from wage employment became more available in the community during the 1960s and 70s, local hunters began to purchase ATVs for use in hunting, fishing, and gathering (Hall 1985:72).

Prior to 1980, most use of ATVs occurred without restriction on Native regional corporation land situated just north of the park boundary. However, the regional corporation surrendered that land to the Park Service in exchange for land with more lucrative petroleum potential on the Arctic coastal plain. With little notice, apparently even to residents of Anaktuvuk Pass, the surrendered areas were now included within the park and became subject to Park Service regulation. At the last minute, easements for continued ATV use were included in the land trade, but local residents soon found these to be inadequate.

Park Service managers looked to ANILCA's section 811 for guidance on the regulation of access. It authorized the use of snow machines, motorboats, "and other means of surface transportation traditionally employed for such purposes by local residents, subject to reasonable regulation" (ANILCA, sec. 811). Congress had provided guidelines to managers about use of some forms of technology for subsistence access; for example, aircraft use was generally not acceptable. However, it was unclear what other forms of "traditional" access could be used, especially those involving new technology. At the same time, the Park Service had a mandate from Congress to protect "wilderness" values, and was concerned about resource damage which might occur from ATV use.

The Park Service subsequently ruled that because ATVs had only limited use prior to the passage of ANILCA they were not "traditional" and thus were prohibited in the park except on existing easements. Anaktuvuk Pass residents objected, pointing to legislative history stating that limitations on subsistence technology are "not intended to foreclose the use of new, as yet unidentified means of surface transportation, so long as such means are subject to reasonable regulation..." (U.S. Congress 1979b:275). Use of ATVs, local residents claimed, was essential to the continuation of traditional patterns of land and resource use (City of Anaktuvuk Pass 1984).

The controversy over the use of ATVs is not yet resolved. Recently, the National Park Service initiated a cooperative research project with residents of Anaktuvuk Pass to determine the vehicular impact on local vegetation and other resources (U.S. Department of the Interior 1986). In addition, negotiations are underway between the Park Service, Nunamiut Corporation, and Arctic Slope Regional Corporation to exchange land and access rights as a means to both protect park values and Anaktuvuk Pass subsistence uses. Because of the Park's wilderness designation, congressional approval for such an exchange would likely be required. The Commission's role in these discussions has been to provide a public forum for airing differing perspectives about traditional use and ATVs, and to lend support to the complex and sensitive negotiations.

A third major controversy relates to eligibility for use of park resources. Congress intended that only those local rural residents (and their descendants) who had customarily and traditionally engaged in subsistence uses of the park be able to continue to do so. However, in implementing ANILCA, the Park Service decided to designate "resident zone communities" adjacent to the park. These communities are required to have a significant concentration of qualified local subsistence users: if so, all residents automatically qualify to use the park for subsistence purposes. The Commission is to play a major role in determining which communities have this concentration of users, and in recommending how eligibility issues are to be addressed.

Use of the "resident zone community" concept avoids requiring each user of the park to obtain an individual subsistence use permit from the Park Service and is in keeping with the intent of Congress to avoid imposing further administrative burdens on local residents. However, some have argued that the zones create unacceptable inequities; that a person could move from Florida to Shungnak for example and could, with no tradition of using the park, automatically qualify as a subsistence user. Environmental organizations have raised this issue, and advocate moving to an individual permit system.

Park managers have expressed concern about the growth of resident zone communities in recent years. Preliminary data suggest, for example, that the population in some resident zone communities near Gates of the Arctic National Park has increased 27 percent between 1980 and 1985 (Waller 1986). The population of communities near other Alaskan parks may have increased as much as 95 percent during the same period. While it is not known if a community's growth necessarily reflects increasing demands upon park resources, managers will certainly be monitoring any resulting resource impacts. For the Gates of the Arctic National Park, the proximity of the Dalton Highway raises questions about the potential for significant change in the socioeconomic and cultural character of local communities.

However, the Commission has endorsed the resident zone concept as a means of resolving local eligibility issues without imposing further administrative burdens on harvesters. It has also noted its responsibility to work with the National Park Service in the years ahead to monitor any changes in the character of local resident zone communities to ensure that Congressional intent is met and that park values are protected (Subsistence Resource Commission 1986).

In summary, the Subsistence Resource Commission for Gates of the Arctic National Park is actively seeking to incorporate local knowledge of resource population dynamics, traditional land use patterns, and subsistence harvest needs into management decision-making. Local peoples' knowledge is essential in applying the concept of "natural and healthy" to resource populations, and in evaluating what uses should be considered "customary and traditional." Commission members provide a vital perspective on cultural values and perceptions about resource management efforts, and about community perceptions of the role of changing technology in traditional pursuits. They also provide a keen awareness of community socioeconomic and cultural factors of significance to issues of subsistence eligibility.

Subsistence Resource Commissions at a Crossroads

Recently, Usher (1986) described efforts underway in northern Canada to foster greater Native involvement in the operations of fish and wildlife management agencies, often referred to as "co-management." He distinguishes between a "state system" of management based upon a common property concept in which the state has full and exclusive responsibility for resource management for the benefit of all citizens, and an "indigenous system" in which "all members of the group are involved with management as well as with harvesting, but leadership and authority within the group are based on the greatest acquisition of knowledge and the demonstrated ability to use it effectively."

Usher describes efforts to improve Native involvement in resource management in Canada, including: 1) incorporation of direct input from local users through decentralization of management systems; 2) establishment of user advisory boards or committees; and 3) encouragement of Native people to become qualified to work as technicians and managers in the state system. Similar efforts are being made in Alaska (Kelso 1982, Langdon 1984, Behnke and Haynes 1986).

Moreover, a growing body of literature suggests that indigenous systems of resource management, and management frameworks in which indigenous systems and state systems work together constructively, may prove to be more effective in addressing Northern resource management issues than are current systems (see Osherenko 1988, Alberta Society of Professional Biologists 1986, Freeman 1981). As Usher notes, while there is considerable room for skepticism about the impact that these efforts may ultimately have on resources, their effectiveness is open to research and verification (Usher 1986:73).

However, Usher expresses concern that strategies for enhancing involvement of Native and other rural people in resource management "do not ... necessarily incorporate elements of the indigenous system as such, much less result in a shift from the state management system to an indigenous system of self-management. On the contrary, they are much more likely to result in the continuation of the state management system in a decentralized but largely unchanged form.... These strategies," he suggests, "add up to a system in which Native harvesters merely provide data, and the state system continues to do the managing and allocation" (ibid).

The question raised here is whether the subsistence resource commissions are simply to be an extension of the existing "state system" of resource management or whether their congressional mandate will result in the meaningful inclusion of the views of local people in park management. In short, will they be vehicles for cooperation or co-optation?

The commissions are now at a crossroads; preparation of the subsistence hunting programs is nearly completed. The manner in which the Secretary of the Interior and the National Park Service respond to those recommendations will be critically important in building upon the efforts made thus far. Steps can be taken at the federal level to respond to Usher's concerns. These include:

1) promptly implementing subsistence hunting program recommendations which meet the guidelines for acceptability specified in ANILCA, and providing a detailed response explaining how they will be implemented. For those not accepted, a written response detailing why they were not should be provided, so that the commission might refine or modify its recommendation(s);

2) taking a broad view of "subsistence hunting" program recommendations, acknow-ledging community views that such a program must integrate concerns about cabin use, access, information and education efforts, local hire and so forth;

3) strengthening the role of commission chairpersons in overseeing budgets and in planning for future commission involvement in park management;

4) providing full and timely administrative and logistical support to the commissions; and

5) seeking to strengthen Native involvement in resource decision-making through cooperative research, planning, and management on park, preserve, and (where appropriate) Native corporation lands (see Berger 1985:165).

Park Service efforts to work cooperatively with Anaktuvuk Pass, the North Slope Borough, and the Bureau of Indian Affairs in conducting research on the impact of all-terrain vehicles demonstrate how local knowledge and Western science can join forces to respond to management needs. The Park Service has also contributed to documentation of traditional knowledge possessed by local elders in communities near the Gates of the Arctic, thus expanding our understanding of local ecological knowledge and Native cultural and historical values.

However, some fear that subsistence resource commissions will not be taken seriously; that managers will treat them as simply one more way to gather public input from special interest groups. Fears have been expressed that the "national interest" in protecting park values will override Native subsistence needs, and that the professional culture of the National Park Service, with its strong tradition of prohibiting consumptive uses of park resources, will bring continued pressure to limit or restrict subsistence.

These fears, however, are countered by some resource managers who believe that park values and subsistence requirements are not incompatible. A park superintendent in Alaska has written:

The new Alaska national parklands created in 1980 by ANILCA are an experiment on a grand scale.... They have set aside some of the largest and most magnificent wildlands remaining in the world and dedicated them not only to protecting the vast natural resources and valuable archaeological resources of the state, but to providing for the continuation of a vanishing lifestyle and the cultures of the Alaska Native people (Shaver 1985).

Other parks in the United States, including Hawaii Volcanoes National Park and Big Cypress National Preserve, have found ways to accommodate limited consumptive uses of park resources by indigenous people. The same applies to many of the newly established national parks in the Canadian North. In Alaska, this accommodation must occur on a significantly larger scale and, in the long term will require meaningful incorporation of the traditional and contemporary knowledge of Native people. With proper support, the subsistence resource commissions can play an important role in this process.

References

Alberta Society of Professional Biologists
1986   Native People and Renewable Resource Management. A.S.P.B. Symposium No. 10. Edmonton.

Anderson, Douglas D. et al.
1977   Kuuvangmiit Subsistence; Traditional Eskimo Life in the Latter Twentieth Century. Washington, D.C.: U.S. Government Printing Office.

Atkinson, Karen
1987   The Alaska National Interest Lands Conservation Act: striking the balance in favor of "customary and traditional" subsistence uses by Alaska Natives. Natural Resources Journal 27(2): 421-440

Behnke, Steven R. and Terry L. Haynes
1986   Local and Native hire in renewable resource management: an Alaskan case. In Native People and Renewable Resource Management. pp. 142-149. Edmonton: Alberta Society of Professional Biologists.

Berger, Thomas R.
1985   Village Journey. New York: Hill and Wang.

Case, David
1985   Alaska Natives and American Laws. Fairbanks: University of Alaska Press.

City of Anaktuvuk Pass
1984   A Statement of Concern From the People of Anaktuvuk Pass Relating to the All Terrain Vehicle (ATV) Easements within the Gates of the Arctic National Park. Unpublished ms. July 10, 1984.

Freeman, Milton M.R. (ed).
1981   Renewable Resources and the Economy of the North. Ottawa: Association of Canadian Universities for Northern Studies and Canada Man and the Biosphere Program.

Freeman, Milton M.R.
1985   Appeal to tradition: different perspectives on Arctic wildlife management. In Native Power: The Quest for Autonomy and Nationhood of Indigenous Peoples. pp. 265-281. Oslo: Universitetsforlaget.

Hall, Edwin S., S. Craig Gerlach and Margaret B. Blackman
1985   In the National Interest: A Geographically Based Study of Anaktuvuk Pass Inupiat Subsistence Through Time. Barrow: North Slope Borough. 2 vols.

Kelso, Dennis D.
1982   Subsistence Use of Fish and Wildlife Resources in Alaska: Consideration in Formulating Effective Management Policies. Transactions of the North American Wildlife and Natural Resources Conference. 47:630-640.

Langdon, Steve
1984   Alaska Native Subsistence: Current Regulatory Regimes and Issues. Anchorage: Alaska Native Review Commission, Vol. XIX, 101 pp.

Lonner Thomas J.
1984   The Spider and the Fly. manuscript. n.d.

Nelson, Richard K., Kathleen Mautner, and G. Ray Bane
1978   Tracks in the Wildland: A Portrayal of Koyukon and Nunamiut Subsistence. Occasional Paper No. 9. Fairbanks: Cooperative Park Studies Unit, University of Alaska.

Osherenko, Gail
1988   Sharing Power with Native Users: Co-management Regimes for Arctic Wildlife. CARC Policy Paper 5. Ottawa: Canadian Arctic Resources Committee.

Pamplin, Lewis
1986   Cooperative Efforts to Halt Population Declines of Geese Nesting on Alaska's Yukon-Kuskokwim Delta. Transaction of the 51st North American Wildlife and Natural Resources Conference.

Shaver, C. Mack
1985   National park values and living cultural parks. Cultural Survival Quarterly 9(1): 51-53.

Stephenson, R.O.
1982   Nunamiut Eskimos, wildlife biologists and wolves. In Wolves of the World: Perspective of Biology, Ecology and Conservation. F.H. Harrington and P.C. Paquet, eds. pp. 434-440. Park Ridge, N. J.: Noyes Publications.

Subsistence Resource Commission for Gates of the Arctic National Park
1986   Final Draft Outline: Subsistence Management Program for Gates of the Arctic National Park. manuscript. June 19, 1986.

University of Alaska
1985   Changing Ownership and Management of Alaska Lands. Anchorage: Institute of Social and Economic Research. Vol. XXII, No. 2.

Usher, Peter
1986   Devolution of power in the Northwest Territories: implications for wildlife. In Native People and Renewable Resource Management. pp. 69-80. Edmonton: Alberta Society of Professional Biologists.

U.S. Congress
1980   Alaska National Interest Lands Conservation Act of 1980. Public Law 96-487.
1979a   Alaska National Interest Lands Conservation Act: Report together with Supplemental and Dissenting View to Accompany HR 39. 96th Congress, 1st session, 1979. H. Rept. 96-97.
1979b   Alaska National Interest Lands: Report together with additional Views to Accompany HR 39. 96th Congress, 1st session. S. Rept. 96-413.
1971   Alaska Native Claims Settlement Act. Public Law 92-203.

U.S. Department of the Interior.
1986   Effects of All-Terrain Vehicle Use on Tundra at Gates of the Arctic National Park and Preserve, Alaska. Research Design. unpublished ms. July 7, 1986, National Park Service.
1985   Draft General Management Plan/Environmental Assessment/Land Protection Plan/Wilderness Suitability Review. Gates of the Arctic National Park and Preserve, Alaska. Anchorage: National Park Service.

Waller, Lou
1986   Personal communication. October 2, 1986. Anchorage: National Park Service offices.

Willis, Frank
1985   Doing Things Right the First Time: The National Park Service and the Alaska National Interest Lands Conservation Act of 1980. Washington, D.C.: Department of the Interior, National Park Service.

An Overview of Adaptive Management of Renewable Resources

Miriam McDonald
University of Alberta

Introduction

Uncertainty is a pervasive feature of ecological systems largely because natural systems are in a constant state of flux; further, the act of management, itself, alters dynamic relationships and modes of behaviour within a system (Walters and Hilborn 1978). Conventionally, resource scientists attempt to control ecological uncertainty by conducting detailed and repeated studies and analyses of ecological systems whereby the problem is reduced to highly specialized levels in an attempt to predict future events with greater certainty.

While standard in terms of conventional modes of scientific inquiry, failure to incorporate uncertainty into the management process has produced two fundamental problems in the development of renewable resource sciences (Walters 1986). First, it has led resource scientists to concentrate primarily on biological and technical harvesting issues, whilst largely ignoring the socio-economic dynamics that are inherent in the utilization of resources. Second, it has inhibited scientific understanding of biological and socio-economic responses to management intervention.

Adaptive management is a new approach emerging in the field of resource sciences (Holling 1978; Walters and Hilborn 1978; Starfield and Bleloch 1983; Walters 1986) that attempts to address problems of uncertainty in recognition that the following features of ecological systems make renewable resources difficult to manage (IIASA 1986: 1-2):

1. sustainable production depends on leaving behind a "capital" stock after each harvesting event, and there are definite limits to the production rates that stocks can maintain,

2. harvesting is normally undertaken by a community or industry of harvesters engaged in a complexity of human ecological relationships, and

3. biological relationships between the size of a managed stock and production rates cannot be predicted in advance from ecological principles, but must be learned through actual experience.

The term "adaptive management" means management of resources in response to change and uncertainty occurring in ecological systems. Instead of assuming almost complete knowledge and use of simplistic, deterministic models to manage resource populations, adaptive management acknowledges the reality of biological and human uncertainties in ecological management systems and presumes almost complete ignorance in terms of their consequences (Walters and Hilborn 1978). Its process, therefore, is based on learning through experience, where management activities become "tools of experimentation" in seeking ways to incorporate uncertainty into the design of resource management programs. Policy decisions are made in response to the effects of past management activities thus establishing a flexible, open-ended process that is adaptive to changing biological and socio-economic relationships within the ecological management system.

The purpose of this paper is to examine the process of adaptive management by determining what it is, how it works and its relevance to the management of animal resources in the Canadian Arctic. The concept of adaptive management will be discussed. Further, the techniques for implementing an adaptive management regime will be examined, and the adaptive management process will be contrasted with the conventional resource management approach. In conclusion, the likely value of adaptive management in the management of Arctic animal resources will be considered.

The Concept of Adaptive Management of Resources

Adaptive management has grown out of concern with practical problems of how to manage fishery, wild animal and land resources (Holling 1978). It is a concept that has risen from fundamental questioning of conventional scientific approaches to the management of renewable resources, and recognition of the need to develop an alternative, pragmatic approach based on discovering how a "partially-observed" system functions (IIASA 1986).

In recognition that the management of renewable resources is "done by man for man," adaptive management is concerned primarily with relationships occurring within a population, between a population and its habitat, and between a population and its users. A basic assumption of adaptive management therefore is that socio-economic dynamics are inherent in the utilization of resources and must be taken into consideration if resource management problems are to be alleviated. Adaptive management practitioners and theorists believe that problems in the resource sciences result from the interaction between ecological and socio-economic systems, and the tendency of scientists and managers to reduce complex ecological-economic relationships into simplified associations (Walters 1986). By concentrating on biological and technical harvesting issues and ignoring the socio-economic implications of management decisions, human resource-use activities are never completely controlled in the conventional, scientific management process (ibid).

Another major assumption of adaptive management is that although everything in nature is ultimately linked, it is not necessary to study all the components of an ecological system before evaluating the behaviour of that system under management. As Walters (1986: 2) asks, "How is anyone going to put the component pieces together, if ever they are all understood?"

In effect, adaptive resource scientists find the reductionist mode of inquiry inadequate, as there is no assurance that understanding how an ecological system functions at a given point of time will provide insight into how it will function under changed circumstances in the future. Furthermore, the act of management itself alters relationships and causes unknown changes within an ecological system, so that systems under study may be changing faster than they can be scientifically understood (Holling 1978; Walters 1986).

Ecological systems are in a state of constant change with annual cycles of growth and production in plants and animals resulting in irregular fluctuations in the size of animal populations. The aim of adaptive management therefore is to "work with nature rather than against it" so that population recovery can be encouraged if collapse were to occur (Walters 1986). Subsequently, long-term management objectives focus on the identification of persistent changes in production processes that can serve as key indicators in assessing the health and status of a population.

As ecological systems are resilient in withstanding considerable stress before their structure is seriously damaged, adaptive resource scientists study the relationship between stress and resilience in order to determine a range of alternative management options. Under this approach, resource scientists, managers and users learn about the potential of animal populations to persist under varying levels of harvest, mainly through direct experience with varied management options rather than through the development of abstract models and theory.

Adaptive management represents a major paradigm shift in the resource sciences by actively seeking ways for dealing directly with uncertainty in the management of renewable resources. Accordingly, renewable resource management moves away from an emphasis on science-based data gathering directed to elaborating better models, in hopes of making more accurate predictions, and toward developing a broader consensus about what the major uncertainties of a particular ecological system are, and the role of on-going management decisions in providing "experiments" needed to resolve the uncertainties.

The goal then, is to develop an understanding of the implications of specific management decisions and to explore the response patterns of systems in order to identify new policy instruments and options. Management, as a result, becomes a continual process of analyzing historic experience in relation to ecological theory and constraints and directing searches for productive and sustainable harvesting policies (Holling 1978).

At the conceptual level, there are three cyclical phases in the adaptive management process (IIASA 1986; Walters 1986). These are:

1. Structural analysis and synthesis to identify a strategic range of alternative management options that are consistent with historical experience yet suggest new opportunities for improved harvest over the long-term. Attempts are made to build predictive models of major processes in an effort to obtain an understanding of the uncertainties involved as well as to provide basic representations of the system against which experience can be tested and expanded. The models, therefore, are to be used as tools for predicting possible outcomes rather than instruments of policy analysis and decision.

2. Systematic development of a range of predictions about key management indicators through use of alternative models and basic management options identified in the first phase. The intent is to gain consensus among actors about the range of future management scenarios and the search for optimum policies that take into account existing uncertainties and the effects of current decisions on uncertainties that future decision-makers will face.

3. Design and implementation of effective monitoring programs to detect system response to management intervention and enable harvesting systems to respond quickly to unexpected changes without undue economic or social hardship.

Implementation of the Adaptive Management Process

Holling (1978) and Walters (1986) maintain there is no "cookbook recipe" to implementing the adaptive management process. Adaptive management, by nature, is a "learning by doing" process in which all management actions are treated as well-designed experiments that will produce short-term system responses and better information for long-term management decisions (Walters and Hilborn 1978). Adaptive management is system-specific and an open-ended process; however, there are distinct phases of activity that guide the process of implementation. These phases are summarized as follows:

Dialogue

- determination of the goals of management
- identification of key questions relating to the goals of management, e.g., what might be done when and on what time scale
- "problem bounding" in terms of reaching consensus on the breadth of factors to be considered, detail of analysis required, spatial scale of the variables measured and time horizon for prediction

Field Study and Analysis

- collection and analysis of data: examination of biological relationships within the ecological system that relate to key questions posed by the goals of management
- identification of the range of predictive outcomes through modelling exercises

Design of Alternative Management Actions

- exploration of alternative management options that can be tested within the range of predictive outcomes, including scientists' explanations to users of new approaches
- development of adaptive experiments for understanding the response of dynamic relationships, within the ecological system, to management intervention

Monitoring and Assessment of Management Actions

- analysis of imposed management actions in relation to existing constraints and observed changes in the system, and in relation to outcomes predicted by ecological theory
- identification of key indicators within the ecological system to ensure the quality of monitoring systems

Evaluation

- determination of likely impacts of alternative management options in view of altered norms of operation and modes of behaviour within the ecological management system
- identification of key questions posed by the management options which initiates a subsequent round of the adaptive management process

Successful implementation of the adaptive management process is dependent on bringing all the actors (namely, resource scientists, managers, users and policy-makers) involved in the management and utilization of a particular resource together, and creating an environment conducive to addressing long-term management concerns. Open communication is integral to guiding field studies, analyses, modelling and consequent judgement about the likely impact of alternative management methods (Holling 1978).

It is also recognized, however, that the diverse range of actors is likely to have conflicting objectives based on their vested interests in the resource (Holling 1978; Bailey 1983; Walters 1986). Dialogue, therefore, is initiated and continues through a series of structured workshops. The workshops are designed to, first, identify the range of ecological and social variables for consideration in management of the resource, and, second, to determine through active discussion alternative methods for management. As the purpose of the workshops is to facilitate communication rather than create forums for various parties to use in promoting their own interests, modelling exercises are regarded as a useful tool (Walters

1986) in that:

1. they serve to establish a broad framework of relationships for organizing a series of more focused workshops and meetings, leading eventually to collective management decision making,
2. other processes for defining uncertainties lack a necessary focus on the definition of management goals, resulting in forums where priority is given to problem analysis rather than to the development of effective resource management systems,
3. models can be used to "challenge scientists and managers to see the problem more broadly" as they require participants to evaluate various management and resource use alternatives without favouring any single hypothesis or previous model, and
4. models can establish explicit links between qualitative data gathered through the accumulated experience of an individual and the decisions made in ecological management practice by relating questions specifically to field observations and management priorities (Starfield and Bleloch 1983).

Adaptive vs. Conventional Resource Management

The differences between adaptive and conventional management of resources are primarily in the techniques of scientific methodology. Essentially, proponents of the adaptive management process find the methods of scientific inquiry in conventional systems of resource management inadequate in dealing with the pervasive feature of uncertainty in ecological systems.

Although scientific resource management is based on general ecological theories, conventional resource scientists and managers tend to rely on Newtonian methods of inquiry by seeking to understand the dynamics of complex ecological systems through detailed analysis of the properties of its components (Holling 1978; Capra 1985; Walters 1986). Walters (1986) finds that, even though most resource scientists are trained as ecologists, the tendency is to reduce complex relationships occurring in harvesting systems to simplified associations or, alternatively, to accumulate large quantities of data upon which conservative policies are based until better biological understanding is ascertained. In contrast, adaptive managers acknowledge the complexity of relationships within an ecological management system and attempt to identify key relationships that can serve as response indicators to management activities.

Both conventional and adaptive managers of renewable resources accept the need for renewable resource management in general terms. There are, however, attitudinal differences (Table 1) and divergent perceptions of the roles of biological uncertainties in the effective management of ecological systems.

According to Walters (1986), conventional attitudes about the objectives of formal policy analysis have risen from the presumption that biological uncertainties are small and can be resolved through careful modelling. Adaptive management attitudes, on the other hand, reflect both recognition and concern for the uncontrolled nature of ecological uncertainties. They also emphasize the development of effective management systems through synthesis of ideas, experience and experimentation.

Interesting differences between convention-

al and adaptive approaches to resource management are also found in the "tactics" employed for policy development and presentation as presented in Table 2. Adaptive management encourages and provides an open forum for the active involvement of actors from all sectors of the resource user-management community, necessarily including users, managers, scientists and policy-makers. In contrast, the design, implementation and evaluation of management strategies in the conventional resource sciences is generally a closed forum, restricted in language and ideology to trained scientists and resource ecologists. Perhaps the greatest ideological divergence between the two systems is reflected in the involvement of a variety of actors and ideas in the adaptive management process to explicitly reveal the uncertainties and difficult choices related to management interventions. Quoting Walters (1986: 352), with regards to the conventional resource management process:

> scientists try to hide their ignorance behind vast tables of statistics, and professional status is wielded like a club at very intelligent people who happen not to carry the standard credentials.

Table 1. Conventional vs. Adaptive Attitudes About the Objectives of Formal Policy Analysis

Conventional	Adaptive
1. seek precise predictions	uncover range of possibilities
2. build prediction from detailed understanding	predict from experience with aggregate responses
3. promote scientific consensus	embrace alternatives
4. minimize conflict among actors	highlight difficult trade-offs
5. emphasize short-term objectives	promote long-term objectives
6. presume certainty in seeking best action	evaluate future feedback and learning
7. define best action from a set of obvious alternatives	seek imaginative new options
8. seek productive equilibrium	expect and profit from change

Source: Walters 1986: 351

Table 2.   Conventional vs. Adaptive Tactics for Policy Development and Presentation

Conventional	Adaptive
1. committee meetings and hearings	structured workshops
2. technical reports and papers	slide shows and computer games
3. detailed facts and figures to back arguments	compressed verbal and visual arguments
4. exhaustive presentation of quantitative options	definition of few alternatives
5. dispassionate view	personal enthusiasm
6. pretense of superior knowledge	invitation to and assistance with alternative assessments

Source: Walters 1986: 352

Conclusion

In this paper, an attempt is made to provide a broad overview of the adaptive management system in terms of what it is, how it works and how it relates to the conventional, scientific system of resource management. In conclusion, brief comments are made on the perceived applicability of adaptive management to the management of living resources in the Canadian Arctic.

The application of an inflexible system of management practices and harvesting regulations in a highly variable environment, such as the Arctic, can be considered inappropriate in light of the sudden, extreme, and unexpected changes in biological productivity that are normal occurrences (Holling 1978; Freeman 1984; Walters 1986). At the same time, however, it would take decades or longer for resource ecologists to analyse in rigorous or acceptable scientific detail, all the variables of Arctic ecological systems that are required to develop a conventional science-based resource management regime, especially if "hedging against uncertainty" was not the pervasive feature (Walters and Hilborn 1978). In this respect then, adaptive management offers an economy of approach that should be attractive to resource scientists with budget constraints, as well as in the best interests of the living resources and the people who depend on the resources for subsistence purposes.

Currently, two systems of resource management operate parallel to each other in the Canadian Arctic: the traditionally based, culturally encoded system of indigenous peoples, and the conventional, science-based system of national and regional state-management agencies (Freeman 1985; Usher 1986). While some cooperative research endeavours have been undertaken in recent years (Gunn et al. 1988; Drolet et al. 1987), and there is growing respect for "traditional" knowledge of the indigenous people, participants of both systems generally experience difficulty in understanding each others' rationale and systems of thought. As a result, the significance of the indigenous system is typically minimized, insofar as the concerns and knowledge of the indigenous people tend to be taken into account only when they can be translated into "scientific language" and validated by strictly scientific methods of inquiry.

The adaptive management process potentially provides a methodological framework in which resource scientists and indigenous peoples can work together to resolve the complexity of resource management issues and problems that prevail in the Arctic. It is an open-ended, systematic process that designs management activities and policies that are responsive to biological changes occurring within a system based on both indigenous knowledge of ecological relationships and scientific processes of knowledge. In seeking the expressed views and active involvement of all people participating in the management and utilization of a resource, adaptive management facilitates a major shift from conventional, reductionist methods of problem analysis prevalent in the resource sciences, towards the discovery and implementation of integrated management systems through the synthesis of ideas, experiences and experimentation (Walters 1986).

Resources

Bailey, James
1984   Principles of Wildlife Management. Toronto: John Wiley and Sons.

Capra, F.
1985   Criteria of systems thinking. Futures, October 1985, pp. 475-478.

Drolet, C. A. , A. Reed, M. Breton and F. Berkes
1987   Sharing Wildlife Management Responsibilities with Native Groups: Case Studies in Northern Quebec. Transactions of 52nd North American Wildlife and Natural Resources Conference: 389-398.

Freeman, M. M. R.
1984   Arctic ecosystems. *In* Handbook of North American Indians. D. Damas ed. Washington, D.C.: Smithsonian Institute, vol. 5: 36-48.

1985   Appeal to tradition: different perspectives on Arctic wildlife management. *In* Native Power. J. Brøsted et al., eds. pp. 265-281. Oslo and Bergen: Universitetsforlaget.

Gunn, A. G. Arlooktoo and D. Kaomayok
1988   The Contribution of the Ecological Knowledge of Inuit to Wildlife Management in the Northwest Territories (this volume).

Holling, C. S. (ed.)
1978   Adaptive Environmental Assessment and Management. Wiley International Series on Applied Systems Analysis, vol. 3. Chicester, UK: Wiley.

IIASA
1986   Adaptive management of renewable resources: overview. Executive Reports. Laxenburg: International Institute for Applied Systems Analysis.

Starfield, A.M. and S.A.L. Bleloch
1983   Expert systems: an approach to problems in ecological management that are difficult to quantify. Journal of Environmental Management 16: 261-268.

Usher, P. J.
1986   The Devolution of Wildlife Management and the Prospects for Wildlife Conservation in the Northwest Territories. Ottawa: Canadian Arctic Resources Committee. Policy Paper 3.

Walters, C. J. and R. Hilborn
1978   Ecological optimization and adaptive management. Annual Review of Ecology and Systematics 9: 157-188.

Walters, C.
1986   Adaptive Management of Renewable Resources. New York: Macmillan Publishing Co.

Self-management and State-management: Forms of Knowing and Managing Northern Wildlife

Harvey A. Feit
McMaster University

Introduction

This paper examines the relationship between local systems of self-management and systems of state-management of wildlife in the Canadian north, placing special emphasis on how knowledge is related to action. Commonalties and differences are explored, as well as the mutual autonomy and mutual inter-dependence of the systems.

The paper begins with a social scientist's perception of state-management of wildlife resources and it seeks reasons why the development of such management concerns has tended to cut state-management off from local self-management. The paper then provides an extended exploration of self-management, in comparison to state-management, and the conclusions present some suggestions concerning their mutual development.

State Mandated Wildlife Management — A Social Scientist's View from the North

Looking from the perspective of several decades, indigenous populations around the circumpolar world have found themselves increasingly encapsulated in nation states. That is, from being wholly autonomous societies in essentially complete control of their own daily lives, and in effective control of the land and resources which they utilized, they have become societies enmeshed in complex relationships to the wider world, and in particular to the national states and to international economies. Some of these linkages have been welcomed, and indeed actively sought, others have been unanticipated or imposed. The process is complicated, and many aspects are beyond the scope of this paper, but it is essential to highlight the changes that are occurring between two societies with unequal resources and sources of power. The power differences are relative, and indigenous societies have shown considerable capacity to reproduce themselves in the context of change. It is also clear that, while the institutions of industrial societies have not always succeeded in bringing about the changes they desired in the North, they are a greater threat to the potential for continued development of indigenous societies, than the reverse. These conflicts and threats are manifest in the uses made of land and natural resources, and, as the national governments of the encapsulating states have extended the land and sea areas open to resource extraction by non-local economic interests, indigenous populations have often resisted and opposed those losses of local control. In those countries where this process has gone forward without direct genocide or forced integration into the national society, part of the indigenous response has been to assert claims of autonomous rights and self-governance.

Into this circumpolar setting of expanding national or international development of land and resources, and of local resistance, the national governments have increasingly inserted environmental scientists, planners and wildlife managers. This may seem a rather stark, and possibly a one-sided perspective from which to view the development of northern conservation and wildlife management, but I think it accurately reflects something of how this development looks when perceived in the North, as opposed to alternative perspectives developed by wildlife specialists in the south. From this northern perspective government mandated wildlife research and management is often seen as part of a process of intrusion, enhancing centralization of control rather than contributing to local autonomy and self-governance. This is not of course necessarily the intention of the individual wildlife biologists and managers themselves, but it is part of the context in which they work. Those wildlife specialists who see and are concerned by this process often are able to moderate the impacts of their own undertakings, but without altering the context. The reaction of indigenous hunters to wildlife professionals is not in my experience typically hostile, but they are cautious and deeply concerned about the implications of state-mandated wildlife management for their own local practices. And such concerns are not without foundation, for they emerge from previous experience, and they are consistent with what appears to have been happening over many years in the south.

The developmental history of the conservation professions and movements follows the destruction of significant habitat and the decimation of wildlife in the regions of North America which were settled and exploited in the last century; their development was motivated in part by the desire to conserve part of what remained, and, where it was possible, to promote rehabilitation. The task was not an easy one, nor has it been characterized by steady success, but rather by uneven and hard-won progress. Many important habitats and some important species have been conserved, and public awareness of the value of nature has been greatly enhanced in the last eighty years, and especially in the last twenty. Indeed, the development of ecological and conservation sciences has been one of the truly important developments of the 20th century.

Important as these developments have been, they are still in their adolescence when viewed from the perspective of the weight they carry in the practical arenas of economic and political decision making. It is no accident, nor is it just a rhetorical strategy, that most of the public education about conservation has come about by publicizing the losses of habitats and wildlife.

While the practical accomplishments to date are important; a simply descriptive account of the main features of the last decades would, it seems to me, have to emphasize the continuing loss (of extent and quality) of agricultural land and forested resources, the growing awareness and continued polluting of the seas and the air, and the general deterioration of the urban environments by complex chemical pollutants. The ecological sciences have shown these trends cannot continue at the present pace for very much longer without significantly escalating impacts. In response to the difficulties of generating effective changes in these trends, the conservation-directed policies and programs of national and international agencies have tended to move from local, regional and national problems to consider world-wide threats to the future viability of planet-wide systems. Examples include concern with the world-wide rate of species extinctions, acid rain, pollution of the seas, reduction in the ozone layer, airborne particulate pollution, the effect of deforestation on oxygen balance, and the environmental consequences of nuclear accidents. Without questioning the validity of examining these issues, it is important to note that the scale of the issues being discussed, and the rhetoric of conservation in the public and policy-making arenas, have escalated because the problems are still increasing. Thus, the development of environmental and conservation issues in the last few years has been toward world-wide problems which require national and international responses.

This overview indicates that the intransigence of the problems has moved the primary focus of conservation concerns away from the local level to the international and global levels, toward a focus on governmental policy makers and bureaucrats as the primary agents for action. However, it is important to note that this trend does not reflect any ineffectiveness of local-level responses to environmental management at the local or regional levels. Rather it responds to the need for a response to the continuing environmental deterioration which follows from the generally limited priority given to environmental and ecological issues in national and international economies and policy making.

As a consequence, these recent approaches tend not to encourage or support local initiatives, local control of environments and resources, and local conservation measures as a primary goal and strategy. There are some counter trends within the professions and organizations, some of which are noted below; but it appears that the overall trend has not been toward local management. In general, where local management has become a concern it tends to be legitimated and viewed from the point of view of its contribution to national and international management planning.

It will be argued that these directions are insufficient when dealing with the North and other regions in which local communities or regional societies predominate, and where long-term occupation and use of lands and wildlife by socially organized communities of resource users continues. Furthermore, while the present governmental strategies being followed are essential, they are held to be insufficient, and fail to advance opportunities for conservation in the Canadian North through forms of local management by the Northern communities themselves. Many indigenous groups in the Canadian North assert that they do presently manage renewable resources without depending on the intervention of national or provincial governments. Those which do not assert this tend to claim that they could do so in the future; both groups assert that they did manage renewable resources over a long historical period. These claims are based on forms of self-management.

Self-management, State-management and Co-management — Definitions

The term self-management is used in a specific sense, namely, as the local or regional level systems for regulating the use of wildlife and/or for managing the wildlife themselves, which originate and are legitimated and practiced by local or regional societies, or groups of resource users. Self-management systems do not depend on recognition by any other governmental or administrative authority for their existence or essential operation. They do not therefore depend on the delegation of responsibility or authority, nor on the legal recognition of rights to such practices by the courts, legislation or other legal instruments of the state; although each of these latter may compliment self-management and/or enhance the possibilities for the effective practice of self-management. Self-management may be recognized by the state by any of these means, but this does not create or define self-management, quite the contrary, it is a form of giving recognition within an encapsulating legal, political and administrative system to a set of practices whose origins, capabilities, and legitimacy are established by local social groups.

Self-management in short is the direct exercise of effective managerial and regulatory practices with respect to wildlife and land. The legitimacy and authority for such practices are determined at the local level by reference to community-based systems of knowledge, values and practice. Furthermore, they are especially embedded in local practices and knowledge with respect to world view, property rights, social authority, and the definition of the sacred.

Self-management in this sense is therefore a part of local or regional-level societies and cultures — whether these be indigenous peoples or communities of resource users, such as outport fishermen. Self-management occurs whether practices be "traditional" or recently developed. It is necessary to emphasize this latter point, because self-management is not only found in the contexts of isolated societies, but also where the effects of the nation state and of the world economic systems are widespread.

Thus, the fact that self-management by definition has a source independent of state authority does not imply that it exists in social communities which are independent of such authorities, or that it can itself exist today without relations to state authority. Indeed, it can be argued that the existence, or at least the development, of certain forms of self-management have their origins or development in the local resistance to state forms of management. This emphasizes that self-management is closely related to state management and co-management, but also why they must be distinguished.

State management is management deriving from the authority of the law of a nation state, usually from the constitutional powers exercised by legislatures or executives. State management in North America is typified by several characteristics. The day to day administration of state management in North America is not usually in the hands of groups of resource users, but is conducted by a highly professionalized group of administrators and scientists. State management tends to emphasize national or provincial/territorial interest over local interests, because of the structure of legislative power by which state management is established. State management therefore also operates within a legal system which has placed greater weight on non-wildlife resources such as forests and minerals than it does on wildlife, thus complimenting the state-level priority on development.

Unfortunately, the administrative departments with responsibilities for wildlife management generally exercise limited political weight within their respective governmental structures, although they are often staffed by very dedicated personnel. Thus, state management, even in its most successful forms, tends to involve conflict and complex negotiation among units within the state structure that legitimates it. Therefore the mix of resource policies which governments adopt tend to involve significant compromises on the goals and means of conservation. These are a necessary cost of having some effectiveness, but whether they are an acceptable cost may differ from a local or a national viewpoint. State management therefore tends to generate conflicts with local conservation interests, because it is at the local level that the major costs of these compromises are generally felt.

It must be emphasized however that state management, like self-management does vary through time and geographically. Thus in some continental European states the legally constituted management authorities are considerably less centralized. For example, in France conservation and management of wildlife is legally the responsibility of local and regional communal associations comprising land owners, resource users, and the local population; enforcement is in significant degree also locally organized (Doumenq 1981). Such a system has certain affinities with self-management, although it is also fundamentally different because authority is derived from national institutions, and local associations are parts of regional and national federations. Nevertheless, it is interesting to note that these various communal and localized forms of wildlife management can be found in some modern nation-state administrations, and that North American state practices are not the sole options. That this is the case has become apparent due to the development of new forms of co-management in North America.

Co-management as generally defined involves some working arrangement between state-mandated agents and individuals or groups of wildlife users who themselves have a role in managing the resources (Pinkerton, in press). Co-management may involve various linkages with self-management systems, or the resource users who participate in co-management may be individuals whose mandate and authority does not derive from local institutions, but from the appointment to the co-management body itself. Nevertheless, co-management may serve as an important institution, linking self managers and state managers. Indeed, there is increasing evidence that local-level systems for control of wildlife resources operate in diverse parts of the world, and with respect to diverse species (cf. McCay and Acheson 1987).

Local systems of self-management of fisheries have been described in the south Pacific islands and in Africa; local self-management of terrestrial wildlife has been described in African communities, in India, New Guinea, Malaysia, and Australia; forest management has been described in North American Native communities, Australian Aboriginal communities, in India and in Indonesia; and general land use and management has been described in Africa, the Middle East, India, New Guinea, and Australia, among others (see references cited below). Many types of research have touched on these issues, and the themes of local knowledge and practice of wildlife resource management are increasingly being discussed through the work of various international agencies, such as the International Union for Conservation of Nature and Natural Resources (IUCN), the International Union of Biological Sciences, UNESCO Man and Biosphere Programme, the United Nations Environment Programme and others. While a comprehensive survey of the research being done is beyond the scope of these comments, the extent of such work is now substantial, as indicated by recent collected volumes of papers (McCay and Acheson 1987; Williams and Hunn 1982; McNeeley and Pitt 1985; Ruddle and Johannes 1985; and Hanks 1984), and by the non-North American monograph length studies cited in the bibliography (Conklin 1975; Marks 1976, 1984; Nietschmann 1973; Johannes 1980).

Within northern Canada, northern Quebec has probably been the most intensively studied region, but studies conducted in northern Ontario, Alberta, British Columbia, the Northwest Territories, Yukon, and Alaska show similar results. Research on northern North American indigenous communities has examined culturally distinctive social methods of regulating access to resources, sustainable yield harvesting strategies, social systems of production, distribution and consumption affecting resource use practices, customary law and systems of rights regulating decision-making and control of resources, and systems of language, ritual and spiritual beliefs which shape the interpretation of environmental experience and knowledge. A more limited, but nevertheless important set of studies, have compared and tested actual resource use practices with their biological outcomes, and with recognized management objectives (references provided below).

It is unknown just how widespread such systems are at present. The most plausible assumption, however, is that in one form or another, they must have been quite widespread. This is so for two reasons. First, as indicated below, there is no reason not to expect that indigenous peoples, any less than peoples of European descent, would develop a realistic body of knowledge about an environment with which they intensively interact, or that they would use that knowledge to conserve or manage resources which they value.

Furthermore, indigenous groups' survival seems ample testimony to a recognizable level of accomplished knowledge; which is not to say, perfect knowledge. Survival is not just testimony of knowledge, but of the effective application of knowledge to management practices. It is one of the legacies of the research on the evolution of human societies that it is now recognized that hunting and gathering practices and societies have been the primary means of human subsistence and of human social life for fully nine-tenths of the period during which there has been human life on the earth. Moreover, it has been found that hunting and gathering societies which have survived to the present are highly adaptive societies.

It now seems clear that human hunters have had for millennia the capability to deplete some of the important wildlife resource populations which they have been using, given the use of fire and the capability to drive herds of animals into surrounds or over precipices. But in the light of this finding, it is also clear that most wildlife populations survived in significant degree their use by these hunters. And although not all wildlife populations may have survived use by hunting and gathering societies, the extent of surviving wildlife populations reported during the early centuries of European expansion implies that some forms of self regulation by the hunters must have occurred, and probably were common. Indeed, the fact that wildlife depletion has almost certainly intensified, rather than declined, during the transition to urbanized state-level societies, is not just a result of demographic and technological changes, but of the changes in social organization and in particular of the increased social scale that is at a core of the declining capability for local self-regulation in industrialized societies.

The reasonableness of the assumption that systems of self-management must have been widespread and common throughout human prehistory, makes it essential to examine their continued presence in the contemporary world, where their existence and functioning can be researched. This is particularly important in areas such as the Canadian North where there has generally been only limited disruption of the environment, limited management by the state, and limited although growing competition for resources.

This paper examines what is known of local self-management of wildlife, particularly in the Canadian North, and where it is appropriate it compares self-management with government management on two dimensions: first the structures of knowledge which underlie effective management and, second, the historical practices of management.

Culture and Environmental Knowledge

A substantial literature has been published on the systems of environmental knowledge among peoples from diverse cultures around the world.

Human beings strive to create knowledge, a coherent world, out of their complex and continuously novel experience, and only through such an organization of knowledge, or culture, does human action and survival appear possible. By means of cultural ordering, the always unique experiences and the always unique situations for action are reduced to a limited range of items, events, and contexts, to which relatively standardized understandings, rules and behaviors can apply. Cultures are diverse, but each creates structures of knowledge and practice which permit an ordered life, and each culture is learned, shared and reproduced in a human social group. Thus, the very considerable knowledge possessed by other societies is not identical to Western knowledge, for it is embedded in its own distinctive cultural system. That is, the knowledge is the result of a process of interpreting phenomenal experience, and it is both "natural" and fundamentally and inseparably cultural as well. The meaning of the categories lies not in any denotative pointing to phenomenal reality, but in the system of categories as symbols. Thus, specific types of plants and animals are associated with other types in different groupings in each culture, and each may be associated with different feelings, usages, moral categories. That is, we both discover nature and create a meaningful world in the same process, and we cannot separate the two processes.

For the Waswanipi Cree, for example, the classification of animals involves a hierarchy which links animals to men and both to spirits and to God. Animals are social beings, not cut off from humans as part of a natural order separated from human society. And Waswanipi therefore interpret animal actions as the results of willful choice on the part of the animals. Animals in turn are interpreted as social beings capable of interpreting and understanding the actions of men. The Waswanipi hunters say that they only catch an animal when the animal gives itself to them, or is given them by God and the spirits. They are given animals because they respectfully ask for what they need to survive, and their requests are heard. And they are under reciprocal obligation for what they receive, and treat the animals with respect in the way they hunt, butcher, consume and use the animal bodies. This respect is expected and appreciated by the animals, whose souls survive to be reborn again. With the rebirth of animals, respectful and thankful men may find the animals and the food they need to survive for the duration of their own lives, and to raise their children in turn. When hunters act properly, animals souls survive, and animals continue to be reborn, in health and numbers, and humans too lead healthy lives. The balance is reciprocal. It is stated that hunters have the skill and technology to kill too many animals, and it is part of the responsibilities of the hunter not to kill more than he is given. How signs from the animals and the spirits tell him how many can be taken will be indicated briefly below, but these signs involve complex observation and interpretation of weather, snow, vegetation and animal population parameters, all of which are considered as communications from animals and the spirits.

This understanding is decidedly different from that achieved by Western science. However, both construct and incorporate vast bodies of knowledge about northern environments and both involve construction of models to give meaning to those worlds. Western science constructs and uses an organismic model, which ecology has been increasingly applying to the natural world, the ecosystem model. Thus ecological models break down the barriers erected prior to the 19th century between the organic and the inorganic world, and these models show how animal and habitat are incorporated in a complex system not unlike that of an organism. The Cree for their part construct a social world, a world which they have extended to all potentially active entities in their experience. Both models constitute a world of complex reticulate causalities, linking the human, the organic and the inorganic. Both models anticipate the possibility and the desirability of a balanced participation of humans in their worlds. Both models organize extensive factual information in a form which tends to motivate appropriate action. And both models tend to help humans understand their worlds and acknowledge responsibility for it.

This conclusion, that all systems of human knowledge are created by similar processes and are more alike than the focus on their surface differences appears to indicate, makes clear that all human systems of knowledge incorporate considerable information and warrant thoughtful study and practical respect.

The Practice of Self-management

While general knowledge establishes the basic structures of the world in which we live, specific knowledge of the particular contexts and situations in which we must act is continually being sought and used. Current information on the condition and history of game populations is essential in order to apply generalized knowledge and principles to particular circumstances, and wildlife managers are continually collecting such knowledge. This is as true for local level managers as for state-mandated managers.

For example, as previously reported (Feit 1986b), information on the composition of beaver colonies is continually collected by Waswanipi hunters from signs of the beaver around the sites, from the sizes and sexes of the beaver caught, and from information collected in the process of butchering beaver. Waswanipi hunters work with a model of the growth of beaver colonies: first year colonies are comprised of founding couples, second year colonies are typically comprised of six beaver, namely adults with kits of the year, and third year or older colonies typically have 10 to 12 beaver comprised of adults with yearlings plus kits of the year (Feit 1978). The latter composition is considered potentially stable through out-migration of the two year old beaver.

Knowledge of beaver colonies being hunted, of their age and sex composition is sought in order to determine how many beaver are present and how many may be taken. Knowing the history and age of a colony gives some idea of the possible composition, according to the model, but this must be adapted to particular instances. Tooth marks on wood cuttings around a pond, how bank burrows far from the lodge are used, and other indicators all provide useful information on whether kits or yearlings may be present. The size of the last cohort born to a mating female can be determined if she is caught, because women look for placental scars on the uterus when butchering beaver. Hunters never know for sure how many beaver there are in a lodge, but they make increasingly accurate estimates as their observations increase, and as they watch for signs of the activities of the remaining beaver, and as they learn from the trapping process which ages and sexes of animals are definitely present. Furthermore trends in the numbers of colonies, in the abandonment of sites, the size of cohorts, and in the numbers of unmated beavers are continually being noted.

When the Cree hunters who were in charge of specific hunting territories were interviewed in land use surveys in the 1970s it was found that they could not only mark on a map beaver lodges occurring in a hunting territory in excess of 300 km^2 but many could indicate how many beaver of each age and sex category had been harvested the last time a lodge was trapped, and some could indicate how many of each age group they thought were still to be found at the colony. This inventory often involved a report on 50 to 100 beaver colonies. The hunters were the first to say that they were not absolutely certain of these numbers, but they would discuss the observations and assumptions they made in order to make these estimates.

For moose similar patterns of monitoring go on, although for a more dispersed population. The numbers of occupied moose yards, the size of yarding groups, the frequency with which females are accompanied by young, the frequency of twin young are all noted and discussed by hunters (Feit 1987b).

In both cases the parameters monitored are all ones which wildlife biologists have found to be important indicators of the condition of the game populations and useful indicators for management decisions concerning the sustainability of present harvests (Feit 1978). Absolute numbers are not recorded, but trends in the basic parameters are noted and discussed by Waswanipi hunters. These trends are not understood in the same way by scientists, because for the Cree these indicators are treated as a form of social communication, a message from the animals concerning their willingness to continue to be harvested. Nevertheless, the consequences for the planning of future harvest levels are not entirely dissimilar for the Cree as for other wildlife managers.

However, the level of information available to the Cree is fundamentally different from that available to the scientist/managers. The scientist/managers typically have results from only periodic surveys of one or more parameters, measured by sampling over a very extensive area. And to interpret these data they typically use generalized ranges derived from the few intensive scientific surveys conducted in more or less comparable environments. For example, when beaver quotas were being set in the 1960s in northern Quebec the assumed number of beaver per lodge was based on data from Michigan and Alaska collected in the 1940s and early 1950s.

When research was undertaken to directly measure the size of beaver colonies by a government scientist in the 1970s, a number of colonies were trapped out in order to estimate their composition; local Cree were neither interviewed nor was their assistance enlisted. The number of beaver the scientist trapped out,

and his estimate of the size of the colonies was distinctly lower than the average number of beaver the Cree removed from the colonies which they thought they had successfully trapped out. The scientific study appeared to say more about the trapping abilities of the researcher than about the beaver. The result, unfortunately, also says something about the way some wildlife biologists treat local knowledge and experience. The knowledge available to local managers and to state-mandated managers is different, but if the effort is made to share both types of information it would often be found that they are mutually informative.

Social Organization of Knowledge

The monitoring of indicators, and the type of information the hunters use is not universally available within a local community, for it is knowledge which typically is synthesized only by a limited number of people who generally are leaders in hunting activities. These may be hunting-territory bosses, or the leaders of hunting parties or camps.

The social distribution of knowledge is related in part to the conditions required for creating such knowledge in the first place. The James Bay Cree system of monitoring certain manageable wildlife populations, for example, requires that hunting leaders gain knowledge of the wildlife populations either on appropriately sized areas of land, or, in the case of migratory or widely ranging species, that they distinguish recurrent natural population sub-units within the migrating population. The recognition of such natural population units have been reported among Cree goose hunters (Berkes 1982; Scott 1986). For such wide ranging and migratory species, information may also depend on sharing knowledge among several hunting leaders.

Thus, Cree hunting bosses are aided in their judgments of the significance of trends in the wildlife populations on their hunting lands by hearing from others whether similar trends are occurring elsewhere. For knowledge of current trends to be meaningful, it is also necessary that hunting leaders know the history of the wildlife populations which they are observing. This permits evaluating the duration and intensity of the trends, as well as making it possible to relate different points in the development of the trends to specific changes in the environment, or to the history of harvesting intensity. Furthermore, in a region noted for its variability, it is useful to know something of the range of past variability, and also of the climatic or vegetational conditions, if any, which may be associated with some of the variability.

Finally, the hunt leaders find it useful to know the history of the harvests taken from a given population, because this is the variable which they have some influence or control over, and they need to judge the significance of past and current harvest levels for the trends being observed. Hunting leaders actively collect and are given such information. Hunting leaders typically see or hear about the harvests taken by all or most of the other hunters using their territory or living in their camp. The gathering of knowledge is thus not simply an individual affair, it is a socially structured process in which a group of hunting leaders or elders have extended access to the available information. In turn these leaders are expected under appropriate circumstances to impart useful or interesting explanations to others concerning the behavior of wildlife populations in their territory.

Such leaders not only are expected to synthesize knowledge, they usually expect and are expected to play the key role in social decision-making concerning the future harvests. These roles may vary from community to community and from activity to activity, and may range from providing wise counsel to other hunters, to being able to actually direct hunting activities. In James Bay Cree society such direction is typically conducted in extremely subtle ways, so as not to interfere with the autonomous responsibility of each hunter; nevertheless, there are recognized bosses or leaders for most intensive harvesting activities, and there is a complex system of hunting territories and goose hunting camps which are supervised by hunting bosses who are usually elders.

The application of such knowledge may conserve animals, it may anticipate or respond to declines in game populations and help prevent further declines, it may increase the efficiency of the harvest, or decrease the uncertainty of a harvest. Often people speak as if it does several of these things together, depending on the circumstances and the knowledge possessed by the hunt leaders.

Both hunting knowledge and hunting practices are therefore part of a complex social system in the societies in which these patterns have been examined, and probably more widely in the arctic and sub-arctic regions. Several researchers have noted the important connection between knowledge and hunting practices and a brief summary of the conclusions the researchers drew from their detailed studies may demonstrate the linkages.

Martin Weinstein, a biologist, concluded from a study (1976) of wildlife resource use at Fort George (now Chisasibi) Quebec, that hunters base their strategies "on knowledge of the behavior of the resource species and information about local animal population size and movements." Bruce Winterhalder, an ecological anthropologist interested in the application of optimal foraging theories to human hunters, researched micro-level strategies at Muskrat Dam Lake in Ontario and concluded that "gathering, assessing, and updating environmental information and developing the skills necessary to apply the rules require extensive experience. Cree foraging is the knowledgeable application of simple rules in an always changing and immensely intricate setting" (1983b).

Fikret Berkes, an environmental scientist, summarized a study (1977) of fishery resource use in Chisasibi by noting that the fishery "was characterized by a high degree of order, social regulation of the fishing effort and the gillnet mesh size, and practices that were identified as adaptations to the subarctic ecosystem." He noted that Cree controlled the magnitude of the harvest and the species and size composition of the catch. He also noted that the fishermen can alter the scarcity-abundance patterns of the stocks.

Anthropologist Adrian Tanner's study of religious ideology and hunting practices at Mistassini, Quebec, led him to conclude (1979) that much "of the religious thought of the hunters is concerned with the state of the natural environment, with how the environment may be controlled, and with the reason for failure when hunters are unable to exercise that control."

Anthropologist Colin Scott's studies of geese hunting at Wemindji showed that foremost "in hunters' minds as they seek understanding of changes in goose behavior is the extent to which their own activities are responsible" (1983). In a more recent paper (1986) he noted among other strategies that there is a rotation and "resting" of hunting sites. He noted a series of other rules for hunting behavior, which minimize stress on the migrating population, while encouraging geese to return to an area and thereby enhancing long-term availability of the population to the Cree.

My own research at Waswanipi Quebec has led me to conclude that the relative stability of both populations and harvests of moose and beaver over a ten to fifteen year period are significant evidence of a real level of success of Waswanipi conservation and management practices, as well as of the potential sustainability of the harvest levels being practiced in a harvesting system which emphasizes the rotational use of hunting territories (1986a, 1986b, 1987b).

Studies in the Western subarctic have been less extensive, but tend to parallel aspects of the conclusions cited above (see especially Lewis 1977, 1982; Brody 1981; Nelson 1982, 1983). Studies in Alaska have complimented those in Canada, indicating the forms of social integration of wildlife resource use practices with the wider economic, social and cultural systems of local communities (see for example Worl 1979, 1980; Langdon and Worl 1981; Fienup-Riordan 1983; Lonner 1986; Wolfe 1986; Wolfe and Ellanna 1983; Wolfe et al. 1984). The Alaskan studies also show the development of new and effective local-level conservation institutions and practices in response to both growing local concerns to protect wildlife populations and to growing intrusion by outside agencies (see Freeman in press; Feldman 1986).

The relative uniformity of conclusions of these studies with respect to the concern of Native hunters for their environments, their effective creation and use of important bodies of environmental knowledge, and their systematic attempts to apply such knowledge to wildlife resource harvesting practices in such a way as to manage or conserve resources should not surprise us. It only makes good sense for people who want and expect to see continuing generations maintain close ties to the animals and the land they occupy and use. We do not need to exaggerate their success to note the intensity of the effort, and the fact that it is often, although not always, successful.

These results from the Canadian North are echoed, at least in part, at the recent symposia and volumes on traditional knowledge and conservation in local communities around the world, although it is worth noting that the Canadian research represents, in some respects, the scientific forefront. These studies report a recent resurgence in awareness and appreciation of traditional resource systems, and they note that while destructive practices and effective efforts to conserve natural resources co-existed in most societies, this does not diminish the need to recognize and take account of the traditional methods of management and conservation (see especially Johannes 1983; McNeely and Pitt 1985).

Such forms of self-management have often been overlooked, because they depend on social institutions and practices unfamiliar in our own society, and fundamentally different from forms of bureaucratic decision-making and highly specialized fields of responsibility which characterize state-mandated wildlife management systems. The growing awareness of self-management systems raises questions about the history and future of such systems.

Histories of Management

In the cases where we know the history of self-management practices we know that they are highly adaptive and resilient systems of wildlife use and management. Thus, among the James Bay Cree, where we know some of the practices in reasonable detail over several decades, and where there is evidence that these systems extend back several centuries, there is good evidence indicating that the practices have been changing and are adapted to continually altering circumstances. Human populations have grown ten-fold in the last eight decades, transportation and harvesting technologies have been greatly enhanced, competing Euro-Canadian wildlife users have entered the region, the Cree have been partially sedentarized and participate in public education systems and wage economies, the fur trade has been monitized and has become more competitive, and wildlife resources have been constantly impacted as forests age, and forestry, mineral and hydroelectric development occurs. Through all of these changes self-management practices have continued to be valued, changed, maintained and relatively effective. These systems have also been extended to apply to significant new resources, such as moose, as well as adapted to previously managed resources. In short, it has been shown that "traditional" local self-management can be adaptive in complex and sometimes rapidly changing conditions, although this is not to say that there have not been problems as well.

The historical record also shows that there have been occasions throughout the Canadian North during which local management has not been effective; however, because this literature is not systematic, it cannot be easily evaluated. One study (Feit 1986b), detailing the depletion of beaver in the Waswanipi area in the 1930s will be discussed here because some of the conclusions which emerge from this case merit consideration as possible general hypotheses which warrant examination more widely.

The first important conclusion from this case was that the breakdown of self-management was not an "all or nothing" event. The study showed that breakdown can occur only partially, for example it may be specific practices for a particular species that are no longer effective, and it may be temporary and related to specific circumstances. Indeed, partial rather than global problems are more likely, because breakdown of management of one species may put increased importance on the management of other species critical to the users.

Furthermore, management breakdown was accompanied by remedy seeking, and a search for ways to re-establish management of the affected resources, and these remedies were effective. The history of self-management is not therefore a history of continual success, but neither is it a history of continual and cumulative failures. Rather it is a history of the efforts to adapt and maintain self-management to changing circumstances, and it is a history of various forms of disruption and renewal of self-management systems.

The histories of self-management therefore may provide an improved understanding of the conditions which lead to the maintenance, breakdown, and re-establishment of self-management practices, and indeed this should be one of the important goals of ongoing and future research. These questions are just beginning to be examined, yet some other preliminary hypotheses can be suggested. It appears that self-management is promoted where local communities or groups have continuing control of access to and use of the managed resources. It is also promoted where these communities retain continuing and long-term interest in the resource, and if they develop alternative and conflicting interests self-management may be weakened. Where the future of the resource appears to be uncertain, despite continuing local interest in it, breakdown may be promoted. In the latter case, as opposed to the case where a change in their interests occurs, efforts to re-establish the conditions for self-management may be common.

In the present context therefore, changes in technology or demography are not in themselves the sources of breakdown, and although they do require adaptations, such adaptations have been made repeatedly in the past. On the other hand, there are more subtle factors with potentially more serious consequences requiring relatively new forms of adaptations. For example, self-management may be disrupted when the institutions or means for gathering and applying information essential to the management of the resource are not effectively maintained or adapted to changing conditions, particularly where new education systems interfere with inter-generational patterns of education and information transmission. The interest of some sectors of the indigenous communities in wildlife may also be changed as efforts grow to create resource-based employment opportunities for a sector of the population which will not be living full-time as subsistence harvesters. Self-management also depends on the maintenance of social systems defining work group organization and property rights and their legitimation and sanction. And, these social practices can be altered, for example, by the need to incorporate part-time hunters into the social system regulating hunting. They can also be altered by the need to create new structures and practices for exchanges between those in the communities with more adequate cash incomes, who can capitalize hunting, and those who may be short of capital, but want to be intensively engaged in hunting. In the North at the present time there appears to be a range of social experiments and explorations, as communities respond to these relatively new changes.

A pattern of successes and failures of self-management should not be surprising in so changing an environment as the North. And, lest we judge it too rigidly, we must note that it should not surprise us either that scientifically based, state-mandated management has also had an uneven record of accomplishment in the North. Unfortunately, there are few extended studies of the lessons to be learned from the experiences of state-mandated wildlife management in the Canadian North, nor very much independent evaluative research on specific management cases. While the available research is clearly incomplete, important recent research has begun to identify some of the accomplishments, problems and possibilities inherent in governmental wildlife management policy-making in the North (e.g., McCandless 1985). Some of this research has identified areas in which scientific wildlife management has encountered recurring difficulties relating to indigenous management systems, and while not being competent to adequately review the accomplishments of scientific management in the North, it is important to note the general problems scientific managers have had relating to local self-management.

Milton Freeman has noted two important reasons for repeated problems. One is that frequently used scientific models require information and knowledge which often far exceeds that available, and the managerial response has often been to depend very heavily on assumptions to fill the gaps. This often proves inadequate in an environment where so much basic knowledge is still lacking. Freeman then goes on to note that in some of these cases, indigenous peoples had criticisms of the assumptions used by scientists, and at a local and specific level they formulated knowledge which conflicted with those assumptions, but which did not enter into the state managers' decisions (1985b). Thus scientific or state management has often cut itself off from this significant source of knowledge, under conditions in which it can ill afford not to use all the available information.

In a number of recent papers Peter Usher has argued that wildlife management scientists are themselves largely unaware of the ways that their own scientific enterprise often presupposes and incorporates culturally specific ideas and values which are scientifically unexamined, such as the notions of property and individuality, which are simply assumed in our society and our political institutions (Usher 1986). Usher points out that one of the implications of these features of managers' thought and training is to limit effective appreciation of indigenous knowledge and practices, as the latter are based on distinctive social forms of knowledge and practice, and on collective or communal rights to land and resources. Not only do indigenous systems become difficult to understand, but their existence becomes difficult to recognize at all.

My own observations confirm the consequences of recurring failures of state-mandated managers to take adequate account of local cultures and resource use and management practices. I have seen several instances where objectives have not been achieved by state-sponsored management policies directed at local peoples. In these cases the state managers neither understood the difficulties such rules created for local resource users, nor did they appreciate why such rules could be perceived as lacking legitimacy. In either case, limited enforcement capability led to avoidance strategies on the part of the local resource users which often had impacts quite at variance with either the state management plans, or with normal local management practices.

Thus while the available research on state-mandated wildlife management in the Canadian North is probably less developed than the research into local level management systems, we can see that its own historical record points to both successes and to much needed development and unfulfilled potentials and promises.

Prospects and Conclusions

The question then is how to go forward from here, and the answer I believe must include the continued development of forms of self-management as well as improved forms of state-level wildlife management. And if I may be permitted a potentially provocative assessment, I would hypothesize that on the ground at present, local-level self-management is more widespread, and that it is presently the more effective at conserving the resources, than is state-mandated wildlife management. I believe this assessment is supported by a series of studies which indicate how government-sponsored conservation efforts have been repeatedly subordinated to the interests of the development of non-living resources, and how they have been limited by the modest support being made available by government wildlife-resource management in the North (for example, Usher and Beakhust 1973; Freeman and Hackman 1975; Theberge 1981; Lonner 1986). But whether my hypothesis about their relative presence on the ground is true or not, both self-management and state-management systems will be needed in the future.

Even where self-management is effective today, it is no longer typically sufficient to all the problems local wildlife managers face today in its present forms. Local wildlife-resource uses are only rarely isolated from the impacts of the international economic system or of state policy-making with respect to wildlife and development. National and international commercial interests, sport interests, non-renewable resource developments are all often beyond the direct influence of the practitioners of traditional self-management systems. This is not to say, that there have not been effective local responses in various circumstances. Nevertheless, traditional forms of self-management must respond to these threats to wildlife resources and to environments by extending self-management to new forms which regulate the actions of individuals and agencies outside the local or regional groups. This provides an incentive to change, if for no other reason than that many of the forms of wildlife management and environmental protection now needed are difficult to respond to effectively at the scale of the existing systems of self-management, and require institutions and practices at a regional or wider scale. Such institutions and practices can develop as forms of self-management, but they also constitute an incentive towards co-management, or a combination of the two.

With respect to the future development of self-management systems, the main point I would make is that self-management practices have histories, and from those histories we can learn something of the conditions under which self-management is maintained, under which it may breakdown, and we can also learn something of the conditions which can facilitate and enhance self-management in the future.

Given that self-management has a reality and a history, then I think that history also shows us that self-management exists today in a milieu in which there are also real pressures for strengthening state-mandated management as well as for instituting forms of co-management. With respect to state management, it clearly needs to be linked to self-management systems to fill gaps in knowledge, to determine realistic objectives, to fit local practices, and to build ties to local communities where policy decisions must be respected in order to be effectively implemented.

With respect to forms of co-management, they are especially likely to be promoted in part through the negotiation of aboriginal rights, but they are needed in the short run and without waiting for the outcomes of those negotiations. In the future, it will be important not only to continue development of the concepts and practical structures of co-management, but also some form of clear recognition that co-management arrangements themselves derive from the systems of knowledge and social rights of the groups agreeing to co-manage with the state, as well as from the legal system of the state.

While a co-management system is likely to be given legal force within the structures of the state, co-management which is capable of being recognized as legitimate and effective in the North will in most cases have to be based on and express forms of pre-existing self-management. Various principles of international as well as constitutional law need to be mobilized to give adequate recognition to the dual sources, state and local, for co-management in the Northern context.

The thrust of this analysis is that both self-managing and state level managing systems exist, and have a future; and that in a real and practical sense they are now inseparably inter-linked, and in many ways they are necessary to each other.

Given these conclusions, two questions seem central to further analyses. One is whether the pressures for change will result in extensive co-management systems, or whether they will result in a little co-management and much more expanded self-management. A complimentary question is whether co-management will in the long term come to constitute a form of co-optation and domination, which will weaken self-management and self-governance. I think that the answer will depend on whether forms of co-management can be developed which effectively recognize the autonomy of self-managers, and their participation with equal authority, legal standing, resources, and respect.

Bibliography

Alberta Society of Professional Biologists
1986   Native People and Renewable Resource Management. Edmonton: ASPB.

Asch, Michael
1986   Wildlife, domestic animals and the Dene aboriginal rights claim. Paper read at the 4th International Conference on Hunting and Gathering Societies, London: September 8-13, 1986.

Berkes, Fikret
1977   Fishery resource use in a subarctic Indian community. Human Ecology 5:289-307.
1979   An investigation of Cree Indian domestic fisheries in Northern Quebec. Arctic 32:46-70.
1981   The role of self-regulation in living resources management in the North. In Renewable Resources and the Economy of the North. pp. 143-160. M.M.R. Freeman, ed. Ottawa: Association of Canadian Universities for Northern Studies.
1981   Fisheries of the James Bay area and northern Quebec: a case study in resource management. In Renewable Resources and the Economy of the North. M.M.R. Freeman, ed. Ottawa: Association of Canadian Universities for Northern Studies.
1982   Waterfowl management and northern Native peoples with reference to Cree hunters of James Bay. Musk-Ox 30:23-35.
1984   Alternative styles in living resources management: the case of James Bay, Quebec. Environments 16(3)114-123.
1985a   The common property resource problem and the creation of limited property rights. Human Ecology 13(2):187-208.
1985b   Fishermen and "the tragedy of the commons." Environmental Conservation 12(3):199-206.
1987   Common property resource management and Cree Indian fisheries in subarctic Canada. In Capturing the Commons. pp. 66-91. B.J. McCay and J.M. Acheson, eds. Tuscon: University of Arizona Press.

Berkes, Fikret and Milton M.R. Freeman
1986   Human ecology and resource use. In Canadian Inland Seas. I.P. Martini, ed. pp. 425-455. Amsterdam: Elsevier Science Publishers.

Berlin, Brent
1973   Folk systematics in relation to biological classification and nomenclature. Annual Review of Ecology and Systematics 4:259-271.

Berlin, Brent, Dennis E. Breedlove and Peter H. Raven
1974   Principles of Tzeltal Plant Classification. New York: Academic Press.

Black, Mary B.
1967   An ethnoscience investigation of Ojibwa ontology and world view. Ph.D. Dissertation. Stanford University.

1977   Ojibwa power belief system. *In* The Anthropology of Power. R.D. Fogelson and R.N. Adams, eds. pp. 141-151. New York: Academic Press.

Brelsford, T.
1980   Subsistence protections: The political and administrative struggles in Alaska and James Bay, Quebec. *In* Papers of the 2nd International Conference on Hunting and Gathering Societies. pp. 207-261. Quebec: Université Laval.

Brody, Hugh
1981   Maps and Dreams: Indians and the British Columbia Frontier. Vancouver, B.C.: Douglas and McIntyre.

Brokensha, David, D.M. Warren, Oswald Werner, eds.
1980   Indigenous Knowledge Systems and Development. Washington, D.C.: University Press of America.

Bulmer, Ralph
1967   Why is the cassowary not a bird? A problem of zoological taxonomy among the Karam of the New Guinea Highlands. Man (N.S.) 2(1):5-25.
1968   The strategies of hunting in New Guinea. Oceania 38:302-318.
1970   Which came first, the chicken or the egghead? *In* Echanges et communications. J. Pouillon and P. Maranda, eds. pp. 1069-1091. Hague: Mouton & Co., Vol. II.
1974   Folk biology in the New Guinea Highlands. Social Science Information 13(4-5):9-28.

Clad, James C.
1985   Conservation and indigenous peoples: a study of convergent interests. *In* Culture and Conservation. J.A. McNeely and David Pitt, eds. pp. 45-67. London: Croom Helm.

Conklin, Harold C.
1954a   The relation of Hanunoo culture to the plant world. Ph.D. Dissertation, Yale University.
1954b   An ethnoecological approach to shifting cultivation. Transactions of the New York Academy of Science, Series 2, 17(2):133-142.
1972   Folk classification: a topically arranged bibliography of contemporary and background references through 1971. New Haven: Yale University, Dept. of Anthropology.
1975/1957 Hanunoo agriculture. Northford, Conn.: Elliot's Books.

Craik, B.
1975   The formation of a goose hunting strategy and the politics of hunting group. *In* Proceedings of the Second Congress, Canadian Ethnology Society. J. Freedman and J. Barkow, eds. pp. 450-465. Ottawa: National Museum of Man.

Dahl, A.L.
1985   Traditional Environmental Management in New Caledonia: A Review of Existing Knowledge. Noumea, New Caledonia: SPREP Secretariat.

Douglas, Mary
1970   Natural Symbols. Explorations in Cosmology. New York: Vintage.

1975   Environments at risk. *In* Implicit Meanings. M. Douglas, ed. pp. 230-248. London: Routledge & Kegan Paul.

Douglas, Mary, ed.
1973   Rules and meanings. The anthropology of everyday knowledge. Harmondsworth: Penguin.

Doumenq, Michel
1981   Les associations communales de chasse agréés. Paris: Comité National d'Information Chasse Nature.

Draz, Omar
1985   The Hema system of range reserves in the Arabian Peninsula: its possibilities in range improvement and conservation projects in the Near East. *In* Culture and Conservation. J.A. McNeely and D. Pitt, eds. pp. 109-121. London: Croom Helm.

Feit, Harvey A.
1973   The ethno-ecology of the Waswanipi
        Cree: or how hunters can manage their
        resources. *In* Cultural Ecology:
        Readings on Canadian Indians and
        Eskimos. B. Cox, ed. pp. 115-125.
        Toronto: McClelland and Stewart.
1978   Waswanipi Realities and Adaptations:
        Resource Management and Cognitive
        Structure. Ph.D. Thesis, McGill
        University.
1982   The future of hunters within nation
        states: anthropology and the James Bay
        Cree. *In* Politics and History in Band
        Societies. E. Leacock and R.B. Lee, eds.
        pp. 373-417. Cambridge: Cambridge
        University Press.
1984   Conflict arenas in the management of
        renewable resources in the Canadian
        North: perspectives based on conflicts
        and responses in the James Bay region,
        Quebec. *In* National and Regional
        Interests in the North. pp. 435-458.
        Ottawa: Canadian Arctic Resources
        Committee.
1986a   Hunting and the quest for power, the
        James Bay Cree and white men in the
        twentieth century. *In* Native Peoples: The
        Canadian Experience. R.B. Morrison
        and C.R. Wilson, eds. pp. 171-207.
        Toronto: McClelland and Stewart.
1986b   James Bay Cree Indian management
        and moral considerations of fur bearers.
        In Native People and Renewable
        Resource Management. pp. 49-65.
        Edmonton: Alberta Society of
        Professional Biologists.
1987a   Waswanipi Cree management of land
        and wildlife: Cree cultural ecology
        revisited. *In* Cultural Ecology. Bruce
        Cox, ed. 2nd ed. pp. 75-91. Toronto:
        McClelland and Stewart.
1987b   North American Native Hunting and
        Management of Moose Populations.
        Swedish Wildlife Research, Supplement
        1: 25-42.
In press The power and the responsibility:
        implementation of the wildlife hunting
        provisions of the James Bay and northern
        Quebec Agreement. *In* James Bay and
        Northern Quebec Agreement, Ten Years
        After. Sylvie Vincent, ed.

Feldman, Kerry D.
1986   Subsistence beluga whale hunting in
        Alaska: a view from Escholtz Bay. *In*
        Contemporary Alaskan Native
        Economies. Steve J. Langdon, ed. pp. 153-
        171. Lanham: University Press of
        America.

Fienup-Riordan, Ann
1983   The Nelson Island Eskimo: Social
        Structure and Ritual Distribution.
        Anchorage: Alaska Pacific University
        Press.

Foster, Janet
1978   Working for Wildlife. Toronto:
        University of Toronto Press.

Freeman, Milton M.R.
1979   Traditional land users as a legitimate
        source of environmental expertise. *In*
        The Canadian National Parks: Today
        and Tomorrow — Conference II, Ten
        Years Later. G. Nelson, et al. eds. pp.
        345-369. Waterloo: Waterloo University
        Studies in Land Use, History and
        Landscape Change.
1985a   Effects of petroleum activities on the
        ecology of arctic man. *In* Petroleum
        Effects in the Arctic Environment. F.R.
        Engelhardt, ed. pp. 245-273. London:
        Elsevier.
1985b   Appeal to tradition: different perspectives
        on arctic wildlife management. *In*
        Native Power: The Quest for Autonomy
        and Nationhood of Indigenous Peoples.
        Jens Brøsted et al., eds. pp. 265-281.
        Bergen: Universitetsforlaget.
1986   Renewable resources, economics and
        Native communities. *In* Native People
        and Renewable Resource Management.
        pp. 29-37. Edmonton: Alberta Society of
        Professional Biologists.
In press The Alaskan Eskimo whaling com-
        mission: successful co-management of a
        stressed resource. *In* Cooperative
        Management of Local Fisheries. E.
        Pinkerton, ed. Vancouver: University of
        British Columbia Press.

Freeman, Milton M.R. and Linda Hackman
1975   Bathurst Island, N.W.T.: A Test Case of
        Canada's Northern Policy. Canadian
        Public Policy 1:402-414.

Gadgil, Madhav
1985   Social restraints on resource utilization: the Indian experience. *In* Culture and Conservation. J.A. McNeely and D. Pitt, eds. pp. 135-154. London: Croom Helm.

Geertz, Clifford
1966   The impact of the concept of culture on the concept of man. *In* New Views of the Nature of Man. John Platt, ed. pp. 93-118. Chicago: University of Chicago Press.

Hallowell, A.I.
1926   Bear ceremonialism in the Northern hemisphere. American Anthropologist 28:1-175.
1955   Culture and Experience. Philadelphia: University of Pennsylvania Press.
1976   Contributions to anthropology — selected papers of A. Irving Hallowell. Chicago: University of Chicago Press.

Hanks, J., ed.
1984   Traditional Life-styles, Conservation and Rural Development. Gland: International Union for the Conservation of Nature and Natural Resources, Commission on Ecology Papers No. 7.

Hays, Samuel P.
1969 [1959] Conservation and the Gospel of Efficiency. New York: Atheneum.

Hutchins, Peter W.
In press The law applying to trapping of furbearing animals by aboriginal peoples — a case of double jeopardy. *In* Wild Furbearer Management and Conservation in North America. M. Novak and J.A. Baker, eds. Toronto: Ontario Ministry of Natural Resources, Wildlife Branch.

Johannes, R.E.
1978   Traditional marine conservation methods in Oceania and their demise. Annual Review of Ecology and Systematics, 9:349-364.
1980   Words of the lagoon: fishing and marine lore in the Palau district of Micronesia. Berkeley University of California Press.

Johannes, R.E. et al.
1983   Traditional knowledge and management of marine coastal systems. Special Issue of Biology International.

Kemp, William
1971   The flow of energy in a hunting society. Scientific American 224(3):104-115.

Klee, Gary A.
1985   Traditional marine resource management in the Pacific. *In* Culture and Conservation. J.A. McNeely and D. Pitt, eds. pp. 193-202. London: Croom Helm.

Krech, Shepard III, ed.
1981   Indians, Animals, and the Fur Trade. Athens: University of Georgia Press.

Kwapena, Navu
1984   Traditional conservation and utilization of wildlife in Papua New Guinea. *In* Traditional Life-styles, Conservation and Rural Development. J. Hanks, ed. pp. 22-26. Gland: IUCN.

Langdon, Steve J.
1986   Contradictions in Alaskan Native economy and society. *In* Contemporary Alaskan Native Economies. S.J. Langdon, ed. pp. 29-46. Lanham: University Press of America.

Langdon, Steve J. and R. Worl
1981   Distribution and Exchange of Subsistence Resources in Alaska. Juneau: Alaska Department of Fish and Game, Subsistence Division, Technical Report No. 55.

LeJeune, Roger
1965   Répertoire préliminaire des poissons du Nottaway. Le Naturaliste canadien 92(2):69-75.

Lewis, H.
1977   Maskuta: The ecology of Indian fires in northern Alberta. Western Canadian Journal of Anthropology 7:15-52.
1982a   Fire technology and resource management in aboriginal North America and Australia. *In* Resource Managers: North American and Australian Hunter-Gatherers. N.M. Williams and E.S. Hunn, eds. pp. 45-67. Boulder: Westview Press.
1982b   A Time for Burning: Traditional Indian Uses of Fire in the Western Canadian Boreal Forest. Edmonton: University of Alberta, Boreal Institute for Northern Studies.

Lonner, Thomas, D.
1986   Subsistence as an economic system in Alaska: Theoretical observations and management implications. *In* Contemporary Alaskan Native Economies. Steve J. Langdon, ed. pp. 15-27. Lanham: University Press of America.

Magnin, Etienne
1964   Premier inventaire de la faune ichtyologique du lac et de la rivière Waswanipi. Le Naturaliste canadien 91(11):273-308.

Marks, S.
1976   Large Mammals and a Brave People: Subsistence Hunters in Zambia. Seattle: University of Washington Press.
1977   Hunting behavior and strategies of the Valley Bisa in Zambia. Human Ecology 5(1):1-36.
1984   The Imperial Lion. Human Dimensions of Wildlife Management in Central Africa. Boulder: Westview Press.

Martin, Calvin
1978   Keepers of the Game: Indian-Animal Relationships and the Fur Trade. Berkeley: University of California Press.

McCandless, Robert G.
1985   Yukon Wildlife: A Social History. Edmonton: University of Alberta Press.

McCay, Bonnie J.
1980   A fishermen's cooperative, limited: Indigenous resource management in a complex society. Anthropological Quarterly 53:29-38.

McCay, Bonnie J. and James M. Acheson, eds.
1987   Capturing the Commons. Tucson: University of Arizona Press.

McNeely, J.A. and Pitt, D.
1985   Culture and Conservation: The Human Dimension in Environmental Planning. London: Croom Helm.

Nelson, Richard K.
1982   A conservation ethic and environment: The Koyukon of Alaska. *In* Resource Managers: North American and Australian Hunter-Gatherers. N.M. Williams and E.S. Hunn, eds. pp. 211-228. Boulder: Westview.

1983   Make Prayers to Raven: A Koyukon View of the Northern Forest. Chicago: University of Chicago Press.

Nelson, R.K., K. Mautner and G. Bane
1978   Tracks in the Wildland: A Portrayal of Koyukon and Nunamiut Subsistence. Fairbanks: University of Alaska, Cooperative Parks Study Unit.

Nietschmann, B.
1972   Hunting and fishing focus among the Miskito Indians, eastern Nicaragua. Human Ecology 1(1):41-66.
1973   Between land and water. The subsistence ecology of the Miskito Indians, eastern Nicaragua. New York: Seminar Press.

Ovington, J.D.
1984   Aboriginal people — guardians of a heritage. *In* Traditional Life-styles, Conservation and Rural Development. J. Hanks, ed. pp. 36-39. Gland: IUCN.

Pinkerton, Evelyn
In press Attaining better fisheries management through co-management: prospects and problems. *In* Cooperative Management of Local Fisheries. E. Pinkerton, ed.

Pitt, David
1983   Culture and conservation: an action/research plan. Gland: International Union for Conservation of Nature and Natural Resources, Commission on Environmental Planning.
1985   Towards ethnoconservation. *In* Culture and Conservation. J.A. McNeely and D. Pitt, eds. pp. 283-295. London: Croom Helm.

Polunin, Nicholas V.C.
1985   Traditional marine practices in Indonesia and their bearing on conservation. *In* Culture and Conservation. J.A. McNeely and D. Pitt, eds. pp. 155-179. London: Croom Helm.

Pulae, M.
1985   Customary law relating to the environment, South Pacific region: An overview. Noumea, New Caledonia: SPREP Secretariat.

Reichel-Dolmatoff, G.
1976   Cosmology as ecological analysis: a view from the rain forest. Man 11(3):307-318.

Roussow, George
1957   Some considerations concerning sturgeon spawning periodicity. Journal of the Fisheries Research Board of Canada 14(4):553-572.

Ruddle, K. and Johannes, R.E., eds.
1985   The traditional knowledge and management of coastal systems in Asia and the Pacific. Jakarta: UNESCO, Regional Office for Science and Technology for Southeast Asia.

Salisbury, R.F.
1986   A Homeland for the Cree: Regional Development in James Bay, 1971-1981. Montreal: McGill-Queen's Press.

Scott, C.H.
1979   Production and exchange among Wemindji Cree: egalitarian ideology and economic base. Culture 11(3):51-64.
1983   The semiotics of material life among Wemindji Cree hunters. Ph.D. Dissertation. McGill University, Montreal.
1984   Between "original affluence" and consumer affluence: domestic production and guaranteed income for James Bay Cree hunters. In Affluence and Cultural Survival. Richard F. Salisbury, ed. Proceedings of the spring meeting of the American Ethnological Society, 1981.
1984   Signs of reciprocity: James Bay Cree construction of exchanges with Canada geese. Paper presented to the Toronto Semiotic Circle, November meeting, 1983, and to the Canadian Ethnology Society Annual Meeting, Symposium: Information, Imagination, Adaptation: World View and Adaptive Strategy Among Hunting and Gathering People, May 7-11, 1984, University of Montreal.
1986   The socio-economic significance of waterfowl among Canada's aboriginal Cree: Native use and local management. Paper given at the 19th International Council for Bird Preservation World Conference, Kingston, Ontario, June.

Siechowicz, K.
1982   "We are all related here": The social relations of land utilization in Wunnummin Lake, Northwestern Ontario. Ph.D. Thesis, University of Toronto.

Tanner, A.
1973   The significance of hunting territories today. In Cultural Ecology: Readings on the Canadian Indians and Eskimos. B. Cox, ed. Toronto: McClelland and Stewart.
1979   Bringing home animals. Religious ideology and mode of production of the Mistassini Cree hunters. St. John's: Memorial University, Institute of Social and Economic Research.
1983   Algonquian land tenure and state structures in the North. Canadian Journal of Native Studies 3(2):311-320.

Theberge, J.B.
1981   Commentary: conservation in the North — an ecological perspective. Arctic 34(4):281-285.

Thomas, Keith
1983   Man and the Natural World. Changing Attitudes in England 1500-1800. Harmondsworth: Penguin.

Usher, P.J.
1981   Sustenance or recreation? The future of Native wildlife harvesting in northern Canada. In Renewable Resources and the Economy of the North. Milton M.R. Freeman, ed. pp. 56-71. Ottawa: Association of Canadian Universities for Northern Studies.
1984   Property rights: The basis of wildlife management. In National and Regional Interests in the North. pp. 389-415. Ottawa: Canadian Arctic Resources Committee.
1986   The devolution of wildlife management and the prospects for wildlife conservation in the Northwest Territories. Ottawa: Canadian Arctic Resources Committee, Policy Paper No. 3.

Usher, P.J. and G. Beakhust
1973   Land Regulation in the Canadian North. Ottawa: Canadian Arctic Resources Committee.

Vayda, A.P., Carol J. Pierce Colfer and Mohamed Brotokusumo
1985   Interactions between people and forests in East Kalimantan. In Culture and Conservation. J.A. McNeely and D. Pitt, eds. pp. 211-227. London: Croom Helm.

Webb, L.J. and D.M. Smith
1984   Ecological guidelines and traditional empiricism and rural development. *In* Traditional Life-styles, Conservation and Rural Development. J. Hanks, ed. pp. 99-105. Gland: IUCN.

Weinstein, M.S.
1976   What the land provides. An examination of the Fort George subsistence economy and the possible consequences on it of the James Bay hydroelectric project. Montreal: Grand Council of the Crees of Quebec.

Williams, Nancy and Eugene S. Hunn, eds.
1982   Resource managers: North American and Australian hunter-gatherers. Washington: American Association for the Advancement of Science.

Winterhalder, B.
1981a   Optimal foraging strategies and hunter-gatherer research in anthropology: Theory and models. *In* Hunter-Gatherer Foraging Strategies. B. Winterhalder and E.A. Smith, eds. pp. 13-35. Chicago: University of Chicago Press.
1981b   Foraging strategies in the boreal forest: an analysis of Cree hunting and gathering. *In* Hunter-Gatherer Foraging Strategies. B. Winterhalder and E.A. Smith, eds. pp. 66-98. Chicago: University of Chicago Press.
1983a   History and ecology of the boreal zone in Ontario. *In* Boreal Forest Adaptations. A.T. Steegman, Jr., ed. pp. 9-54. New York: Plenum.
1983b   Boreal foraging strategies. *In* Boreal Forest Adaptations. A.T. Steegman, Jr., ed. pp. 201-241. New York: Plenum.
1983c   The boreal forest, Cree-Ojibwa foraging and adaptive management. *In* Resource Dynamics and the Boreal Zone. R.W. Wein, R.R. Riewe, and I.R. Methuen, eds. pp. 331-345. Ottawa: Association of Canadian Universities for Northern Studies.

Wolfe, Robert J.
1986   The economic efficiency of food production in a Western Alaska Eskimo population. *In* Contemporary Alaskan Native Economies. Steve J. Langdon, ed. pp. 101-120. Lanham: University Press of America.

Wolfe, Robert J. and Linda J. Ellanna, eds.
1983   Resource Use and Socioeconomic Systems: Case Studies of Fishing and Hunting in Alaskan Communities. Juneau: Alaska Department of Fish and Game, Division of Subsistence, Technical Paper No. 61.

Wolfe, Robert J. et al.
1984   Subsistence Based Economies in Coastal Communities of Southwest Alaska. Juneau: Alaska Department of Fish and Game, Division of Subsistence, Technical Report No. 95.

Worl, Rosita
1980   The north slope Inupiat whaling complex. *In* Alaska Native Culture and History. Y. Kotani and W.B. Workman, eds. Osaka: National Museum of Ethnology, Senri Ethnological Studies, 4:305-320.

Yupiktak Bista
1974   A Report on Subsistence and the Conservation of the Yupik Life Style. Bethel: Yupiktak Bista.

Acknowledgement

This paper draws on research funded by the Social Sciences and Humanities Research Council of Canada (Grants 410-81-0241, 410-84-0547, and 410-87-0715), and by the Arts Research Board of McMaster University. I wish to thank both agencies.

Wildlife Management in the North American Arctic: The Case For Co-Management*

Gail Osherenko
The Center for Northern Studies
Wolcott, Vermont

Introduction

Two models of wildlife management are in common use throughout Alaska and the Canadian North, an indigenous system and a state system, but the former has limited application and the latter has never worked well. This paper identifies the problems associated with the dualism and argues that co-management arrangements in which governmental authorities share power with indigenous user groups offer the best prospect for solving these problems. The paper examines three existing wildlife co-management regimes: the Beverly and Kaminuriak Barren ground caribou management regime in the central Canadian Arctic, the Northern Quebec beluga management regime, and the Yukon-Kuskokwim Delta goose management regime in Alaska.

The essay concludes with an account of lessons to be drawn from existing co-management regimes. Only by involving indigenous user groups in management decisions will co-management alleviate the programs associated with the clash of indigenous and state systems and meld the two into a single ecologically sound, efficient, equitable, and enduring system.

* This paper, in extended form, is published as Sharing power with native users: co-management regimes for Arctic wildlife. CARC Policy Paper 5. Ottawa: Canadian Arctic Resources Committee, 1988.

The Two Systems

In order to understand the current problems, we begin with brief characterizations of the two ideal types, the state system and the indigenous system.

The state system features written laws, rules, and regulations made and administered by governments to manage common property resources. As Usher (1986) puts it:

> The state manages for certain levels of abundance on a technical basis, and then allocates shares of this abundance to users on an economic and political basis. The system of knowledge is based on a scientific accumulation, organization, and interpretation of data, and management problems are resolved in a technical, ahistorical, and "value-free" framework. This system of management is bureaucratic, which is to say hierarchically organized and vertically compartmentalized. For example, managers are distinct from harvesters, authority is centralized and flows from the top down, and separate units are designated to manage individual components of the environment.

The state system arose from the needs of non-Native cultures to maintain wildlife populations as well as to allocate wildlife resources among different groups of users. In the far North, however, agencies have found it difficult to apply the state system. In some cases, application of laws and regulations is relaxed, and authorities make few attempts to enforce the written rules.

The state system allows for consultation of user groups, but does not accord users a broader role in management.

The indigenous system of wildlife management is a collection of unwritten rules or social norms that govern Native hunting, fishing, and trapping. The rules have been handed down by example and orally for generations. For the most part, compliance, based on cultural values, ethics, and even taboos, has been high.

Because the system is seldom codified in Native communities, much less incorporated into laws and regulations made by non-Native society (the state system), wildlife managers sometimes conclude that Native communities have no self-imposed rules to control human behaviour and ensure conservation of marine and terrestrial animals. Yet a recognition of human dependance on and respect for animals underlies the indigenous system. Whether people live in communities of 85 or 3,000, they depend on wild animals for food. Hunting not only provides preferred food, it is often a preferred occupation that confers respect and prestige in the community. Research, management, and harvesting are inseparable in the indigenous system. Knowledge, which comes from travelling, searching, hunting, butchering, and eating, is shared constantly within the household, the kinship group, and the community (Usher 1986). The indigenous system often makes use of conservation measures, including setting aside sanctuaries to allow certain animal populations time to recover from hunting or trapping pressure. Chuckchi in Siberia, for example, traditionally banned hunting at several walrus hauling-out sites on the coast of Chukotka. Cree trappers regularly "let the land rest" in places where they perceive a need to allow beaver and other species to recover from trapping pressure (Berkes 1985).

A key problem for the indigenous system arises when rules, once widely followed, are no longer passed down to the younger generation. Children learn values in school that conflict with values essential to their Native culture—values that stress individuality and competition over community and co-operation. As well, new authority figures (school teachers, outside experts) begin to displace the elders, reducing the likelihood of compliance with previously held social norms. Additionally, students attending conventional schools have few opportunities to learn the skills of the land from their elders, and inadequate training has left a younger generation of hunters who often don't have the skill to maintain high rates of retrieval. Even so, most anthropologists working in the North confirm the continued vitality of Native cultures and note that social norms and practices are changing or evolving rather than dying. We must not be too quick, therefore, to jump to the conclusion that customary law is no longer protecting wildlife in the Arctic.

Problems of Dualism

A number of problems arise from clashes between these two systems of wildlife management. The state system is fundamentally ill-suited to Native communities. It often relies on cumbersome procedures (licenses and fees, harvest tickets and reports) which are impractical to administer in Native communities (especially where many hunters are not fluent in the language in which the rules are printed). The state system emphasizes individual bag limits rather than community needs as well as seasonal limits and gear restrictions that are often at odds with subsistence practices. Ultimately, it enforces by fine, forfeiture, seizure, and even personal confinement rather than social pressure to conform to community standards (Schaeffer et al. 1986). Understandably, compliance with such formal rules is low; by some estimates, only 15-20 percent of the active hunters in northwest Alaska obtain hunting licenses (ibid). Public authorities, recognizing some of these problems with the state system, have adapted the system somewhat to meet indigenous needs. For example, regulators try to match seasonal restrictions with the users' seasonal needs, the Northwest Territories Department of Renewable Resources issues (annual) general hunting licenses to Natives (permitting them to hunt in any season for subsistence needs and to trap in accord with seasonal restrictions), and agencies in northern Quebec do not impose regulations on Native users except in cases of conservation need and then only after consultation with the users. These adjustments solve some of the problems of dualism, but they fail to give indigenous users a sense of ownership in the decision-making process and do not address the difficult issues that arise when state managers fear over-exploitation of a species.

In a few cases, the failure to develop a workable wildlife management system and a legal regime that melds indigenous and state systems has contributed to declines in populations of highly migratory species which both systems aim to protect. Two of the co-management regimes examined in this essay arose out of wildlife population crises.

Wildlife research as well as harvest data is essential to early detection of species' declines. However, information obtained when either system operates alone is incomplete and can lead to inaccurate conclusions. The data on which to base sound management decisions cannot be collected without co-operation of user groups. Correspondingly, information obtained through western scientific research can be useful to Native communities.

Where co-operation rather than confrontation occurs, by contrast, the frontiers of knowledge about wildlife can expand rapidly. University-trained researchers create excellent synchronic data sets covering wide geographic areas (well beyond the limits of knowledge likely to be available in remote Native communities). For their part, Natives provide remarkably accurate diachronic data for particular localities and specific stocks of animals about which knowledge has been transmitted orally for a hundred years or more. But the two sets of data must be integrated to produce a full picture of the wildlife population dynamics and to generate assessments credible to both communities (Drolet et al. 1987).

Finally, the costs of imposing the state system on communities that neither understand nor accept it are significant. Some regulations and procedures are so unenforceable that by policy (or individual discretion) public authorities ignore them, thereby undercutting the credibility of the entire system. The clash of systems of wildlife management in the far North results in serious compliance problems, ecological crises, inadequate research data that can lead to inaccurate conclusions, and unnecessary political and financial costs.

The Co-Management Solution

Co-management regimes represent a practical solution to the problems encountered by the standard arrangements. A co-management regime is an institutional arrangement in which government agencies with jurisdiction over resources and user groups enter into an agreement covering a specific geographic region and make explicit 1) a system of rights and obligations for those interested in the resource, 2) a collection of rules indicating actions that subjects are expected to take under various circumstances, and 3) procedures for making collective decisions affecting the interests of government actors, user organizations, and individual users (Young 1977, 1982). Co-management does not require government agencies to relinquish or transfer any legal jurisdiction or authority; it does require public authorities to share decision-making power with user groups. Administrators often object to any suggestion that the arrangement implies an equal partnership between governmental agencies and user organizations. In each of the arrangements discussed here, however, public authorities have openly acknowledged that they cannot manage the relevant wildlife species without the co-operation of the user groups, and they have, therefore, accorded user groups a substantial role in management decisions, a role beyond that of "consultant" or "advisor." The role of the user group or joint government/ user board created by the agreement may be termed advisory, but if the user group does not concur in major management decisions regarding the relevant species, the co-management regime will fall apart and the user group will no longer be obligated to participate or comply with regime rules.

Seven wildlife co-management regimes have been created in the North American Arctic to solve problems caused by clashes between indigenous and state systems of wild management, and several others are in vari stages of conception. These vary substantially i the degree of power accorded to the participating user groups. In addition to the three cases examined in this essay, several other examples exist in Alaska and Canada, including joint US-Canada co-management arrangements for such transborder migratory species as polar bear and caribou. (See Figure 1.)

The three case studies of wildlife co-management regimes that follow demonstrate that while co-management regimes between government agencies and indigenous users may employ varying organizational structures, successful co-management regimes always give the indigenous users a sense of ownership in the system.

Co-management of Caribou in the Central Canadian Arctic

In the late 1970s, biologists thought the Kaminuriak and Beverly herds had dropped to as low as a tenth and a third, respectively, of their previous populations.

In 1979, representatives of five government agencies revitalized a long-standing Administrative Committee on Caribou Conservation as a Caribou Management Group but concluded that they could not effectively manage the herds without involving Native users—Inuit of the Keewatin, Chipewyan Dene and Metis of border communities in Manitoba, Saskatchewan and the South Slave region of the NWT, and some northern Cree. In 1981, representatives of these Native groups proposed a user's caribou management board with government officials having only advisory status. In June 1982, the governments responded by agreeing to create a 13-member Caribou Management Board (CMB) composed of eight Native user representatives and five government officials. The board is the organizational vehicle for collective decision-making regarding caribou management.

The agreement provides a theoretical basis for ecologically sound management. The board's members represent users throughout almost the entire ranges of the Beverly and Kaminuriak herds (with the exception of some

he North where the herds' ranges
ore northern herds). The CMB's
sdiction is not defined by
ological boundaries.

is unique in its user-oriented
as well as its user-dominated
co sition. The board is responsible for coordinating management of the herds "in the interest of traditional users and their descendants, who are or may be residents on the range of the caribou, while recognizing the interest of all Canadians in the survival of this resource" (Caribou Management Agreement 1986). The agreement did not transfer jurisdiction or authority for wildlife management to the board, but assigned the board the responsibility "to develop and make recommendations to the appropriate governments and to groups of traditional caribou users for the conservation and management of the Beverly and Kaminuriak herds ... and their habitat in order to restore the herds, as far as reasonably possible, to a size and quality which will sustain the requirements of traditional users" (Ibid). Strictly speaking the CMB is advisory. In reality, governments have, to date, followed the board's advice on matters of species management, although not on habitat protection. In addition to its advisory role, the board has responsibility for monitoring caribou habitat and conducting an information programme.

All five signatory government agencies share the base costs of operating the regime. The total budget for board expenses and caribou management programmes under the caribou management plan will be about $1.3 million (Canadian) in 1987, a reasonable expense in relation to a resource that produces two million pounds of meat with an estimated value of $15 million (Canadian) annually. This regime is more secure financially than either of the other co-management regimes examined in this essay.

Now in its fifth year of operation, the CMB is often heralded as a model of successful co-management in the North. In order to evaluate whether it deserves this reputation, we must ask whether the signatories have forged a partnership that avoids the usual problems of

Figure 1. Co-Management Regimes for Arctic Wildlife

Regime	Year Created	Wildlife Covered	Location	Participants
James Bay & Northern Quebec hunting, fishing and trapping regime	1975	all marine and terrestrial species	James Bay & Northern Quebec	Province of Quebec (4) * Government of Canada (4) Inuit (3) Cree (3) Naskapi (2)
Alaskan whaling regime	1981	bowhead whales	Bering & Beaufort Seas; Alaskan whaling communities	National Oceanic and Atmospheric Administration (NOAA) Alaska Eskimo Whaling Commission (AEWC)
Beverly & Kaminuriak caribou management regime	1982	Beverly and Kaminuriak caribou herds	central Canadian Arctic	Indian Affairs and Northern Development Canada (1) Environment Canada (1) Manitoba Dept. of Natural Resources (1) Saskatchewan Dept. of Parks (1) NWT Dept. of Renewable Resources (1) Inuit of Keewatin (2) Chipewyan Bands of Northern Manitoba and Cree-Metis community of Brochet, Man. (2) user communities of Saskatchewan (2) user communities south and east of Great Slave Lake in NWT (2)
Inuvialuit wildlife harvesting and management regime	1985	all fauna in a wild state other than reindeer	Inuvialuit Settlement Region within the NWT; northwestern NWT	Wildlife Management Advisory Council: •Environment Canada (1) •Government of NWT (2) •Inuvialuit Game Council (represents community Hunters and Trappers Committees) (3) Fisheries Joint Management Committee: •Dept. Fisheries and Oceans Canada (2) •Inuvialuit Game Council (2)
Beluga management regime	1986	belugas (white whales) of eastern James Bay, Hudson Strait, and Ungava Bay	northern Quebec	Dept. of Fisheries and Oceans Canada (DFO) Anguvigaq (regional wildlife organization) Anguvigapiks (local wildlife committees)
Canadian Porcupine caribou herd management regime	1986	Porcupine caribou herd	northwestern Canada (parts of Yukon Territory and NWT)	Government of the Yukon Territory (1) Dept. of Renewable Resources, NWT (1) Indian Affairs and Northern Development Canada (1) Environment Canada (1) Council for Yukon Indians (1) Inuvialuit Game Council (1) Dene Nation (1) Metis Assoc. of NWT (1)
Pacific walrus regime	1987	Pacific walrus	Coastal areas of northwestern Alaska	U.S. Fish & Wildlife Service (FWS) Alaska Dept. of Fish & Game (ADF&G) Eskimo Walrus Commission

*Numbers in parentheses indicate the number of representatives on the regimes' governing boards.

dualism and creates an ecologically sound, efficient, equitable, and enduring management system.

From the outset, the board questioned the population predictions of biologists and deferred discussion of hunting quotas. Instead, it emphasized harvest studies to be conducted by Native communities with government funds. It initiated estimates of user needs (numbers of caribou required by hunters to support their families), and improved caribou population surveys employing aerial photography, studies of herd recruitment, distribution, overlap, and mixing. The board determined what the optimum herd size would be (e.g., 300,000 for each herd, or 330,000 for the Beverly herd if it is to be used by the people of Fort Chipewyan) and that emergency action to protect the herds would only be necessary if either herd fell below fifty percent of that number. While these decisions were being made, caribou populations showed signs of a substantial increase. Improved census-taking techniques documented that both herds were sizable and increasing. This made difficult allocation issues unnecessary, at least for the time being.

Freed from any immediate crisis, the CMB has been able to address problems of caribou habitat protection and predation as well as to plan for the future. Since users had long attributed decreased caribou numbers in northern Manitoba and Saskatchewan to habitat destruction caused by fires, the board initiated a study of the effects of fire on caribou and habitat and recommended that governments implement a short-term fire management strategy on the winter ranges. The board's recommendations for permanent protection of the calving grounds have not yet produced results, but the board has achieved some influence over industrial activities. For example, the Government of the Northwest Territories (GNWT) and DIAND have established Caribou Protection Areas and have limited construction, mining, and other potentially damaging exploration activities in or near critical areas during calving, immediate post-calving and migration periods. At its August 1987 meeting, the board finally approved its long-term management plan, which is to be subject to annual review.

The CMB has taken steps to avoid misuse of caribou and ecological problems as well as to reduce tensions between indigenous and state systems by ensuring that traditional knowledge of caribou is transmitted to younger generations along with relevant biological training. The board ordered the development of an innovative elementary and high school education programme that has been adapted for use in adult education. And the board has initiated programmes to reduce waste through user education.

The caribou management regime ended "a long period of claim and counterclaim (that had) fostered a climate of confrontation" (Ibid). Now, government scientists and managers work co-operatively with Native users through the mechanisms of the regime. Native knowledge regarding caribou health, numbers, migratory patterns, and behavior over the last several centuries is now integrated with techniques of biologists for gathering current data. In the view of the Executive Secretary of the board, Native board members, who are all knowledgeable hunters, have provided remarkable expertise to governments from the first meeting. Reporting on harvested numbers of caribou improved dramatically following creation of the board; e.g., known harvest figures doubled for the 1981-82 period over previous estimates.

Although tensions between government agencies and Native users have largely subsided, non-Native users, not directly represented on the CMB, have voiced their discontent with the regime.

The CMB has not been severely tested by the kind of controversy that would erupt should current caribou populations plunge. Nevertheless, the board's ability to avert a perceived ecological crisis and to move forward to long-range management planning is a testament to its success. Overall, the CMB has avoided problems of compliance with state-imposed hunting restrictions, reduced the possibility of future ecological crises, increased user-government cooperation, dramatically increased education and information to users of all kinds, improved the quality and content of research, and avoided unreasonable political and economic costs.

What accounts for these successes? Above all, the agreement provides a significant role for indigenous users. Although the CMB's authority is technically advisory, its decisions, at least on wildlife conservation issues, are taken seriously by the relevant governments. This may be due in part to fortunate political circumstances. One of the government parties to the regime, the GNWT, represents a predominantly Native population holding a majority of seats in the Legislative Assembly. In recent years, Natives have, at different times, held the minister and deputy minister posts in the Department of Renewable Resources of the GNWT, the agency with authority to regulate caribou hunting. Today, much of the caribou research is conducted by the GNWT, and relations between the GNWT researchers and user communities are good. Thus, in addition to the dominance of Native user representatives on the board and the user-oriented objectives of the regime, the political context in which the regime operates helps to ensure its success in creating a partnership between government and user groups.

Decision making by the board is not polarized into users versus government, a strong indicator of effective partnership between user groups and governmental agencies. The agreement calls for consensus decision making whenever possible, an acknowledgement of the value of the indigenous system.

Another reason for the board's success in creating "ownership" by the user groups is its extensive network of communication with local communities. The long-term plan calls for a budget of $123,000 (Canadian) annually for board liaison activities including video and audio tapes, press releases, annual reports in English and Native languages, community meetings, and visits to communities by individual board members. Every household in the region receives the bi-monthly newsletter, *Caribou News*, that has become a vehicle for discussion of important topics. Each issue contains some articles in Native languages.

Another key component in this regime's success is continuity of member representation and staff which has enabled the CMB to operate efficiently. The board Chairman, the representative of the Metis Association of the NWT, has served at the board's pleasure since the establishment of the board. Five of the eight original Native members were still serving after four years, as were two of the five original government representatives (and one of the government alternates). And one individual has filled the paid position of Executive Secretary from the outset. The board has demonstrated creativity and flexibility in responding quickly to changing economic and environmental conditions. When the board learned that aerial transport was leading to excessive and wasteful caribou hunts, it called for hunters to wait 12 hours after landing to begin hunting. When economic conditions changed making the regulations not only unnecessary but also burdensome to subsistence hunters, the Board rescinded its former ruling. The ability of the CMB to function effectively presents a marked contrast to the Hunting Fishing and Trapping Coordinating Committee (CC) created under the James Bay and Northern Quebec Agreement (JBNQA) discussed briefly in the next case. The success of the CMB may be due to its more limited focus on a single species. However, the question

of the differences in performance of the CMB and the CC requires further study and is relevant to the question of whether new co-management regimes covering all wildlife in a particular geographic region can be designed effectively.

The biggest threat to the regime comes from the apparent unwillingness of public authorities to act on the CMB's advice with regard to habitat protection. This undermines the good faith efforts of participants to the regime and raises questions concerning the commitment of government parties to the regime. As well, governments' failure to provide fire protection to the caribou range and to permanently protect regularly used calving grounds as recommended by the board may contribute to ecological crises in the future that the board is powerless to prevent. In another period of declining populations, users would be unlikely to accept harvest restrictions when declines may have been triggered by the unwillingness of governments to prevent habitat destruction.

Co-management of Beluga Whales in Northern Quebec

After scientists documented a need to reduce hunting in northern Quebec to conserve beluga whales, the Department of Fisheries and Oceans (DFO), encouraged and advised Anguvigaq, a Native organization composed of hunters, to create and implement a beluga management plan. In August 1986, DFO adopted that plan as its own, thereby creating an informal co-management arrangement later formally approved by the Hunting, Fishing and Trapping Coordinating Committee for the region.

DFO has jurisdiction to manage marine resources throughout Canada, subject to a broad co-management regime for two-thirds of northern Quebec. That regime was created in 1975 as part of a comprehensive land claims agreement, the James Bay and Northern Quebec Agreement (JBNQA) between the federal government, the Province of Quebec, and Native peoples (Inuit of Northern Quebec and Cree of James Bay). The agreement guarantees Natives priority in harvesting all species for subsistence in conformity with the principle of conservation and exclusive rights to harvest certain species.

The agreement also prevents any federal or provincial regulation of Native wildlife harvesting except when necessary for conservation purposes, interpreted by DFO to involve both ecological protection and maximum sustainable use. General principles of the JBNQA state that regulation of Native harvesting shall be minimal and less restrictive than regulation of non-Native harvest activities.

The agreement created a Hunting, Fishing and Trapping Coordinating Committee of 16 members—half government and half Native representatives. All hunting, fishing, and trapping regulations relating to Native people proposed by government agencies must be submitted to the coordinating committee for its advice before enactment. Although the coordinating committee's recommendations are only advisory, they are intended to carry great weight with the responsible ministers. The coordinating committee holds lengthy meetings about four times a year, though it met ten times in 1986. The committee has been hampered by the lack of a connecting link to the communities. Federal government representatives have also expressed disappointment that Inuit representatives are not the more experienced hunters who could provide first-hand knowledge of Native practices and needs. The coordinating committee has not become a forum for relaxed communication and co-operation, but rather a political body in which many votes split evenly, the government on one side, the Natives on the other. It is in the context of the failure of this regime to solve the problems caused by the dual indigenous and state systems that the beluga management arrangement developed.

Inuit of northern Quebec harvest several hundred belugas annually; for them it is nutritionally and culturally an important harvest. However, in 1983, research indicated depletion of the whale stocks had occurred. At about this time, the Inuit regional government and Makivik Corporation formed Anguvigaq Wildlife, Inc., a Native organization devoted to wildlife management, composed of representatives of wildlife committees established in every community of Northern Quebec. DFO welcomed Anguvigaq because it solved the problem of identifying appropriate individuals with whom to work at the community level.

DFO officials also provided a contract for Anguvigaq to carry out harvest studies, and discussed research plans with the local communities. Initial exchanges of information among hunters, government researchers, and managers led DFO to publish an information booklet on the biology and management of Arctic seals and whales (Breton et al. 1984). Hunters and managers discussed the research data and management options for beluga whales and agreed to work co-operatively toward the common goals of ensuring beluga conservation and sustained harvesting.

DFO chose to guide the users by providing information on the species and management techniques and encouraging the users to adopt management measures. DFO avoided imposition of regulations, contingency plans, or enforcement actions, options which are allowed as a last resort under the JBNQA. The local wildlife committees adopted rules protecting beluga females accompanied by calves and requiring hunters to harpoon before shooting to improve rates of retrieval. The latter rule, if followed, would entail a significant change in modern hunting practice. Two Ungava Bay communities established a beluga sanctuary within which "no one may attempt to hunt, disturb or harass any whales...." In 1986, three years after the first meetings concerning beluga management, the wildlife committees and Anguvigaq established harvest quotas for each of three regions and for each community. These quotas limit the harvest to 200 belugas, a significant reduction from a mean annual catch of 310 between 1981 and 1985. Although DFO identified numerous management techniques for protecting belugas (including closed seasons and managing specific areas by selective closings), the hunters decided to use quotas to reduce the harvest in all regions. In this way, hunters explained to DFO managers, Inuit would share management responsibility as they have always shared food. Although hunters had been uncomfortable about counting belugas early in the research phases (stating how many animals you expect to kill shows disrespect for the prey), they have adopted a management system dependent on counting yet hinged on an important Inuit value, sharing.

The Northern Quebec Beluga Management Plan (1986) is a compilation of the specific local management plans and agreements adopted by each local wildlife committee and the executive members of Anguvigaq, as well as the few laws applying to belugas throughout Canada and specifically in northern Quebec. The management plan, in effect, spells out the regime's rules as well as the rights and obligations of those interested in using the resource. In 1987, after meetings in every Inuit community, Anguvigaq and DFO adopted a management plan for 1987 and 1988 which refines the previous plan

Although not formalized by an agreement, DFO has forged an innovative partnership with the user groups that, hopefully, will avert problems of compliance, ecological crisis, inadequate or inaccurate harvest and research data, and unnecessary political and economic costs. The communities of northern Quebec have begun to reduce their harvest. In the most critical region, Ungava Bay, they have not terminated the harvest as recommended by biologists, but they have set their own quotas for all communities and, in the first year, stayed within the overall harvest limit. Participating communities pressured the one community that most resisted restrictions the first year, and now that community is more willing to co-operate. Since this is the first subsistence activity to be actively managed in the region, DFO believes that hunters, who at first did not respect the system, need time to adjust to it.

Information and education, rather than regulation and enforcement, are the main management tools of this regime. Personal communication between the managers and researchers and the users plays a major role. Secondary schools throughout the region use the beluga pamphlet in an ecology class, and the regional school board plans to introduce it into adult education classes in the future.

The informal arrangement between DFO and Anguvigaq has proven more efficient and effective than the formal mechanism of the Coordinating Committee. While it has not entirely removed tensions between government regulators and users, especially regarding research, it has reduced hostility and increased communication between the two. In fact, participants in the beluga regime are now preparing to finalize a cooperative management plan for walrus as well.

The arrangement for beluga management nested within the larger hunting, fishing, and trapping regime for northern Quebec has solved many of the problems of dualism, but Anguvigaq's participation in the regime is not entrenched and its funding is not guaranteed. Though the communication and co-operation already begun appear likely to continue, clear authority and secure funding for the Inuit organization most responsible for creating a management plan and reducing hunting pressure on beluga whales would strengthen this fledgling co-management arrangement.

Co-management of Migratory Geese in Alaska's Yukon-Kuskokwim Delta

In 1984, the U.S. Fish and Wildlife Service (FWS), fish and game departments in Alaska and California, and organizations representing tribal governments in southwestern Alaska formed a co-management regime to deal with declines in four species of migratory waterfowl along the Pacific flyway. The coastal plain of the Yukon-Kuskokwim Delta (Y-K Delta) in southwestern Alaska is the nesting grounds for virtually all cackling Canada geese and Pacific flyway white-fronted geese, and a large proportion of the emperor goose and black brant breeding populations (Pamplin 1986). The region is also the homeland and hunting grounds of approximately 18,000 Yup'ik Eskimos of Alaska. Since 1918, the Migratory Bird Treaty Act (MBTA) has banned taking any of these birds or their eggs between 10 March and 1 September. The closed season would virtually prohibit spring and summer Native egging and hunting as the relevant species arrive in the delta in mid-late April and fly south in late September or early October. However, geese are an important source of fresh meat and eggs for Natives during the time between sealing and salmon fishing. A sizable hunt as well as egg collection has always occurred.

The four species of geese have all suffered sharp declines in population over the last 20 years, declines attributed to harvesting in the Y-K Delta together with sport hunting along the flyway, loss of habitat, pollution, and natural predation (Ohlendorf et al. 1984, Reisner 1987).

Government managers eventually recognized the impossibility of protecting the geese without co-operation from Native users. In 1982, FWS solicited co-operation from delta hunters in reducing the harvest of white-fronted geese, and many hunters voluntarily co-operated. Beginning with the Hooper Bay Agreement in 1984, government agencies and Native organizations created a co-management regime for the Y-K Delta which, when modified in 1985, became known as the Yukon-Kuskokwim Delta Goose Management Plan (YKDGMP) (Pamplin 1986). This document, signed by FWS, the Alaska Department of Fish and Game (ADF&G), the California Department of Fish and Game (CDFG), the Association of Village Council Presidents (AVCP), a Native organization representing tribal governments in southwestern Alaska, and its Waterfowl Conservation Committee (WCC), establishes the rights and obligations of the parties, rules regarding sport and subsistence hunting, and procedures for collective decision making. The agreement, updated in 1986 and 1987, has not been renegotiated for 1988 and is enmeshed in disputes over interpretation of a recent court decision.

Parties to the YKDGMP aim to restore and maintain the four species at "optimum population levels." The plan specifies population objectives for each species, minimum population levels below which hunting should be halted, and midrange levels at which hunting may resume.

In Alaska, the regime relies largely on voluntary compliance with hunting restrictions and depends on social control mechanisms of the indigenous communities. Government and user groups formed an Information and Education Task Force to explain the need for and provisions of the YKDGMP and to encourage compliance with it (Blanchard 1987, Pamplin

1986). The task force has produced materials for television, radio, newspapers, magazines, and school programmes. It arranges meetings in villages and schools, holds environmental education workshops for teachers, and (together with the National Audubon Society) sponsored a poster contest.

Some of these same agencies signed a supplemental agreement in March 1985 that deals with monitoring, verification, and enforcement of hunting restrictions. All suspected violations must be reported to the FWS Refuge manager and AVCP. Representatives of the four signatories then meet jointly with the village government where an incident occurs.

Government agencies are obligated to supply Native parties with research data and include AVCP and WCC in discussions of biological research and all phases of goose management. And the parties agreed to co-operate to develop a comprehensive plan to improve migratory bird scientific research.

State and federal public authorities question the term "co-management" in so far as it implies joint management authority. They prefer to refer to the YKDGMP as "co-operative management and improved communication." While the agreement does not transfer management authority to Native organizations or even give them equal power, it does create obligations and expectations for all parties. If one party withdraws from the YKDGMP or fails to fulfill its obligations, presumably, the other parties are also freed from their obligations to co-operate. Thus, the definition of co-management employed here, applies to the YKDGMP.

The YKDGMP has resolved many of the problems that existed prior to this regime. In four years, hunters have reduced their take of all four targeted species and government/Native communication and co-operation have improved markedly. Harvest studies estimated a 56 percent overall reduction from 1980 to 1985 in Native harvests, and the reduction appears to continue. Yup'ik hunters have reduced the number of goose eggs taken from over 15,000 in 1981 to about 1,600 in 1986. This demonstrates a remarkable change in behavior attributable, in large measure, to the YKDGMP.

The regime survived a major test in 1986 when AVCP and WCC agreed to a total ban on harvest of emperor geese. (Taking Canadian cackling geese was already prohibited by the YKDGMP.) Researchers reported that emperor geese had dropped below the minimum population level specified in the YKDGMP, a level below which the plan prohibits hunting. Nevertheless, federal managers sought the approval of WCC and AVCP. WCC requested that FWS hold meetings in 13 of the communities most dependent upon emperor geese. Following these meetings, the WCC made the difficult decision (through their usual consensus process) to approve a complete ban. Rather than abandoning the regime or acting unilaterally, all parties concurred in this collective decision.

The main threats to the stability of the regime come from resistance by a powerful sport hunter lobby, reliance on insecure sources of funding for Native participants, and continual tensions between research biologists working in the Y-K Delta and Native users.

Unfortunately, mutual respect for knowledge contributed by each party has been slow to develop in the Y-K Delta. Some Natives believe the decline in geese is related to the arrival of biologists on the delta. In recent years, National Wildlife Refuge managers have reduced the number of research camps and researchers permitted in the delta during the summer, but many Natives question whether the researchers comply with the agreement by all parties to refrain from unnecessarily disturbing the geese. Many elders in particular regard techniques such as capturing and tagging birds or writing on eggs as intrusive and believe that the researchers hamper the birds' reproductive success. Hiring Native assistants has not healed the rift.

A long history of mistrust of wildlife managers is not easily overcome in a few years. The difficulties encountered by researchers in gathering information for the 1986 harvest study (including the refusal of five communities to participate, high turnover of village survey workers, and ambivalence of those questioned with regard to responding to survey questions) demonstrate that mistrust continues. Never-theless, reduced harvests, remarkably high return rates for the 1986 harvest survey forms, and enthusiasm expressed by representatives of all parties to the regime indicate that the regime was working.

Unfortunately, the recent success of two sport hunting organizations in a lawsuit challenging the YKDGMP may effectively terminate the regime. In October 1987, an appellate court declared that FWS's subsistence hunting regulations must conform to the migratory bird treaty between Canada and the U.S. which, unlike later U.S. bilateral treaties with Japan and the Soviet Union, does not allow for Native subsistence harvest of migratory geese (U.S. Ninth Circuit Court of Appeals 1987). Although FWS cannot explicitly authorize closed season hunting, the court's opinion emphasized that FWS has wide discretion over enforcement. In December 1987, FWS proposed an enforcement policy that directs enforcement agents to give priority to regime rules. While law enforcement authorities and the sport hunter lobby push for strict enforcement of the closed season, users and managers hope to reinstitute the YKDGMP. When the geese return in late April, parties to the YKDGMP may return to an era of conflict.

Lessons for the Future

Neither the indigenous system nor the state system alone can protect northern wildlife and ecosystems, much less generate efficient and equitable wildlife management. Government agencies cannot implement and enforce their regulations without Native co-operation, Natives cannot protect the resources nor guarantee access to those resources without cooperation of government agencies. By creating co-management regimes that meld the two systems, both groups gain.

The cases examined in this essay indicate that co-management in the North American Arctic has produced improved communication and understanding between Native users and public authorities. In addition, the cases suggest that co-management has changed hunting practices in the interests of protecting declining species. In the Y-K Delta, users stopped collecting thousands of eggs and reduced harvests of migratory waterfowl covered by the regime. These changes contributed to an increase in the population of Canadian cackler geese in 1986 which reversed a long, serious decline in the species. Inuit in northern Quebec voluntarily cut their harvest of beluga whales by a third. These are impressive changes, especially in light of the history of non-co-operation between government agencies and user groups. The fundamental reason for co-operation is that both sides realize they need each other in order to protect resources they both value.

Since experience with wildlife co-management in the North American Arctic is brief, the conclusions we can draw are necessarily tentative. However, the record does suggest one overriding conclusion. Co-management can help to overcome problems caused by conflicts between indigenous and state systems of wildlife management. To do so, however, government administrators and indigenous users must form a partnership in which the user groups gain a sense of ownership and responsibility for the system's success. To acquire a stake in the success of the regime and a reason to comply with its rules, user groups must take part in a collective decision making process in which all parties concur in major decisions.

The cases suggest that four ingredients are essential to formation of such a partnership:

(1) The regime must have strong support from and a link to the villages. Representation of users on a regional body alone is insufficient to insure that the indigenous system is melded into the regime. The communities have, in some cases, adopted management tools characteristic of the state system, but they must be able to adapt these tools to their own circumstances as well as to employ the techniques of the indigenous system to make the regime work.

(2) Public authorities must grant indigenous users a decision-making role in shaping and operating the regime from research design to enforcement. Participation by Natives as research assistants is useful. But to obtain the benefits of co-operation, biologists must work with Native users to design studies that integrate the indigenous diachronic database with their own synchronic studies. When it becomes

necessary to reduce harvests, indigenous users emphasize information and education activities that establish new behavioral norms rather than the state system's usual enforcement tools. Although users may adopt management techniques such as quotas and bag limits, they are likely to adapt these to suit community lifeways.

(3) Governments must provide adequate funding for the operation of the regime. They must ensure support for participation of local hunter and trapper or wildlife organizations as well as for the joint regional boards that administer the regime or regional Native organizations that represent user communities.

(4) Cultural and linguistic barriers to Native user participation in administrative arrangements must be removed. For example, meetings should take place in northern communities, interpreters should be provided, information should be transmitted in Native languages, and indigenous ways of reaching collective decisions should be incorporated into the management system.

Co-management arrangements already exist for specific populations of caribou, migratory waterfowl, beluga and bowhead whales, and Pacific walrus. However, government officials often jealously guard their authority against encroachment by other agencies, and they are not in the habit of sharing power with those they have authority to regulate. Nevertheless, there is a growing awareness among those wildlife managers who spend time in Native communities that involving Native users in decision making offers the only way to manage wildlife effectively. The success of existing co-management arrangements has convinced many participants in such arrangements to consider handling other wildlife and resource management conflicts through co-management. The real question for the future, therefore, is not whether co-management regimes will increase in number and scope but whether the organizations created to implement them will work effectively. This essay should help those desiring to improve existing arrangements or to design new co-management regimes in the future.

References

Berkes, F.
1985   Fisheries and the "tragedy of the commons." Environmental Conservation 12(3):199-206.

Blanchard, K.
1987   Strategies for the conservation of seabirds on Quebec's North Shore and geese on Alaska's Yukon-Kuskokwim Delta. Transactions, 52nd North American Wildlife and Natural Resources Conference.

Breton, M., T.G. Smith and W. Kemp
1984   Studying and Managing Arctic Seals and Whales. Department of Fisheries and Oceans, Quebec City.

Caribou Management Agreement
1986   Executive Summary of the Long-Term Management Plan for the Beverly and Kaminuriak Caribou Herds, 37-40.

Department of Fisheries and Oceans
1986   Northern Quebec Belugas Management Plan. Quebec City.

Drolet, C.A., A. Reed, M. Breton and F. Berkes
1987   Sharing wildlife management responsibilities with Native groups. Transactions, 52nd North American Wildlife and Natural Resources Conference: 389-398.

Ohlendorf, H., D.J. Hoffman and T. Aldrich
1984   Recent findings and impacts on aquatic birds at Kesterton Reservoir. Paper presented at Agricultural Waste Water Workshop. University of California, Davis.

Pamplin, W.L.
1986   Cooperative efforts to halt population declines of geese nesting on Alaska's Yukon-Kuskokwim Delta. Transactions, 52nd North American Wildlife and Natural Resources Conference.

Reisner, M.
1987   California's vanishing wetlands. Amicus Journal 1:8-15.

Schaeffer, P., D. Barr and G. Moore
1986   Kotzebue Fish and Game Advisory Committee: A Review of the Game Regulations Affecting Northwest Alaska. Kotzebue.

U.S. Ninth Circuit Court of Appeals
1987   Alaska Fish and Wildlife Conservation Fund v. Dunkle, 829 F.2d 933, reversing Alaska Fish and Wildlife Federation and Outdoor Council v. Jantzen, No. CV84-013-V (D.A.K. unreported opin. Jan. 27, 1986), petition for certiorari pending in U.S. Supreme Court.

Usher, P.J.
1986   The Devolution of Wildlife Conservation in the Northwest Territories. Policy Paper No. #3. Canadian Arctic Resources Committee, Ottawa.

Young, O.R.
1977   Resource Management at the International Level: The Case of the North Pacific. London and New York: Francis Pinter and Nicols Publishing.
1982   Resource Regimes: Natural Resources and Social Institutions. Berkeley: University of California Press.

Selected Bibliography of Native Resource Management Systems and Native Knowledge of the Environment

Thomas D. Andrews
Dene/Metis Mapping Project
University of Alberta

Introduction

Over the past ten years there has been a growing awareness of the contribution Native traditional environmental knowledge and management of renewable resources can make to the development of state-based resource management systems and to scientific environmental and ecological research in the North. However, this trend is not restricted to northern regions. In fact there has been an increasing acknowledgement worldwide of the value of traditional indigenous environmental knowledge and resource management systems. This is reflected not only in a vast and expanding professional literature, but also in the recognition of the relevance of traditional knowledge and management systems by some governments (see Sibbeston 1987) and international science-based or development-oriented institutions (e.g., UNESCO, IUCN, FAO).

In North America, this growing awareness is in part due to the negotiation of Aboriginal land claims (e.g., James Bay, Northwest Territories, Yukon, Alaska) and, as well, because of a greater emphasis on community-based research. Perhaps more importantly, it is also the result of a growing realization among Native people of the need to document their traditional systems of management and knowledge of the environment to ensure their active involvement in the redesign of existing state-based management systems holding jurisdiction over their lands (e.g., Barnaby 1987; Kemp 1987; Suluk 1987). It is also, in part, a response by Native people and professional researchers to the impact of existing, but ineffective, management systems on subsistence resources (for example, the Bowhead whaling issue in Alaska; see Bockstoce et al. 1979; North Slope Borough 1980; Oktollik 1985) or to the threat to continued economic viability of Native communities and traditional subsistence activities due to the actions of certain environmental movements (for example, the anti-sealing and anti-trapping campaigns; see Green and Smith 1986; Herscovici 1985). In other regions of the world where developing countries are attempting to establish resource management schemes, indigenous populations are often the only source of sound "scientific" knowledge of resources and the environment (see McNeely and Pitt 1985). The cultural component or "ethnoscience" of local conservation is obviously critically important in these situations, where impact to fragile ecosystems is to be mitigated and managed in any effective way.

This bibliography presents a selective survey of the literature pertaining to Native traditional environmental knowledge and resource management. An attempt has been made to present a comprehensive listing for Canada (with the exception of studies in ethnobotany) and a listing representative of the widest possible range of research and issues for the rest of the world.

Organization

The bibliography contains 246 references arranged by author, date and title. The bibliography is preceded by subject indices which list the entries according to subject, by author and date. This enables the user to search for references on a particular subject (largely geographical) and then find the full citation in the bibliography which follows. The subject index headings include the following information:

Africa and the Middle East

Entries are from the continent of Africa (e.g., Brokensha and Riley 1980; Marks 1984; Tobayiwa 1985), and from southwestern Asia (largely the Arabian peninsula; see Draz 1985).

Alaska and the Continental USA

The majority of the references in this section relate to research conducted in Alaska (e.g., Langdon 1986; Nelson 1983; Worl 1980), though several entries deal with the west coast of the continental United States (e.g., Barsh 1982; Cohen 1986; Richardson 1982).

Australia and Papua New Guinea

Australia and P.N.G. have been included together largely because of geographical proximity and the consequent issues surrounding shared marine resources (i.e., in Torres Strait). The majority of the references refer to knowledge and management of marine and littoral resources and ecosystems, though inland examples are included (see for example: Dwyer 1982; Haines 1982; Hanks, J. 1984; Lewis 1985a; Morauta et al. 1982; Webb 1973).

Canada — Eastern Provinces

A large portion of the entries overall are on research conducted in Canada. By far the greatest number of entries are from eastern Canada, predominantly from the James Bay region in Quebec. The entries by Feit (various) and Berkes (various) are particularly relevant.

Canada — Western Provinces

References from British Columbia and Alberta are included. Research in these provinces has focussed on the knowledge and use of coastal and marine resources (e.g., Cohen and Hansen 1988; Ellis and Swan 1981; Ellis and Wilson 1981), ethnobotany (e.g., Turner, various), the use of fire in managing local environments (see Lewis, various), and traditional management and knowledge of forested and inland ecosystems (e.g., Brody 1981; Ridington 1971).

Canada — Yukon and Northwest Territories

Though this is a vast geographical region, Northern Canada has witnessed comparatively little research into Native traditional environmental knowledge and management systems. Included in this section are entries dealing with traditional knowledge, use and management of arctic sea ice environments and resources (e.g., Arima 1976; Breton et al. 1979; Freeman, various; Suluk 1987), and boreal forest ecosystems (e.g., Basso 1972; Lamont 1977; Smith 1986b; T'Seleie 1985). Also included are entries dealing with examples of successful attempts at co-management (e.g., Gunn et al. 1988; Lloyd 1986) and discussions concerning the role of, and potential for, incorporating traditional knowledge and management systems into evolving state-based management schemes in the North (e.g., Freeman 1986; Usher 1986b).

Greenland and Scandinavia

Three entries are included here; they describe knowledge and management systems among Sámi reindeer herders of northern Norway (Bjorklund 1988) and the knowledge and use of marine and terrestrial resources in Greenland (Christiansen 1964; Freeman 1977).

India and Sri Lanka

In this section several examples of traditional conservation and resource management practices in India and Sri Lanka are presented.

Pacific and South East Asia

There has been considerable research in the field of traditional environmental knowledge and management in this region. It is a geographically large area, and encompasses the south and central Pacific, as well as Indonesia and Thailand. Research has focussed primarily on the knowledge, use and management of marine resources (e.g., Akimichi, various; Hinton 1985; Johannes, various; Ruddle and Johannes 1985), though examples from terrestrial ecosystems are included (e.g., Hanks 1984; McNeely and Pitt 1985; Vayda et al. 1985).

South America

All entries here deal with the use and knowledge of marine resources by Native populations in Brazil (e.g., Cordell 1984) and Nicaragua (e.g., Nietschmann 1972, 1973).

General Overviews, Literature Reviews and Bibliographies

This section presents entries which provide an overall view of traditional knowledge of the environment and management of resources in a variety of contexts worldwide (e.g., Brokensha et al. 1980; Cohen and Hanson 1988; Ruddle and Johannes 1985). Several bibliographies are also included for further references (see Anderson 1983; O'Keefe and Howes 1980; Smith 1986a).

Subject Index

Africa and the Middle East

Berkes and Farvar, in prep.
Brokensha and Riley, 1980
Brokensha et al., 1980
Draz, 1985
Klee, 1980
Marks, 1976
Marks, 1977
Marks, 1984
McNeely and Pitt, 1985
Tobayiwa, 1985

Alaska and the Continental United States

Anderson, 1983
Barsh, 1982
Behnke et al., 1986
Berkes and Farvar, in prep.
Bockstoce et al., 1979
Brelsford, 1980
Brokensha et al., 1979
Caulfield, 1988
Cohen, 1986

Feldman, 1986
Freeman, in prep.b
Freeman and Carbyn, 1988
Green and Smith, 1986
Langdon, 1984
Langdon, 1986
Lewis, 1973
Lewis, 1985b
Lonner, 1986
Magdanz and Olanna, 1984
McCay, 1980
McCay and Acheson, 1987
Minc, 1986
Nelson, 1966a
Nelson, 1966b
Nelson, 1969
Nelson, 1973
Nelson, 1982
Nelson, 1983
Nelson et al., 1982
North Slope Borough, 1980
Oktollik, 1985
Osherenko, 1988a
Richardson, 1982
Smith, S., 1986a
Wheeler, 1988
Williams and Hunn, 1982
Wolfe, 1986
Wolfe and Ellana, 1983
Wolfe and Behnke, 1982
Worl, 1980

Australia and Papua New Guinea

Baines, 1985
Bulmer, 1982
Carrier, 1982
Davis, 1985a
Davis, 1985b
Dwyer, 1982
Grey and Zann, in press
Haines, 1982
Hanks, J., 1984
Hill et al., 1982
Hudson, 1981
Hudson, 1982
Hudson, 1986a
Hudson, 1986b
Johannes, in press
Kowarsky, 1982

Klee, 1980
Kwapena, 1984a
Lasserre and Ruddle, 1983
Lewis, 1982a
Lewis, 1985a
Lewis, in press
Morauta et al., 1982
Nietschmann, 1984
Nietschmann, 1985
Nietschmann and Nietschmann, 1981
Ovington, 1984
Ruddle and Johannes, 1985
Smith, A., 1987
Spring, 1982
Webb, 1973
Williams, 1986
Williams and Hunn, 1982
Wright, 1985

Canada — Eastern Provinces

Berkes, 1977
Berkes, 1979
Berkes, 1980
Berkes, 1981a
Berkes, 1981b
Berkes, 1981c
Berkes, 1982a
Berkes, 1982b
Berkes, 1984
Berkes, 1987
Berkes, 1988
Berkes and Freeman, 1986
Berkes and Farvar, in prep.
Black, 1967
Boyd, 1979
Brelsford, 1980
Brice-Bennett, 1977
Cohen and Hanson, 1988
Craik, 1975
Drolet, 1986
Drolet et al., 1987
Feit, 1973
Feit, 1978
Feit, 1979
Feit, 1982
Feit, 1984
Feit, 1985
Feit, 1986a
Feit, 1986b

Feit, 1987
Feit, 1988a
Feit, 1988b
Feit, in press a
Feit, in press b
Feit, in press c
Freeman, 1977
Freeman and Carbyn, 1988
Green and Smith, 1986
Herscovici, 1985
Hutchins, in press
Kemp, 1987
Makavik Corp., 1984
Martin, 1978
Nakashima, 1986
Pinkerton, in press
Ridington, 1988
Salisbury, 1986
Salisbury et al., 1972
Scott, 1982
Scott, 1983
Scott, 1987
Steegman, 1983
Tanner, 1973
Tanner, 1979
Tanner, 1983
Weinstein, 1976
Weinstein, 1977
Williams and Hunn, 1982
Winterhalder, 1980
Winterhalder, 1981a
Winterhalder, 1981b
Winterhalder, 1983a
Winterhalder, 1983b
Winterhalder, 1983c

Canada — Western Provinces

Arima, 1975-6
Berringer, 1982
Brody, 1981
Cohen and Hanson, 1988
Ellis and Swan, 1981
Ellis and Wilson, 1981
Green and Smith, 1986
Kennedy and Bouchard, 1974
Kennedy and Bouchard, 1976
Lewis, 1977
Lewis, 1980
Lewis, 1982a

Lewis, 1982b
Pinkerton, 1983
Pinkerton, 1988
Pinkerton, in press
Richardson, 1982
Ridington, 1971
Ridington, 1988
Turner, 1973
Turner, 1974
Turner, 1975
Turner, 1978
Turner, 1979
Turner and Bell, 1971
Turner and Efrat, 1982
Turner et al., 1980
Turner et al., 1983
Waquan, 1986
Weinstein, 1985

Canada — Yukon and Northwest Territories

Arima, 1976
Basso, 1972
Barnaby, 1987
Berkes and Freeman, 1986
Berkes and Farvar, in prep.
Bockstoce et al., 1979
Bodden, 1981
Breton et al., 1984
Brody, 1981
Cohen and Hanson, 1988
Cruikshank, 1981
DeLancey, 1985
DeLancey and Andrews, 1988
Feit, 1988
Freeman, 1975
Freeman, 1976
Freeman, 1979
Freeman, 1984a
Freeman, 1984b
Freeman, 1985
Freeman, 1986
Freeman, in prep. a
Freeman and Carbyn, 1988
Green and Smith, 1986
Gunn et al., 1988
Hanks and Winter, 1986
Herscovici, 1985
Lamont, 1977
Lloyd, 1986

McCandless, 1985
Nelson, 1966a
Nelson, 1969
Osherenko, 1988b
Poole, 1981
Riewe and Gamble, 1988
Sabo and Sabo, 1985
Sibbeston, 1986
Smith, S., 1986b
Suluk, 1987
T'Seleie, 1985
Usher, 1981
Usher, 1984
Usher, 1986a
Usher, 1986b
Usher, 1987

Greenland and Scandinavia

Bjorklund, 1988
Christiansen, 1964
Freeman 1977

India and Sri Lanka

Alexander, 1977
Berkes and Farvar, in prep.
Brokensha et al., 1980
Gadgil, 1985
McNeely and Pitt, 1985
Sankhala, 1985

Pacific and South East Asia

Akimichi, 1978
Akimichi, 1981
Akimichi, 1986
Berkes and Farvar, in prep.
Brokensha et al., 1980
Chapman, 1985
Dahl, 1985
Hanks, J., 1984
Hill, 1978
Hinton, 1985
Johannes, 1975
Johannes, 1978
Johannes, 1981a
Johannes, 1981b
Johannes, 1981c
Johannes, 1982
Johannes, 1984

Johannes, 1985
Johannes et al., 1983
Klee, 1976
Klee, 1980
Klee, 1985
Lasserre and Ruddle, 1983
McNeely and Miller, 1984
McNeely and Pitt, 1985
Pernetta and Hill, 1984
Polunin, 1985
Pulae, 1985
Ruddle and Akimichi, 1984
Ruddle and Johannes, 1985
Sya'rani and Willoughby, 1985
Vayda et al., 1985
Watson, 1982
Zann, 1985

South America

Berkes and Farvar, in prep.
Brokensha et al., 1980
Cordell, 1984
Nietschmann, 1972
Nietschmann, 1973
Nietschmann, 1974

*General Overviews, Literature Reviews and
Bibliographies*

Acheson, 1981
Anderson, 1983
Baines, 1985
Berkes, 1985
Berkes and Farvar, in prep.
Bodley, 1988
Brokensha et al., 1980
Chapman, 1985
Clad, 1985
Cohen, 1986
Cohen and Hanson, 1988
Dahl, 1985
DeLancey and Andrews, 1988
Feit, 1988a
Feit, 1988b
Freeman, 1979
Freeman and Carbyn, 1988
Green and Smith, 1986
Hanks, J., 1984
Johannes et al., 1983
Klee, 1980

Kwapena, 1984b
Leff, 1985
Lewis, 1985b
Martin, 1978
McCay, 1980
McCay and Acheson, 1987
McDonald, 1988
McNeely and Miller, 1984
McNeely and Pitt, 1985
Morauta et al., 1982
Nelson, 1966a
Nelson, 1966b
Nowick, 1985
O'Keefe and Howes, 1980
Osherenko, 1988a
Pinkerton, 1988
Pinkerton, in press
Pitt, 1985
Ruddle and Johannes, 1985
Smith, S., 1986a
Usher, 1981
Usher, 1984
Waldram, 1987
Webb and Smith, 1984

Bibliography

Acheson, J.M.
1981   Anthropology of fishing. *Annual Review of Anthropology*, 10:275-316.

Akimichi, Tomoya
1978   The ecological aspect of Lau (Solomon Islands) ethnoichthyology. *Journal of the Polynesian Society*, 87:301-326
1981   Perception and function: traditional resource management in three Pacific Islands. *Resource Management and Optimization*, 1(4):361-378.
1986   Conservation of the sea: Sawatal, Micronesia. *In* Atholl Anderson (ed.), *Traditional fishing in the Pacific: ethnographical and archaeological papers from the 15th Pacific Science Congress,* Pacific Anthropological Records, No. 37. Honolulu, Hawaii. pp. 15-33.

Alexander, P.
1977   Sea tenure in Sri Lanka. *Ethnology,* 16:231-253.

Anderson, D.B.
1983   Regional subsistence bibliography, interior Alaska. *Technical Report Number 2,* Division of Subsistence, Alaska Department of Fish and Game, Juneau.

Arima, Eugene Y.
1975-6 Notes on the southern west coast (Nootka) Native environment and exploitative techniques for the P'a:chi"da?atH of Port San Juan. Unpublished ms., National Museum of Man and Parks Canada.
1976   Views on land expressed in Inuit oral tradition. *In* M.M.R. Freeman, (ed.), *Report: Inuit land use and occupancy project.* Department of Indian Affairs and Northern Development, Ottawa. vol. 2: 217-222.

Baines, G.
1985   Draft programme on traditional knowledge for conservation. *Tradition, conservation and development: occasional newsletter of the Commission on Ecology's Working Group on Traditional Ecological Knowledge,* 3:5-13.

Barnaby, Joanne
1987   University research and the Dene Nation, a summary of a presentation at the ACUNS meetings in Yellowknife. *In* W. Peter Adams (ed.), *Education, research, information systems and the North.* ACUNS, Ottawa. 27 pp.

Barsh, Russel L.
1982   The economics of a traditional coastal salmon fishery. *Human Organization* 41(2):170-176.

Basso, Keith H.
1972   Ice and travel among the Fort Norman Slave: folk taxonomies and cultural rules. *Language in society,* 1:31-49.

Behnke, Steven R. and Terry L. Haynes
1986   Local and Native hire in renewable resource management: an Alaskan case. *In* J. Green and J. Smith (eds.), *Native People and renewable resource management.* Proceedings of symposium of the Alberta Society of Professional Biologists, Edmonton. pp. 142-149.

Berkes, Fikret
1977   Fishery resource use in a subarctic Indian community. *Human Ecology,* 5(4):289-309.
1979   An investigation of Cree Indian domestic fisheries in northern Quebec. *Arctic,* 32(1):46-70.
1980   Issues and perspectives in fish and wildlife management in the James Bay area. *Bulletin of the Canadian Society of Environmental Biologists,* 37(2):95-101.
1981a   Fisheries of the James Bay area and northern Quebec: a case study in resource management. *In* M.M.R. Freeman (ed.) *Proceedings: First International symposium on renewable resources and the economy of the North.* Association of Canadian Universities for Northern Studies and the Man and the Biosphere Program, Ottawa. pp. 143-160.
1981b   The role of self-regulation in living resource management in the North. *In* M.M.R Freeman, (ed), *Proceedings: First International symposium on renewable resources and the economy of the North.* Association of Canadian Universities for Northern Studies and the Man and the Biosphere Program, Ottawa. pp. 166-178.
1981c   Some environmental and social impacts of the James Bay hydroelectric project, Canada. *Journal of Environmental Management,* 12:157-172.
1982a   Waterfowl management and northern Native peoples with reference to Cree hunters of James Bay. *Musk-Ox,*

30:23-36.

1982b   Preliminary impacts of the James Bay Hydroelectric Project, Quebec, on estuarine fish and fisheries. *Arctic*, 35:524-530.

1984   Alternative styles in living resources management: the case of James Bay. *Environments*, 16(3):114-123.

1985   Fishermen and "the tragedy of the commons." *Environmental Conservation*, 12(3):199-206.

1987   Common property resource management and Cree Indian fisheries in subarctic Canada. *In* B.J. McCay and J.M. Acheson, (eds.), *Capturing the Commons.* University of Arizona Press, Tuscon. pp. 66-91.

1988   Environmental philosophy of the Chisasibi Cree people of James Bay. *In* M.M.R. Freeman and L.N. Carbyn (eds.) *Traditional knowledge and renewable resource management*, Boreal Institute for Northern Studies, Occasional Publication No. 23, Edmonton.

Berkes, F. and M.M.R. Freeman
1986   Human ecology and resource use *In* I.P. Martini (ed), *Canadian Inland Seas.* Elsevier. pp. 425-455.

Berkes, F. and M. Taghi Farvar
in prep *Community-based sustainable development: the ecology of common property resources.* Cambridge University Press.

Berringer, Patricia A.
1982   Northwest coast traditional salmon fisheries systems of resource utilization. M.A. thesis, Department of Anthropology and Sociology, University of British Columbia, Vancouver.

Bjorklund, Ivar
1988   Sámi Reindeer pastoralism as an indigenous resource management system in northern Norway. *In* M.M.R. Freeman and L.N. Carbyn (eds.), *Traditional knowledge and renewable resource management in northern regions.* Boreal Institute for Northern Studies, Occasional Publication No. 23, Edmonton.

Black, Mary B.
1967   An ethnoscience investigation of Objibwa ontology and world view. Ph.D. dissertation. Stanford University.

Bockstoce, J.R., M. Freeman, W.S. Laughlin, R.K. Nelson, M. Orbach, R. Peterson, J.G. Taylor and R. Worl
1979   Report of the panel to consider cultural aspects of aboriginal whaling in North America. *Reports of the International Whaling Commission, Special Issue 4.* Cambridge. pp. 35-49.

Bodden, Kenneth R.
1981   The economic use by Native peoples of the resources of the Slave River Delta. M.A. thesis, Department of Geography, University of Alberta, Edmonton.

Bodley, John H. (ed.)
1988   *Tribal Peoples and Development Issues: A Global Overview.* Mayfield Publishing Company, California. 421 pp.

Boyd, H.
1979   Waterfowl hunting by Native peoples in Canada: The case of James Bay and northern Quebec. *In XIII International Congress of Game Biologists,* Atlanta. pp. 463-473.

Breton, M., T.G. Smith and B. Kemp
1984   *Studying and managing arctic seals and whales: the views of scientists and Inuit on biology and behavior of arctic seals and whales, harvesting sea mammals, management and conservation for the future.* Department of Fisheries and Oceans, Canada. Minister of Supply and Services. Ottawa, Canada.

Brelsford, T.
1980   Subsistence protections: the political and administrative struggles in Alaska and James Bay, Quebec. *In Papers of the 2nd International Conference on Hunting and Gathering Societies,* Université Laval, Department of Anthropology, Quebec. pp. 207-261.

Brice-Bennett, C. (ed.)
1977   *Our footprints are everywhere.* Labrador Inuit Association, Nain, Labrador.

Brody, Hugh
1976   Land occupancy: Inuit perceptions. *In* M.M.R. Freeman, (ed.), *Report: Inuit land use and occupancy project.* Department of Indian Affairs and Northern Development, Ottawa. Vol. 2:193-201.

1981 *Maps and dreams: Indians and the British Columbia frontier*. Douglas and McIntyre, Toronto.

Brokensha, David W., D.M. Warrens and Oswald Werner (eds.)
1980 *Indigenous knowledge systems and development*. University Press of America, Lanham. 466 pp.

Brokensha, David W. and B.W. Riley
1980 Mbeere knowledge of their vegetation and its relevance for development: a case study from Kenya. *In* D.W. Brokensha et al. (eds.), *Indigenous knowledge systems and development*. University Press of America, Lanham. pp. 113-129.

Bulmer, R.N.H.
1982 Traditional conservation practices in Papua New Guinea. *In* L. Morauta, J. Pernetta and W. Heaney (eds.), *Traditional conservation in Papua New Guinea: implications for today*. The Institute of Applied Social and Economic Research, Monograph 16, Boroko. pp. 59-79.

Caufield, Richard
1988 The role of subsistence resource commissions in the management of Alaska's new National Parks. *In* M.M.R. Freeman and L.N. Carbyn (eds.), *Traditional knowledge and renewable resource management in northern regions*. Boreal Institute for Northern Studies, Occasional Publication, No. 23, Edmonton.

Carrier, J.G.
1982 Conservation and conception of the environment: A Manus Province case study. *In* L. Morauta, J. Pernetta and W. Heaney (eds.), *Traditional conservation in Papua New Guinea: implications for today*. The Institute of Applied Social and Economic Research, Monograph 16. Boroko. pp. 39-43.

Chapman, Margaret D.
1985 Environmental influences on the development of traditional conservation in the south Pacific region. *Environmental Conservation*, 12(3):217-230.

Christiansen, Hans C.
1964 *Laerbo I Fangst for Syd- og Nordgrønland* [Textbook of hunting and fishing for south and north Greenland]. Den kongelie grønlanske Handel, Copenhagen.

Clad, James C.
1985 Conservation and indigenous peoples: A study of convergent issues. *In* J.A. McNeely and D. Pitt (eds.), *Culture and Conservation: The Human Dimension in Environmental Planning*. IUCN/ Croom Helm, London. pp. 45-62.

Cohen, Fay G.
1986 *Treaties on trial: the continuing controversy over northwest Indian fishing rights*. University of Washington Press, Seattle. 229 pp.

Cohen, Fay G. and A.J. Hanson (eds.)
1988 *Community-based resource management in Canada: an inventory of research and projects*. Canadian Commission for UNESCO, Man and the Biosphere Program, Ottawa. (In press).

Cordell, J.C.
1984 Traditional sea tenure and resource management in Brazilian coastal fishing. *In* J.H. Kapetsky and G. Lasserre (eds.), *Management of coastal lagoon fisheries*. General Fisheries Council for the Mediterranean, Studies and Reviews No. 61, FAO, Rome. pp. 429-438.

Craik, Brian
1975 The formation of a goose hunting strategy and the politics of the hunting group. *In* J. Freedman and J.H. Barkow (eds.), *Proceedings of the second conference, Canadian Ethnology Society*. National Museum of Man, Mercury Series No. 28, Ottawa. pp. 450-465.

Cruikshank, Julie
1981 Legend and landscape: convergence of oral and scientific traditions in the Yukon Territory. *Arctic Anthropology*, 18(2):67-93.

Dahl, A.L.
1985 Traditional environmental management in New Caledonia: a review of existing knowledge. South Pacific Environment Programme, *Topic Review* No. 18, UNEP, Nairobi. 17 pp.

Davis, S.

1985a Aboriginal knowledge and use of the coast and sea in Northern Arnhem Land. *In* K.N. Bardsley, J.D.S. Davie and C.D. Woodroffe (eds.), *Coasts and tidal wetlands of the Australian monsoon region*. ANURU Mangrove No. 1, Darwin. pp. 297-312.

1985b Traditional management of the littoral zone among the Yolngu of northern Australia. *In* K. Ruddle and R.E. Johannes (eds.), *The traditional knowledge and management of coastal systems in Asia and the Pacific*. UNESCO, Regional Office for Science and Technology for Southeast Asia, Jakarta. pp. 101-124.

DeLancey, Debbie

1985 Trapping and the Aboriginal economy. *Information North,* Winter, 1985: 5-12.

DeLancey, D. and T.D. Andrews

1988 Denendeh (Western Arctic). *In* Fay G. Cohen and A.J. Hanson (eds.), *Community-based resource management in Canada: An inventory of research and projects*. Canadian Commission for UNESCO, Man and the Biosphere Program, Ottawa. (in press).

Draz, Omar

1985 The Hema system of range reserves in the Arabian Peninsula: Its possibilities in range improvement and conservation projects in the Near East. *In* J.A. McNeely and D. Pitt, (eds.), *Culture and Conservation*. Croom Helm, London. pp. 109-121.

Drolet, C.A.

1986 Land claims settlements and the management of migratory birds, a case history: the James Bay and Northern Quebec Agreement. *Transactions of the North American Wildlife and Natural Resources Conference,* 51: 511-515.

Drolet, C.A., A. Reed, M. Breton and F. Berkes

1987 Sharing wildlife management responsibilities with Native groups: case histories in northern Quebec. *Transactions of the North American Wildlife and Natural Resources Conference,* 52:389-398.

Dwyer, P.D.

1982 Wildlife conservation and tradition in the highlands of Papua New Guinea. *In* L. Morauta, J. Pernetta and W. Heaney (eds.), *Traditional conservation in Papua New Guinea: implications for today*. The Institute of Applied Social and Economic Research, Monograph 16. Boroko. pp. 173-189.

Ellis, David W. and Luke Swan

1981 *Teachings of the tides: uses of marine invertebrates by the Manhousat people*. Theytus Books, Nanaimo, B.C. 118 pp.

Ellis, David W. and Solomon Wilson

1981 *The knowledge and usage of marine invertebrates by the Skidegate Haida people of the Queen Charlotte Islands*. Monograph Series No. 1, The Queen Charlotte Museum Society, Queen Charlotte City. 40 pp.

Feit, Harvey A.

1973 The ethno-ecology of the Waswanipi Cree, or how hunters can manage their resources. *In* Bruce Cox, (ed.), *Cultural Ecology: Readings on Canadian Indians and Eskimos*. McClelland and Stewart, Toronto. pp. 115-125.

1978 Waswanipi realities and adaptations: resource management and cognitive structure. Ph.D. Dissertation, McGill University, Montreal.

1979 Political articulations of hunters to the state: means of resisting threats to subsistence production in the James Bay and Northern Quebec Agreement. *Etudes/Inuit/Studies,* 3(2):37-52.

1982 The future of hunters within nation states: anthropology and the James Bay Cree. *In* E. Leacock and R. Lee (eds.), *Politics and history of Band societies,* Cambridge University Press. Cambridge. pp. 373-417.

1984 Conflict arenas in the management of renewable resources in the Canadian north: perspectives based on conflicts and responses in the James Bay region, Quebec. *In National and Regional Interests in the North*. Canadian Arctic Resources Committee, Ottawa. pp. 435-468.

1985 Legitimation and autonomy in James Bay Cree responses to hydroelectric development. *In* N. Dyck (ed.), *Indigenous peoples and the nation state: fourth world politics in Canada, Australia and Norway*. Memorial University, Institute for Social and Economic

Research, St. John's. pp. 27-66.

1986a James Bay Cree Indian management and moral considerations of fur-bearers. *In* J. Green and J. Smith, (eds.), *Native people and renewable resource management*. Proceedings of the 1986 symposium of the Alberta Society of Professional Biologists, Edmonton. pp. 49-65.

1986b Hunting and the quest for power: the James Bay Cree and Whiteman in the twentieth century. *In* R.B. Morrison and C.R. Wilson (eds.), *Native peoples: the Canadian experience*. McClelland and Stewart, Toronto. pp. 171-207.

1987 Waswanipi management of land and wildlife: Cree ethno-ecology revisited. *In* B. Cox, (ed), *Native People, Native Lands: Canadian Indians, Inuit and Metis*. Carleton Library Series, No. 142. Carleton University Press, Ottawa. pp. 75-91.

1988a Self-management and State-management: forms of knowing and managing northern wildlife. *In* M.M.R. Freeman and L.N. Carbyn (eds.), *Traditional knowledge and renewable resource management in northern regions*. Boreal Institute for Northern Studies, Occasional Publication, No. 23, Edmonton.

1988b Local-level resource management studies/projects in the James Bay region. *In* Fay G. Cohen and A.J. Hanson (eds.), *Community-based resource management in Canada: an inventory of research and projects*. Canadian Commission for UNESCO, Man and the Biosphere Program, Ottawa. (in press)

in press a. James Bay Cree self-governance and management of land and wildlife. *In* E. Wilmsen, (ed.), *We are here: Social history and Politics of Forager land rights*. University of California Press, Berkeley.

in press b. North American Native hunting and management of moose populations. Second International Moose Symposium Proceedings, *Swedish Wildlife Research*, Uppsala.

in press c. The power and the responsibility: implementation of the wildlife hunting provisions of the James Bay and Northern Quebec Agreement. *In* Sylvie Vincent, (ed.), *James Bay and Northern Quebec Agreement, Ten Years After*.

Feldman, Kerry D.
1986 Subsistence Beluga whale hunting in Alaska: a view from Escholtz Bay. *In* Steve Langdon (ed.), *Contemporary Alaskan Native Economies*. University Press of America, Lanham. pp. 153-171.

Freeman, Milton M.R.,
1975 Assessing movement in an Arctic caribou population. *Journal of Environmental Management* 3:251-57.

1976 *Report: Inuit Land Use and Occupancy Project*. Department of Indian and Northern Affairs, 3 vols. Ottawa.

1977 A cultural ecologic analysis of harp seal hunting in the Eastern Canadian Arctic, Northern Labrador and West Greenland. Unpublished manuscript, 95 pp. Deposited in the Boreal Institute Library, Edmonton.

1979 Traditional land users as a legitimate source of environmental expertise. *In* R.D. Needham, S.H. Nelson and R.C. Scace (eds.), *The Canadian National Parks: Today and Tomorrow, Conference II, Ten Years After*, vol. 1, Studies in Land Use History and Landscape Change, No. 7, Waterloo. pp. 345-369.

1984a New/Old approaches to renewable resource management in the North. Paper presented at the twenty-third annual meeting, western Regional Science Association, Monterey California.

1984b Contemporary Inuit exploitation of the sea-ice environment. *In* Alan Cooke and E. Van Alstine (eds.), *Sikimuit: "the people of the sea ice."* A workshop, Montreal, Quebec, April 1982. Canadian Arctic Resources Committee, Ottawa.

1985 Appeal to tradition: different perspectives on arctic wildlife management. *In* Jens Brøsted, Jens Dahl, Andrew Gray et al. (eds.), *Native Power: the quest for autonomy and nationhood of indigenous peoples*. Universitetsforlaget AS, Bergen, Norway. pp. 265-281.

1986 Renewable resources, economics and Native communities. *In* J. Green and J. Smith (eds.), *Native People and renewable resource management*. Proceedings of the 1986 symposium of the Alberta Society of Professional Biologists, Edmonton. pp. 29-37.

in prep.a. Graphs and Gaffs: A cautionary tale in the common property debate. *In* F. Berkes and M. Taghi Farvar (eds.), *Community-based sustainable develop-*

ment: the ecology of common property resources. Cambridge University Press.

in prep.b. The Alaska Eskimo Whaling Commission: Successful co-management under extreme conditions. *In* E. Pinkerton, (ed.), *Cooperative management of local fisheries.* University of British Columbia Press, Vancouver.

Freeman, M.M.R. and Ludwig N. Carbyn (eds.)
1988 *Traditional knowledge and renewable resource management in northern regions.* Boreal Institute for Northern Studies, Occasional Publication, No. 23, Edmonton.

Gadgil, Madhav
1985 Social restraints on resource utilization: The Indian experience. *In* J.A. McNeely and D. Pitt (eds.), *Culture and Conservation.* Croom Helm, London. pp. 135-154.

Green, J. and J. Smith
1986 *Native people and renewable resource management.* Proceedings of the 1986 Symposium of the Alberta Society of Professional Biologists, Edmonton.

Grey, F. and L. Zann
in press *Traditional knowledge of the marine environment in northern Australia.* Proceedings of a workshop, Townsville, 1985. Great Barrier Reef Marine Park Authority.

Gunn, Anne, G. Arlootoo and D. Kaomayak
1988 The contribution of ecological knowledge of Inuit to wildlife management in the Northwest Territories. *In* M.M.R. Freeman and L.N. Carbyn (eds.), *Traditional knowledge and renewable resource management in northern regions.* Boreal Institute for Northern Studies, Occasional Publication No. 23, Edmonton.

Haines, A.K.
1982 Traditional concepts and practices in inland fisheries management. *In* L. Morauta, J. Pernetta and W. Heaney (eds.), *Traditional conservation in Papua New Guinea: implications for today.* The Institute of Applied Social and Economic Research, Monograph 16. Boroko. pp. 279-291.

Hanks, J. (ed.)
1984 *Traditional lifestyles, conservation and rural development.* Proceedings of a symposium, Bandung, Indonesia, 1982. Commission on Ecology Papers No. 7. IUCN, Gland.

Hanks, C. and B.J. Winter
1986 Local knowledge and ethnoarchaeology: an approach to Dene settlement systems. *Current Anthropology,* 27(3):272-275.

Herscovici, Alan
1985 *Second nature: the animal rights controversy.* CBC Enterprises, Toronto. 254 pp.

Hill, H.B.
1978 The use of nearshore marine life as a food resource by American Samoans. Miscellaneous Working Paper, Pacific Islands Program, University of Hawaii.

Hill, L., J. Pernetta and B. Rongap
1982 The traditional knowledge base: implications and possibilities for contemporary Papua New Guinea. *In* L. Morauta et al. (eds.), *Traditional conservation in Papua New Guinea: implications for today.* The Institute of Applied Social and Economic Research, Monograph 16. Boroko. pp. 349-362.

Hinton, Peter
1985 An approach to the study of traditional systems of coastal resources management in Thailand. *In* K. Ruddle and R.E. Johannes (eds.), *The traditional knowledge and management of coastal systems in Asia and the Pacific.* UNESCO, Regional Office for Science and Technology for Southeast Asia, Jakarta.

Hudson, B.E.T.
1981 The dugong conservation, management and public education programme in Papua New Guinea: working with people to conserve their dugong resources. *In* H. Marsh (ed.), *The Dugong.* James Cook University, Townsville. pp. 70-79.
1982 Dugong myth and management in Papua New Guinea. *In* L. Morauta et al. (eds.), *Traditional conservation in Papua New Guinea: implications for today.* The Institute of Applied Social and Economic Research, Monograph 16. Boroko. pp. 311-315.
1986a The hunting of dugong at Daru, Papua

New Guinea, during 1978-1982: community management and education. *In* A.K. Haines et al. (eds.), *Torres Strait Fisheries Seminar.* Port Moresby, P.N.G., 1985. pp. 77-94.

1986b Dugongs and people. *Oceanus,* 29(2):100-106.

Hutchins, Peter W.

in press The law applying to trapping of furbearing animals by aboriginal peoples — a case of double jeopardy. *In* M. Novak and J.A. Baker (eds.), *Wild furbearer management and conservation in North America.* Ontario Ministry of Natural Resources, Wildlife Branch, Toronto.

Johannes, R.E.

1975 Exploitation degradation of shallow marine food resources in Oceania. *In* R.W. Force and B. Bishop (eds.), *The impact of urban centers in the Pacific.* Pacific Science Association, Honolulu. pp. 47-79.

1978 Traditional marine conservation methods in Oceania and their demise. *Annual Review of Ecology and Systematics,* 9:349-364.

1981a *Words of the lagoon: Fishing and marine lore in the Palau district of Micronesia.* University of California Press, Berkeley.

1981b Making better use of existing knowledge in managing Pacific island reef and lagoon ecosystems. South Pacific Environment Programme, *Topic Review,* No. 4, UNEP, Nairobi. 18 pp.

1981c Working with fisherman to improve coastal tropical fisheries and resource management. *Bulletin of Marine Science,* 31(3):673-680.

1982 Traditional conservation methods and protected marine areas in Oceania. *Ambio,* 11(5):258-261.

1984 Marine conservation in relation to traditional life-styles of tropical artisanal fisherman. *In* J. Hanks (ed.), *Traditional life-styles, conservation and rural development.* Proceedings of a symposium, Bandung, Indonesia, 1982. Commission on Ecology Papers No. 7, IUCN. pp. 30-35.

1985 The value today of Islander's traditional knowledge of their natural resources. *Pandanus Periodical* No. 7.

in press Research on traditional tropical fisheries: some implications for Torres Strait and Australian Aboriginal fisheries. *In* F. Grey and L. Zann (eds.), *Traditional knowledge of the marine environment in northern Australia.* Proceedings of a workshop, Townsville, 1985. Great Barrier Reef Marine Park Authority, Townsville.

Johannes, R.E. et al.

1983 Traditional knowledge and management of marine coastal systems. *Biology International,* Special Issue 4.

Kemp, William B.

1987 Makavik Research Department and the development of Inuit-based research and scientific education. *In* W. Peter Adams (ed.), *Education, research, information systems and the North.* ACUNS, Ottawa. pp. 39-42.

Kennedy, Dorothy I.D. and Randy Bouchard

1974 Utilization of fishes, beach foods, and marine mammals by the Tl'uhus Indian people of British Columbia. Unpublished m.s., British Columbia Indian Language Project, Victoria, British Columbia.

1976 Utilization of fishes, beach foods, and marine mammals by the Squamish Indian people of British Columbia. Unpublished m.s., British Columbia Indian Language Project, Victoria, British Columbia.

Kowarsky, J.

1982 Subsistence hunting of sea turtles in Australia. *In* K.A. Bjorndal (ed.), *Biology and conservation of sea turtles.* Smithsonian Institution Press, Washington, D.C. pp. 305-313.

Klee, Gary A.

1976 Traditional time reckoning and resource utilization. *Micronesia* 12(2):211-246.

1980 *World systems of traditional resource management.* V.H. Winston and Sons, New York. (ed.). 290 pp.

1985 Traditional marine resource management in the Pacific. *In* J.A. McNeely and D. Pitt (eds.), *Culture and Conservation.* Croom Helm, London. pp. 193-202.

Kwapena, Navu

1984a Traditional conservation and utilization of wildlife in Papua New Guinea. *In* J. Hanks (ed.), *Traditional life-styles,*

conservation and rural development.
Commission on Ecology Papers No. 7,
IUCN, Gland. pp. 22-26.

1984b   Wildlife conservation by the people. *In*
J.A. McNeely and K.R. Miller (eds.),
*National Parks, Conservation and
Development: The Role of Protected Areas
in Sustaining Society.* Smithsonian
Institution Press, Washington, D.C. pp.
315-321.

Lamont, S.M.
1977   The Fisherman Lake Slave and their
environment: a study of floral and
faunal resources. M.A. thesis,
Department of Plant Ecology, University
of Saskatchewan, Saskatoon. 368 pp.

Langdon, Steve J.
1984   Alaskan Native subsistence: current
regulatory regimes and issues. *Alaskan
Native Review Commission*, Volume XIX,
Anchorage. 101 pp.

1986   *Contemporary Alaskan Native economies.*
University Press of America, Lanham,
(ed.). 194 pp.

Lasserre, Pierre and K. Ruddlé,
1983   Traditional management of marine
coastal systems. *Biology International,*
Special Issue 4.

Leff, Enrique
1985   Ethnobotany and anthropology as tools
for a cultural conservation strategy. *In*
J.A. McNeely and D. Pitt (eds.), *Culture
and conservation: the human dimension in
environmental planning.* IUCN, Croom
Helm, London. 308 pp.

Lewis, Henry T.,
1973   *Patterns of Indian burning in California:
ecology and ethnohistory.* Ballena Press,
Ramona, California.

1977   Maskuta: the ecology of Indian fires in
northern Alberta. *Western Canadian
Journal of Anthropology*, 7:15-52.

1980   Indian fires of spring. *Natural History,*
89:76-83.

1982a   Fire technology and resource manage-
ment in aboriginal North America and
Australia. *In* N.M. Williams and E.S.
Hunn (eds.), *Resource managers: North
American and Australian hunter-
gatherers.* American Association for the
Advancement of Science, Selected
Symposium, No. 67, Westview Press,
Colorado.

1982b   *A time for burning: traditional Indian uses
of fire in western Canadian boreal forest.*
Occasional publication no. 17, Boreal
Institute for Northern Studies,
Edmonton.

1985a   Burning the "Top End": kangaroos and
cattle. *In* J.R. Ford (ed.), *Fire ecology
and management in western Australian
Ecosystems.* WAIT Environmental
Studies Group Report No. 14, Western
Australian Institute of Technology,
Perth. pp. 21-32.

1985b   Why Indians burned: specific versus
general reasons. *In* J.E. Lotan, B.M.
Kilgore, W.C. Fischer and R.W. Mutch
(eds.), *Proceedings: Symposium and
Workshop on Wilderness Fire.* Inter-
mountain Forest and Range Experiment
Station, Forest Service, U.S. Department
of Agriculture, Missoula, Montana. pp.
75-86.

in press   Non-agricultural management of
plants and animals: alternative burning
strategies in northern Australia. *In* R.J.
Hudson, K.R. Drew and L.M. Baskin
(eds.), *Wildlife Production Systems.*
Cambridge University Press, Cambridge.

Lloyd, Kevin
1986   Cooperative management of polar bears
on northeast Baffin Island. *In* J. Green
and J. Smith (eds.) *Native people and
renewable resource management.*
Proceedings of the 1986 symposium of the
Alberta Society of Professional
Biologists, Edmonton. pp. 108-116.

Lonner, T.D.
1986   Subsistence as an economic system in
Alaska: theoretical observations and
management implications. *In* S.J.
Langdon (ed.) *Contemporary Alaskan
Native Economies.* University Press of
America, Lanham. pp. 15-27.

Magdanz, Jim and Annie Olanna
1984   *Controls on fishing behavior on the Nome
River.* Technical Paper No. 102. Alaska
Department of Fish and Game, Division
of Subsistence, Nome.

Makivik Corporation
1984   Mitiq: the ecology, use and management
of the Common Eider in northern Quebec.
Kuujjuaq Research Centre, Kuujjuaq. 30
pp.

Marks, S.
1976 *Large mammals and a brave people: subsistence hunters in Zambia.* University of Washington Press, Seattle. 274 pp.
1977 Hunting behavior and strategies of the Valley Bisa in Zambia. *Human Ecology,* 5(1):1-36.
1984 *The Imperial Lion: Human dimensions of wildlife management in Central Africa.* Westview Press, Boulder. 195 pp.

Martin, Calvin
1978 *Keepers of the game: Indian-animal relationships and the fur trade.* University of California Press, Berkeley.

McCandless, Robert G.
1985 *Yukon wildlife: a social history.* University of Alberta Press, Edmonton.

McCay, Bonnie J.
1980 A fisherman's cooperative, limited: indigenous resource management in a complex society. *Anthropological Quarterly* 53:29-38.

McCay, B.J. and J.M. Acheson (eds.)
1987 *The question of the commons: the culture and economy of common property.* University of Arizona Press, Tuscon. 386 pp.

McDonald, Miriam
1988 Traditional knowledge, adaptive management and advances in scientific understanding. *In* M.M.R. Freeman and L.N. Carbyn (eds.), *Traditional knowledge and renewable resource management in northern regions.* Boreal Institute for Northern Studies, Occasional Publication No. 23, Edmonton.

McNeely, J.A. and K.R. Miller (eds.)
1984 *National Parks, Conservation and Development: The Role of Protected Areas in Sustaining Society.* Smithsonian Institution Press, Washington, D.C. 825 pp.

McNeely, J.A. and D. Pitt (eds.)
1985 *Culture and conservation: the human dimension in environmental planning.* IUCN/Croom Helm, London. 308 pp.

Minc, Leah D.
1986 Scarcity and survival: the role of oral tradition in mediating subsistence crises. *Journal of Anthropological Archaeology,* 5:39-113.

Morauta, Louise, J. Pernetta and W. Heaney (eds.)
1982 *Traditional conservation in Papua· New Guinea: implications for today.* The Institute of Applied Social and Economic Research, Monograph 16. Boroko. 392 pp.

Nakashima, D.J.
1986 Inuit knowledge of the ecology of the Common Eider in northern Quebec. *In* Austin Reed (ed.), *Eider ducks in Canada,* Canadian Wildlife Service, Report Series No. 47. pp. 102-113.

Nelson, Richard K.
1966a *Literature review of Eskimo knowledge of the sea ice environment.* Arctic Aeromedical Laboratory, Technical Report 65-7, Aerospace Medical Division, Air Force Systems Command. Fort Wainwright, Alaska.
1966b *Alaskan Eskimo exploitation of the sea ice environment.* Arctic Aeromedical Laboratory, Technical Report 65-19, Fort Wainwright, Alaska. 227 pp.
1969 *Hunters of the Northern ice.* The University of Chicago Press, Chicago. 429 pp.
1973 *Hunters of the Northern forest: designs for survival among the Alaskan Kutchin.* University of Chicago Press, Chicago. 339 pp.
1982 A conservation ethic and environment: the Koyukon of Alaska. *In* N.M. Williams and E.S. Hunn (eds.) *Resource managers: North American and Australian hunter-gatherers.* American Association for the Advancement of Science, Selected Symposium, No. 67, Westview Press, Boulder. pp. 211-228.
1983 *Make prayers to the raven: a Koyukon view of the Northern forest.* University of Chicago Press, Chicago. 292 pp.

Nelson, Richard K., Kathleen H. Mautner and G. Ray Bane
1982 *Tracks in the wildland: a portrayal of Koyukon and Nunamuit subsistence.* Anthropology and Historic Preservation, Cooperative Park Studies Unit, University of Alaska, Fairbanks. 465 pp.

Nietschmann, Bernard
1972 Hunting and fishing focus among the Miskito Indians, eastern Nicaragua.

Human Ecology, 1(1):41-67.
1973 *Between land and water: the subsistence ecology of the Miskito Indians, eastern Nicaragua.* Seminar Press, New York.
1974 When the turtle collapses, the world ends. *Natural History* 83:34-43.
1984 Indigenous island peoples, living resources and protected areas. *In* J.A. McNeely and K.R. Miller (eds.), *National Parks, Conservation and Development: The Role of Protected Areas in Sustaining Society.* Smithsonian Institution Press, Washington, D.C. pp. 333-343.
1985 Torres Strait Islanders sea resource management and sea rights. *In* K. Ruddle and R.E. Johannes, (eds.), *The traditional knowledge and management of coastal systems in Asia and the Pacific.* UNESCO, Regional Office for Science and Technology for Southeast Asia, Jakarta. pp. 125-154.

Nietschmann, Bernard and J. Nietschmann
1981 Good dugong, bad dugong, bad turtle, good turtle. *Natural History,* 90(5):55-62.

North Slope Borough
1980 Resolution on self-regulation of subsistence whaling (Alaska). *The Coastal Zone Management Newsletter* No. 29.

Nowick, P.
1985 Cultural ecology and "management" of natural resources or knowing when not to meddle. *In* J.A. McNeely and D. Pitt (eds.), *Culture and conservation: the human dimension in environmental planning.* IUCN, Croom Helm. London. pp. 269-282.

O'Keefe, L. and M. Howes
1980 A select annotated bibliography: indigenous technical knowledge in development. *In* D.W. Brokensha, D.M. Warrens and Oswald Werner (eds.), *Indigenous knowledge systems and development.* University Press of America, Lanham, MD. pp. 399-413.

Oktollik, John
1985 *The bowhead whale, Balaena mysticetus, management plan of the Alaskan Eskimo Whaling Commission.* Alaskan Eskimo Whaling Commission, Barrow, Alaska.

Osherenko, Gail
1988a Wildlife management in the North American Arctic: the case for co-management. *In* M.M.R. Freeman and L.N. Carbyn (eds.), *Traditional knowledge and renewable resource management in northern regions.* Boreal Institute for Northern Studies, Occasional Publication No. 23, Edmonton.
1988b *Sharing power with Native users: co-management regimes for Arctic wildlife.* CARC Policy Paper 5. Canadian Arctic Resources Committee, Ottawa. 58 pp.

Ovington, J.D.
1984 Aboriginal people — guardians of a heritage. *In* J. Hanks (ed.), *Traditional life-styles, conservation and rural development.* Proceedings of a symposium, Bandung, Indonesia, 1982. Commission on Ecology Papers No. 7, IUCN, Gland. pp. 36-39.

Pinkerton, Evelyn
1983 Taking the Minister to court: changes in public opinion about forest management and their expression in Haida land claims. *B.C. Studies,* 57:68-85.
1988 Local-level management in the British Columbia coastal area. *In* Fay G. Cohen and A.J. Hanson (eds.), *Community-based resource management in Canada: an inventory of research and projects.* Canadian Commission for UNESCO, Man and the Biosphere Program, Ottawa. (in press).
in press *Cooperative management of local fisheries.* University of British Columbia, Vancouver. (ed.)

Pitt, David
1985 Towards ethnoconservation. *In* J.A. McNeely and D. Pitt (eds.), *Culture and Conservation.* Croom Helm, London. pp. 283-295.

Pernetta, J.C. and Lance Hill
1984 Traditional use and conservation of resources in the Pacific basin. *Ambio,* 13(5-6):359-364.

Polunin, Nicholas V.C.
1985 Traditional marine practices in Indonesia and their bearing on conservation. *In* J.A. McNeely and D. Pitt (eds.), *Culture and conservation.* Croom Helm, London. pp. 155-179.

Poole, Peter
1981   Conservation and Inuit hunting; conflict or compatibility? Ph.D. dissertation, Department of Geography, McGill University, Montreal.

Pulae, M.
1985   Customary law relating to the environment, South Pacific region: an overview. SPREP Secretariat, Noumea, New Caledonia.

Richardson, Allan
1982   The control of productive resources on the Northwest coast of North America. *In* N.M. Williams and E.S. Hunn (eds.), *Resource managers: North American and Australian hunter-gatherers.* American Association for the Advancement of Science, Selected Symposium, No. 67, Westview Press, Colorado.

Ridington, Robin
1971   Beaver dreaming and singing. *In* P. Lotz and J. Lotz (eds.), Pilot not commander, Essays in memory of Diamond Jeness. *Anthropologica*, 13(1-2):115-128.
1988   Knowledge, power and the individual in subarctic hunting societies. *American Anthropologist*, 90(1):98-110.

Riewe, Rick and Lloyd Gamble
1988   Inuit and wildlife management today. *In* M.M.R. Freeman and L.N. Carbyn (eds.), *Traditional knowledge and renewable resource management in northern regions.* Boreal Institute for Northern Studies, Occasional Publication No. 23, Edmonton.

Ruddle, K. and T. Akimichi
1984   *Maritime institutions in the western Pacific.* Senri Ethnological Studies 17, National Museum of Ethnology, Osaka, Japan. 329 pp.

Ruddle, K. and R.E. Johannes (eds.)
1985   *The traditional knowledge and management of coastal systems in Asia and the Pacific.* UNESCO, Regional Office for Science and Technology for Southeast Asia, Jakarta.

Sabo III, George and D.R. Sabo
1985   Belief systems and the ecology of sea mammal hunting among the Baffinland Eskimos. *Arctic Anthropology,* 2(2):77-86.

Salisbury, R.F.
1986   *A homeland for the Cree: regional development in James Bay, 1971 - 1981.* McGill-Queens' University Press. 172 pp.

Salisbury, R.F. et al.
1972   *Not by bread alone: subsistence activities of the James Bay Cree.* Indians of Quebec Association, James Bay Task Force, Montreal. 72 pp.

Sankhala, K.S.
1985   People, trees and antelopes in the Indian desert. *In* J.A. McNeely and D. Pitt (eds.), *Culture and conservation: the human dimension in environmental planning.* IUCN, Croom Helm, London. pp. 205-227.

Scott, C.H.
1982   Production and exchange among Wemindji Cree: Egalitarian ideology and economic base. *Culture,* 11(3):51-64.
1983   The semiotics of material life among Wemindji Cree hunters. Ph.D. dissertation. McGill University, Montreal.
1987   The socio-economic significance of waterfowl among Canada's Aboriginal Cree: Native use and local management. *In*: A.W. Diamond and F.L. Filion (eds.), *The value of birds.* ICBP Technical Publication No. 6. pp. 49-62.

Sibbeston, Nick
1987   Economic development and renewable resources in the Northwest Territories. *In* J. Green and J. Smith (eds.), *Native people and renewable resource management.* Alberta Society of Professional Biologists, Edmonton. pp. 153-157.

Smith, A.J.
1987   Usage of marine resources by Aboriginal communities on the east coast of Cape York Peninsula. Final report to the Great Barrier Reef Marine Park Authority, Townsville, June, 1987.

Smith, Shirleen
1986a   *Bibliography of bowhead whales, whaling and Alaskan Inupiat and Yupik whaling communities.* Miscellaneous Publications, Boreal Institute for Northern Studies, Edmonton. 55 pp.
1986b   Value and compensation: subsistence

production in the Dene economy, Fort Good Hope, Northwest Territories. Unpublished M.A. thesis, Department of Anthropology, University of Alberta, Edmonton. 109 pp.

Spring, S.C.
1982 Marine turtle conservation in Papua New Guinea. *In* L. Morauta, et al. (eds.), *Traditional Conservation in Papua New Guinea: implications for today.* The Institute of Applied Social and Economic Research, Monograph 16. Boroko. pp. 303-306.

Steegman, A.T., Jr. (ed)
1983 *Boreal forest adaptations.* Plenum, New York. 356 pp.

Suluk, Donald
1987 Inummariit: An Inuit way of life. *Inuktitut,* 65:4-96.

Sya'rani, L. and N.G. Willoughby
1985 The traditional management of marine resources in Indonesia, with particular reference to central Java. *In* K. Ruddle and R.E. Johannes (eds.), *The traditional knowledge and management of coastal systems in Asia and the Pacific.* UNESCO, Regional Office for Science and Technology for Southeast Asia, Jakarta.

Tanner, Adrian
1973 The significance of hunting territories today. *In* B.Cox (ed.), *Cultural Ecology: Readings on Canadian Indians and Eskimos.* McClelland and Stewart Ltd., Toronto. pp. 101-114.
1979 *Bringing home animals: religious ideology and the mode of production of the Mistassini Cree Hunters.* St. John's Memorial University, St. John's, Newfoundland. 233 pp.
1983 Algonquian land tenure and state structures in the North. *Canadian Journal of Native Studies,* 3(2):311-320.

Tobayiwa, Chris
1985 Shona people, totems and wildlife. *In* J.A. McNeely and D. Pitt (eds.), *Culture and conservation: the human dimension in environmental planning.* IUCN, Croom Helm, London. pp. 229-236.

T'Seleie, Bella
1985 Baseline data: Dene knowledge of behavior patterns in moose, caribou and

fish. Report, Fee-Yee Consulting Ltd., Fort Good Hope, NWT.

Turner, Nancy J.
1973 The ethnobotany of the Bella Coola Indians of British Columbia. *Syesis,* 6:193-220.
1974 Plant taxonomic systems and the ethnobotany of three contemporary Indian groups of the Pacific Northwest (Haida, Bella Coola, and Lillooet). *Syesis,* Vol.7, Supplement 1.
1975 *Food plants of British Columbia Indians. Part 1 — Coastal Peoples.* Handbook 34, British Columbia Provincial Museum, Victoria. 264 pp.
1978 *Food plants of British Columbia Indians. Part 2 — Interior Peoples.* Handbook 36, British Columbia Provincial Museum, Victoria. 259 pp.
1979 *Plants in British Columbia Indian Technology.* Handbook 38, British Columbia Provincial Museum, Victoria.

Turner, Nancy J. and M.A.M. Bell
1971 The ethnobotany of the Coast Salish Indians of Vancouver Island. *Economic Botany,* 25(1):63-104.

Turner, Nancy J., Randy Bouchard and Dorothy I.D. Kennedy
1980 *Ethnobotany of the Okanagan-Colville Indians of British Columbia and Washington.* Occasional Paper No. 21, British Columbia Provincial Museum, Victoria.

Turner, Nancy J. and Barbara S. Efrat
1982 *Ethnobotany of the Hesquiat Indians of Vancouver Island.* Cultural Recovery Paper No. 2, British Columbia Provincial Museum, Victoria.

Turner, Nancy J., John Thomas, Barry F. Carlson and Robert T. Ogilvie
1983 *Ethnobotany of the Nitinaht Indians of Vancouver Island.* Occasional Paper No. 24, British Columbia Provincial Museum, Victoria.

Usher, Peter
1981 Sustenance or recreation? The future of Native wildlife harvesting in northern Canada. *In* M.M.R. Freeman, (ed.), *Proceedings: First International symposium on renewable resources and the economy of the North.* Association of Canadian Universities for Northern

Studies and the Man and the Biosphere Program, Ottawa. pp. 56-71.

1984   Property rights: the basis of wildlife management. *In National and regional interests in the North: third national workshop on people, resources and the environment north of 60.* Yellowknife, NWT, 1-3 June, 1983. Canadian Arctic Resources Committee, Ottawa. pp. 389-415.

1986a   Keynote address: Devolution of power in the Northwest Territories: implications for wildlife. *In* J.Green and J. Smith (eds.), *Native people and renewable resource management.* Proceedings of the 1986 symposium of the Alberta Society of Professional Biologists, Edmonton. pp. 69-80.

1986b   The devolution of wildlife management and the prospects for wildlife conservation in the Northwest Territories. *CARC Policy Paper 3.* Canadian Arctic Resources Committee, Ottawa. 193 pp.

1987   Indigenous management systems and the conservation of wildlife in the Canadian North. *Alternatives,* 14(1):3-9.

Vayda, A.P., Carol J. Pierce Colfer and Mohamed Brotokusumo

1985   Interactions between people and forests in East Kalimantan. *In* J.A. McNeely and D. Pitt (eds.), *Culture and conservation.* Croom Helm, London. pp. 211-227.

Waldram, James B.

1987   Traditional knowledge systems: the recognition of indigenous history and science. *Saskatchewan Indian Federated College Journal,* 2(2):115-124.

Waquan, Chief Archie

1986   Resource co-management in Wood Buffalo National Park: the Cree Band's perspective. *In* J. Green and J. Smith (eds.), *Native People and renewable resource management.* Proceedings of the Alberta Society of Professional Biologists, Edmonton. pp. 69-80.

Watson, Dwight J.

1982   Subsistence fish exploitation and implications for management in the Baram River system, Sarawak, Malaysia. *Fisheries Research,* 1(4):299-310.

Webb, L.J.

1973   "Eat, die and learn" — the botany of the Australian Aborigines. *Australian Natural History,* 17(9): 290-295.

Webb, L.J. and D.M. Smith

1984   Ecological guidelines and traditional empiricism and rural development. *In* J. Hanks (ed.), *Traditional life-styles, conservation and rural development.* IUCN, Commission on Ecology papers No. 7, Gland. pp. 99-105.

Weinstein, Martin

1976   *What the land provides. An examination of the Fort George subsistence economy and the possible consequences on it of the James Bay Hydroelectric Project.* Grand Council of the Crees of Quebec, Montreal. 255 pp.

1977   Hares, lynx and trappers. *American Naturalist,* 111(980):806-808.

1985   Traditional Nishga'a fisheries management. Paper prepared for the Nishga Tribal Council, Nishga Fisheries Management Board's Fisheries Management Workshop, Terrace, B.C., May 27-28, 1985.

Wheeler, Priscilla

1988   Fishery management by traditional means, an Alaskan example. *In* M.M.R. Freeman and L.N. Carbyn (eds.), *Traditional knowledge and renewable resource management in northern regions.* Boreal Institute for Northern Studies, Occasional Publication, No. 23, Edmonton.

Williams, Nancy M.

1986   *The Yolngu and their land: a system of land tenure and the fight for its recognition.* Australian Institute for Aboriginal Studies, Canberra, 264 pp.

Williams, N.M. and E.S. Hunn

1982   *Resource managers: North American and Australian hunter-gatherers.* American Association for the Advancement of Science, Selected Symposium, No. 67, Westview Press, Colorado.

Winterhalder, B.

1980   Canadian furbearer cycles and Cree-Ojibwa hunting and trapping practices. *American Naturalist,* 115:870-879.

1981a   Optimal foraging strategies and hunter-gather research in anthropology: theory and models. *In* B. Winterhalder and E.A. Smith (eds.), *Hunter-gatherer foraging strategies.* University of Chicago

Press, Chicago. pp. 13-35.

1981b Foraging strategies in the boreal forest: an analysis of Cree hunting and gathering. *In* B. Winterhalder and E.A. Smith (eds.), *Hunter-gatherer foraging strategies.* University of Chicago Press, Chicago. pp. 66-98.

1983a The boreal forest, Cree-Ojibwa foraging and adaptive management. *In* R.W. Wein, R.R. Riewe and I.R. Methuen, (eds.), *Resource Dynamics and the Boreal Zone.* Association of Canadian Universities for Northern Studies, Ottawa. pp. 331-345.

1983b Boreal forest strategies. *In* A.T. Steegman, Jr., (ed.) *Boreal forest adaptations.* Plenum, New York. pp. 201-241.

1983c History and ecology of the boreal forest zone in Ontario. *In* A.T. Stegman, Jr. (ed.), *Boreal forest adaptations.* Plenum, New York. pp. 9-54.

Wolfe, Robert J.
1986 The economic efficiency of food production in a western Alaska Eskimo population. *In* Steve J. Langdon (ed.), *Contemporary Alaskan Native Economies.* University Press of America, Lanham. pp. 101-120.

Wolfe, Robert J. and Linda J. Ellana (compilers)
1983 *Resource use and socioeconomic systems: case studies of fishing and hunting in Alaskan communities.* Alaskan Department of Fish and Game, Division of Subsistence, Technical Paper No. 61. Juneau, Alaska. 261 pp.

Wolfe, Robert J. and Steven R. Behnke
1982 Rural Alaska hunting and fishing economics as self-regulating systems. Paper presented to the 33rd Alaska Science Conference, Fairbanks, Alaska.

Worl, Rosita
1980 The north slope Inupiat whaling complex. *In* Y. Kotani and W.B. Workman (eds.), *Alaska Native culture and history.* National Museum of Ethnology, Senri Ethnological Studies, Osaka, 4:305-320.

Wright, A.
1985 Marine resource use in Papua New Guinea: can traditional concepts and contemporary development be integrated? *In* K. Ruddle and R.E. Johannes (eds.), *The traditional knowledge and management of coastal systems in Asia and the Pacific.* UNESCO, Regional Office for Science and Technology for Southeast Asia, Jakarta. pp. 79-99.

Zann, Leon P.
1985 Traditional management and conservation of fisheries in Kiribati and Tuvalu atolls. *In* K. Ruddle and R.E. Johannes (eds.), *The traditional knowledge and management of coastal systems in Asia and the Pacific.* UNESCO, Regional Office for Science and Technology for Southeast Asia, Jakarta. pp. 53-77.

Acknowledgements

I wish to thank Shirleen Smith and Helene Folkman for their assistance in compiling this bibliography. An earlier version of the bibliography was prepared for the Dene Nation, Yellowknife, NWT.